D.

MODERN AGE
1517 A.D.?
THE REFORMATION

THE BUILDING OF CATHEDRALS

THE ENGLISH BIBLE
King James Version
(1611 A.D.)

JOHN BUNYAN (1628-1688 A.D.)

BOOK OF CONCORD
(1580 A.D.)

GUSTAVUS ADOLPHUS (1594-1632 A.D.)

COVERDALE'S ENGLISH BIBLE
(1535 A.D.)

1600 A.D. KING JAMES of England (1566-1625 A.D.)

JOHN KNOX (1505 A.D.-1572 A.D.)

THE GERMAN BIBLE
(Martin Luther's translation:
N. T., 1522; O. T., 1534)

JOHN CALVIN (1509 A.D.-1564 A.D.)

MARTIN LUTHER (1483 A.D.-1546 A.D.)

THE AUGSBURG CONFESSION
(1530 A.D.)

1500 A.D. WILLIAM TYNDALE (1484 A.D.--1536 A.D.)

LUTHER'S CATECHISM
(1529 A.D.)

ULRICH ZWINGLI (1484 A.D.-1531 A.D.)

DIET OF WORMS
(1521 A.D.)

SAVONAROLA (1452 A.D.-1498 A.D.)

THOMAS A KEMPIS (1380 A.D.-1471 A.D.)

LUTHER'S 95 THESES
(1517 A.D.)

1400 A.D.

THE "GUTENBERG" (Latin) BIBLE
(1456 A.D.)

JOHN HUSS (1369 A.D.-1415 A.D.)

THE WYCLIFF MIDDLE ENGLISH
TRANSLATION OF THE BIBLE
(1380 A.D.)

JOHN WYCLIFF (1320 A.D.-1384 A.D.)

1300 A.D.

1200 A.D. FRANCIS OF ASSISI (1182 A.D.-1226 A.D.)

RICHARD, THE LION-HEARTED (1157 A.D.-1199 A.D.)

1100 A.D. BERNARD OF CLAIRVAUX (1091 A.D.-1153 A.D.)

OLAV, King of Norway (995 A.D.-1030 A.D.)

A.D. VLADIMIR, Ruler of Russia (956 A.D.-1015 A.D.)

candinavia (801 A.D.-865 A.D.)

e (742 A.D.-814 A.D.)
pire)

55 A.D.)

THE FIRST HUNDRED YEARS OF LUTHERANISM IN AMERICA

1664—Governor Richard Nicolls grants charter to the Evangelical Lutheran Church of St. Matthew in New York City. (In 1646 this congregation was formed as the "Congregation of the Unaltered Augsburg Confession of Faith.")

1664—The English conquered the Dutch and were more tolerant toward the Lutherans.

1646—The first book translated into an American Indian dialect was Luther's Small Catechism, done by John Campanius.

1642—The first Protestant missionary to the American Indians was the Rev. John Campanius.

1639—The first Lutheran pastor in the United States was the Rev. Reorus Torkillus of Sweden.

1638—The first Lutheran church in America (Old Swedes Church) was erected at Wilmington, Delaware.

1619—The first Lutheran services in America were conducted on Hudson Bay by the Rev. Rasmus Jensen of Denmark.

1564—The first Lutheran Colony in America settled by the French near St. Augustine, Florida.

THE MARCH OF FAITH

The March of Faith

by

INEZ STEEN

Illustrated by

JOHN ELLINGBOE

CHRIST SAID:

"Lo, I am with you always,
even unto the end of the world"

Published by AUGSBURG PUBLISHING HOUSE *Minneapolis*

THE MARCH OF FAITH
Copyright 1939
Augsburg Publishing House

First Printing   October 1939
Second Printing   July 1940

Third Printing

This volume is one in a series of graded Sunday school textbooks issued by The Board of Parish Education, Dr. Jacob Tanner, editor-in-chief

Manufactured in the United States of America
O.'41-8184-30

Table of Contents

Brief Index

(Key to pronunciation: āte, fäther, wē, mĕt, fīle, ōpen, ūse)

Catechism Assignments

The following Catechism and Bible verse assignments are a part of this year's course.

Part One ·· The Ten Commandments

CHAPTER 1

THE FIRST COMMANDMENT

Thou shalt have no other gods before Me.

What does this mean?

Answer: We should fear, love, and trust in God above all things.

Hear, O heavens, and give ear, O earth, for the Lord hath spoken (Is. 1:2).

Thou shalt worship the Lord thy God, and Him only shalt thou serve (Matt. 4:10).

CHAPTER 2

THE SECOND COMMANDMENT

Thou shalt not take the name of the Lord thy God in vain; for the Lord will not hold him guiltless that taketh His name in vain.

What does this mean?

Answer: We should fear and love God so that we do not curse, swear, conjure, lie, or deceive, by His name, but call upon Him in every time of need, and worship Him with prayer, praise and thanksgiving.

Bless, and curse not (Rom. 12:14).

Call upon Me in the day of trouble; I will deliver thee, and thou shalt glorify Me (Ps. 50:15).

CHAPTER 3

THE THIRD COMMANDMENT

Remember the Sabbath day, to keep it holy.

What does this mean?

Answer: We should fear and love God so that we do not despise His Word and the preaching of the same, but deem it holy, and gladly hear and learn it.

Six days thou shalt work, and on the seventh day thou shalt rest (Ex. 23:12).

Thy word have I hid in my heart, that I might not sin against Thee (Ps. 119:11).

CHAPTER 4
THE FOURTH COMMANDMENT

Honor thy father and thy mother, that thy days may be long upon the land which the Lord thy God giveth thee.

What does this mean?

Answer: We should fear and love God so that we do not despise our parents and superiors, nor provoke them to anger, but honor, serve, obey, love, and esteem them.

Children, obey your parents in the Lord, for this is right. Honor thy father and mother which is the first commandment with promise, that it may be well with thee and thou mayest live long on the earth (Eph. 6:1-3).

CHAPTER 5
THE FIFTH COMMANDMENT

Thou shalt not kill.

What does this mean?

Answer: We should fear and love God so that we do our neighbor no bodily harm or cause him any suffering, but help and befriend him in every need.

He that hateth his brother is a murderer, and ye know that no murderer hath eternal life abiding in him (1 John 3:15).

But I say unto you, Love your enemies, and pray for them that persecute you; that ye may be sons of your Father who is in heaven (Matt. 5:44-45).

CHAPTER 6
THE SIXTH COMMANDMENT

Thou shalt not commit adultery.

What does this mean?

Answer: We should fear and love God so that we lead a chaste and pure life in word and deed, and that husband and wife love and honor each other.

Blessed are the pure in heart, for they shall see God (Matt. 5:8).

Let marriage be had in honor among all (Heb. 13:4).

CHAPTER 7
THE SEVENTH COMMANDMENT

Thou shalt not steal.

What does this mean?

Answer: We should fear and love God so that we do not rob our neighbor of his money or property, nor bring them into our possession by unfair dealing or fraud, but help him to improve and protect his property and living.

If any will not work, neither let him eat (2 Thess. 3:10).

It is required in stewards, that a man be found faithful (1 Cor. 9:2).

CHAPTER 8
THE EIGHTH COMMANDMENT

Thou shalt not bear false witness against thy neighbor.

What does this mean?

Answer: We should fear and love God so that we do not deceitfully belie, betray, backbite, nor slander our neighbor, but apologize for him, speak well of him, and put the most charitable construction on all that he does.

A good name is rather to be chosen than great riches (Prov. 22:1).

Lie not one to another (Col. 3:9).

CHAPTER 9
THE NINTH AND TENTH COMMANDMENTS

Thou shalt not covet thy neighbor's house.

What does this mean?

Answer: We should fear and love God so that we do not seek by craftiness to gain possession of our neighbor's inheritance or home nor obtain them under pretense of a legal right, but assist and serve him in keeping the same.

Thou shalt not covet thy neighbor's wife, nor his manservant, nor his maidservant, nor his cattle, nor anything that is thy neighbor's.

What does this mean?

Answer: We should fear and love God, so that we do not estrange or entice away our neighbor's wife, servants, or cattle but seek to have them remain and discharge their duty to him.

The Lord seeth not as man seeth; for man looketh on the outward appearance, but the Lord looketh on the heart (1 Sam. 16:7).

Take heed, and keep yourselves from all covetousness (Luke 12:15).

CHAPTER 10
GOD'S DECLARATION CONCERNING HIS COMMANDMENTS
The Conclusion

What does God declare concerning all these Commandments?

Answer: He says: I the Lord thy God am a jealous God, visiting the iniquity of the fathers upon the children unto the third and fourth generation of them that hate Me; and showing mercy unto thousands of them that love Me and keep my commandments.

What does this mean?

Answer: God threatens to punish all who transgress these commandments. We should, therefore, fear His wrath, and in no wise disobey them. But He promises grace and every blessing to all who keep them. We should, therefore, love Him, trust in Him, and gladly keep His commandments.

The wages of sin is death, but the free gift of God is eternal life in Christ Jesus, our Lord (Rom. 6:23).

Godliness is profitable for all things, having promise of the life which now is, and of that which is to come (1 Tim. 4:8).

CHAPTER 11
THE FIRST ARTICLE — OF CREATION

I believe in God the Father Almighty, maker of heaven and earth.

What does this mean?

Answer: I believe that God has created me and all that exists; that He has given and still preserves to me my body and soul, my eyes and ears, and all my members, my reason and all the powers of my soul, together with food and raiment, home and family, and all my property; that He daily provides abundantly for all the needs of my life, protects me from all danger, and guards and keeps me from all evil; and that He does this purely out of fatherly and divine goodness and mercy, without any merit of worthiness in me; for all of which I am in duty bound to thank, praise, serve, and obey Him. This is most certainly true.

I believe that God has created me and all that exists.

To us there is one God, the Father, of whom are all things, and we unto Him (1 Cor. 8:6).

Holy, holy, holy is the Lord of hosts; the whole earth is full of His glory (Is. 6:3).

CHAPTER 12
THE FIRST ARTICLE — OF CREATION

I believe that God...has given and still preserves to me my body and soul, my eyes and ears, and all my members, my reason and all the powers of my soul, together with food and raiment, home and family, and all my property.

The eyes of all wait for Thee, and Thou givest them their food in due season (Ps. 145:15).

While the earth remaineth, seedtime and harvest, and cold and heat, and summer and winter, and day and night shall not cease (Gen. 8:22).

CHAPTER 13
THE FIRST ARTICLE — OF CREATION

I believe that God... daily provides abundantly for all the needs of my life, protects me from all danger, and guards and keeps me from all evil; and that He does this purely out of fatherly and divine goodness and mercy, without any merit or worthiness in me; for all of which I am in duty bound to thank and praise, serve, and obey Him. This is most certainly true.

Your heavenly Father knoweth that ye have need of all these things (Matt. 6:32).

The Lord is my helper; I will not fear (Heb. 13:6).

O give thanks unto the Lord; for He is good; for His loving-kindness endureth forever (Ps. 106:1).

CHAPTER 14
THE SECOND ARTICLE — OF REDEMPTION

And in Jesus Christ His only Son, our Lord; who was conceived by the Holy Spirit, born of the Virgin Mary; suffered under Pontius Pilate, was crucified, dead, and buried; He descended into hell; the third day He rose again from the dead; He ascended into heaven, and sitteth on the right hand of God the Father almighty; from thence He shall come to judge the quick and the dead.

What does this mean?

Answer: I believe that Jesus Christ, true God, begotten of the Father from eternity, and also true Man, born of the Virgin Mary, is my Lord; who has redeemed me, a lost and condemned creature, bought me and freed me from all sins, from death, and from the power of the devil; not with silver and gold, but with His holy and precious blood, and with His innocent sufferings and death; in order that I might be His own, live under Him in His kingdom, and serve Him in everlasting righteousness, innocence, and blessedness; even as He is risen from the dead, and lives and reigns to all eternity. This is most certainly true.

I believe that Jesus Christ, true God, begotten of the Father from eternity, and also true man, born of the virgin Mary, is my Lord.

This is my beloved Son in whom I am well pleased (Matt. 3:17).

When the fulness of time came, God sent forth His Son, born of a woman (Gal. 4:4).

CHAPTER 15
THE SECOND ARTICLE — OF REDEMPTION

I believe that Jesus Christ...has redeemed me, a lost and condemned creature, bought me and freed me from all sins, from death, and from the power of the devil.

Thou shalt call His name Jesus; for it is He that shall save His people from their sins (Matt. 1:21).

Thanks be to God, who giveth us the victory through our Lord Jesus Christ (1 Cor. 15:57).

CHAPTER 16
THE SECOND ARTICLE — OF REDEMPTION

I believe that Jesus Christ...has redeemed me...not with silver and gold, but with His holy and precious blood, and with His innocent sufferings and death.

Behold the Lamb of God that taketh away the sin of the world (John 1:29).

The blood of Jesus Christ His Son cleanseth us from all sin (1 John 1:7).

CHAPTER 17

THE SECOND ARTICLE — OF REDEMPTION

I believe that Jesus Christ ... has redeemed me ... that I might be His own, live under Him in His kingdom, and serve Him in everlasting righteousness, innocence, and blessedness.

Ye are not your own; for ye were bought with a price; glorify God therefore in your body (1 Cor. 6:19-20).

Christ gave Himself for us, that He might redeem us from all iniquity, and purify unto Himself a people for His own possession, zealous of good works (Titus 2:14).

CHAPTER 18

THE SECOND ARTICLE — OF REDEMPTION

I believe that Jesus Christ ... is risen from the dead, and lives and reigns to all eternity.

The Lord is risen indeed (Luke 24:34).

He is able to save to the uttermost them that draw near unto God through Him, seeing He ever liveth to make intercession for them (Heb. 7:25).

He shall reign for ever and ever (Rev. 11:15).

CHAPTER 19

THE THIRD ARTICLE — OF SANCTIFICATION

I believe in the Holy Spirit; the holy Christian Church, the Communion of Saints; the forgiveness of sins; the resurrection of the body, and the life everlasting.

What does this mean?

Answer: I believe that I cannot by my own reason or strength believe in Jesus Christ my Lord, or come to Him; but the Holy Spirit has called me through the Gospel, enlightened me with His gifts, and sanctified and preserved me in the true faith; in like manner as He calls, gathers, enlightens, and sanctifies the whole Christian Church on earth, and preserves it in union with Jesus Christ in the one true faith; in which Christian Church He daily forgives abundantly all my sins, and the sins of all believers, and at the last day will raise up me and all the dead, and will grant everlasting life to me and to all who believe in Christ. This is most certainly true.

I believe that I cannot by my own reason or strength believe in Jesus Christ my Lord, or come to Him.

The natural man receiveth not the things of the Spirit of God, for they are foolishness unto Him (1 Cor. 2:14).

No man can say, Jesus is Lord, but in the Holy Spirit (1 Cor. 12:3).

CHAPTER 20
THE THIRD ARTICLE — OF SANCTIFICATION

I believe that . . . the Holy Spirit has called me through the gospel, enlightened me with His gifts, and sanctified and preserved me in the true faith.

It is the Spirit that giveth life (John 6:63).

Come; for all things are now ready (Luke 14:17).

CHAPTER 21
THE THIRD ARTICLE — OF SANCTIFICATION

I believe that . . . the Holy Spirit . . . calls, gathers, enlightens, and sanctifies the whole Christian Church on earth, and preserves it in union with Jesus Christ in the one true faith.

There is one body, and one Spirit, even as also ye were called in one hope of your calling; one Lord, one faith, one baptism, one God and Father of all, who is over all, and through all, and in all (Eph. 4:4-6).

CHAPTER 22
THE THIRD ARTICLE — OF SANCTIFICATION

I believe that . . . the Holy Spirit . . . in the Christian Church daily forgives abundantly all my sins, and the sins of all believers.

In Christ we have our redemption, the forgiveness of our sins (Col. 1:14).

If we confess our sins, He is faithful and righteous to forgive us our sins, and to cleanse us from all unrighteousness (1 John 1:9).

CHAPTER 23
THE THIRD ARTICLE — OF SANCTIFICATION

I believe that . . . the Holy Spirit . . . at the last day will raise up me and all the dead, and will grant everlasting life to me and to all who believe in Christ.

The hour cometh, in which all that are in the tombs shall hear His voice, and shall come forth; they that have done good, unto the resurrection of life; and they that have done evil, unto the resurrection of judgment (John 5:28-29).

Blessed are the dead who die in the Lord from henceforth (Rev. 14:13).

CHAPTER 24

THE LORD'S PRAYER

Our Father, who art in heaven.

Hallowed be Thy name.

Thy kingdom come.

Thy will be done on earth, as it is in heaven.

Give us this day our daily bread.

And forgive us our trespasses, as we forgive those
who trespass against us.

And lead us not into temptation.

But deliver us from evil.

For Thine is the kingdom, and the power, and the
glory, for ever and ever. Amen.

THE INTRODUCTION

Our Father, who art in heaven.

What does this mean?

Answer: God thereby tenderly encourages us to believe that He is truly our Father, and that we are truly His children, so that we may boldly and confidently come to Him in prayer, even as beloved children come to their dear father.

Ask, and it shall be given you; seek, and ye shall find; knock, and it shall be opened unto you (Matt. 7:7).

Whatsoever ye shall ask in My name, that will I do, that the Father may be glorified in the Son (John 14:13).

Your Father knoweth what things ye have need of, before ye ask Him (Matt. 6:8).

CHAPTER 25

THE FIRST PETITION

Hallowed be Thy name.

What does this mean?

Answer: God's name is indeed holy in itself; but we pray in this petition that it may be hallowed also among us.

How is this done?

Answer: When the Word of God is taught in its truth and purity and we, as God's children, lead holy lives, in accordance with it. This grant us, dear Father in heaven! But whoever teaches and lives otherwise than God's Word teaches, profanes the name of God among us. From this preserve us, heavenly Father!

Ye shall be holy; for I the Lord your God am holy (Lev. 19:2).
Sanctify them in the truth; Thy word is truth (John 17:17).

CHAPTER 26
THE SECOND PETITION

Thy kingdom come.

What does this mean?

Answer: The kingdom of God comes indeed of itself, without our prayer; but we pray in this petition that it may come also to us.

How is this done?

Answer: When our heavenly Father gives us His Holy Spirit, so that by His grace we believe His holy Word, and live a godly life here on earth, and in heaven for ever.

The kingdom of God is not eating and drinking, but righteousness and peace and joy in the Holy Spirit (Rom. 14:17).
The kingdom of God is within you (Luke 17:21).
Of His kingdom there shall be no end (Luke 1:33).

CHAPTER 27
THE THIRD PETITION

Thy will be done on earth, as it is in heaven.

What does this mean?

Answer: The good and gracious will of God is done indeed without our prayer; but we pray in this petition that it may be done also among us.

How is this done?

Answer: When God destroys and brings to naught every evil counsel and purpose of the devil, the world, and our own flesh, which would hinder us from hallowing His name, and prevent the coming of His kingdom; and when He strengthens us and keeps us steadfast in His Word and in faith, even unto our end. This is His good and gracious will.

I know the thoughts that I think toward you, saith the Lord, thoughts of peace, and not of evil (Jer. 29:11).

This is the will of God, even our sanctification (1 Thess. 4:3).

CHAPTER 28
THE FOURTH PETITION

Give us this day our daily bread.

What does this mean?

Answer: God indeed gives daily bread to all men, even to the wicked, without our prayer; but we pray in this petition that He would lead us to acknowledge our daily bread as His gift, and to receive it with thanksgiving.

What is meant by daily bread?

Answer: Everything that is required to satisfy our bodily needs; such as food and raiment, house and home, fields and flocks, money and goods; pious parents, children, and servants; godly and faithful rulers, good government; seasonable weather, peace and health; order and honor; true friends, good neighbors, and the like.

The eyes of all wait for Thee; and Thou givest them their food in due season (Ps. 145:15).

Giving thanks always for all things in the name of our Lord Jesus Christ to God, even the Father (Eph. 5:20).

CHAPTER 29
THE FIFTH PETITION

And forgive us our trespasses, as we forgive those who trespass against us.

What does this mean?

Answer: We pray in this petition that our heavenly Father would not regard our sins nor because of them deny our prayers; for we neither merit nor are worthy of those things for which we pray; but that He would grant us all things through grace, even though we sin daily, and deserve nothing but punishment. And certainly we, on our part, will heartily forgive, and gladly do good to those who may sin against us.

Who can discern his errors? Clear Thou me from hidden faults (Ps. 19:12).

For if ye forgive men their trespasses, your heavenly Father will also forgive you. But if ye forgive not men their trespasses, neither will your Father forgive your trespasses (Matt. 6:14-15).

CHAPTER 30
THE SIXTH PETITION

And lead us not into temptation.

What does this mean?

Answer: God indeed tempts no one to sin; but we pray in this petition that God would so guard and preserve us, that the devil, the world, and our own flesh may not deceive us, nor lead us into error and unbelief, despair, and other great and shameful sins; but that, when so tempted, we may finally prevail and gain the victory.

My son, if sinners entice thee, consent thou not (Prov. 1:10).

Watch, and pray, that ye enter not into temptation (Matt. 26:41).

CHAPTER 31
THE SEVENTH PETITION

But deliver us from evil.

What does this mean?

Answer: We pray in this petition, as in a summary, that our heavenly Father would deliver us from all manner of evil, whether it affect body or soul, property or reputation, and at last, when the hour of death shall come, grant us a blessed end, and graciously take us from this world of sorrow to Himself in heaven.

The Lord shall keep thee from all evil (Ps. 121:7).

The Lord will deliver me from every evil work, and will save me unto His heavenly kingdom (2 Tim. 4:18).

THE CONCLUSION

For Thine is the kingdom, and the power, and the glory, for ever and ever. Amen.

What does the word "Amen" mean?

Answer: It means that I should be assured that such petitions are acceptable to our heavenly Father, and are heard by Him; for He Himself has commanded us to pray in this manner, and has promised to hear us. Amen, Amen, that is, Yea, yea, it shall be so.

Hallelujah, salvation, and glory, and power, belong to our God (Rev. 19:1).

CHAPTER 32
THE SACRAMENT OF BAPTISM

I.

What is Baptism?

Answer: Baptism is not simply water, but it is the water used according to God's command and connected with God's Word.

What is this Word of God?

Answer: It is the Word of our Lord Jesus Christ, as recorded in the last chapter of Matthew: "Go ye, therefore, and make disciples of all the nations, baptizing them into the name of the Father and of the Son and of the Holy Spirit."

II.

What gifts or benefits does Baptism bestow?

Answer: It works forgiveness of sins, delivers from death, and the devil, and gives everlasting salvation to all who believe, as the word and promise of God declare.

What is this word and promise of God?

Answer: It is the word of our Lord Jesus Christ, as recorded in the last chapter of Mark: "He that believeth and is baptized shall be saved; but he that disbelieveth shall be condemned."

As many of you as were baptized into Christ did put on Christ (Gal. 3:27).

CHAPTER 33

III.

How can water do such great things?

Answer: It is not the water, indeed, that does such great things, but the Word of God, connected with the water, and our faith which relies on that Word of God. For without the Word of God, it is simply water and no baptism. But when connected with the Word of God, it is a baptism, that is, a gracious water of life and a washing of regeneration in the Holy Spirit, as St. Paul says to Titus, in the third chapter: "According to His mercy He saved us, through the washing of regeneration and renewing of the Holy Spirit, which He poured out upon us richly, through Jesus Christ our Savior; that, being justified by His grace, we might be made heirs according to the hope of eternal life. This is a faithful saying."

Be baptized, and wash away thy sins (Acts 22:16).

IV.

What does such baptizing with water signify?

Answer: It signifies that the old Adam in us, together with all sins and evil lusts, should be drowned by daily sorrow and repentance, and be put to death; and that the new man should daily come forth and rise, to live before God in righteousness and holiness for ever.

Where is it so written?

Answer: St. Paul, in the sixth chapter of the Epistle to the Romans, says: "We were buried therefore with Him through baptism into death: that like as Christ was raised from the dead through the glory of the Father, so we also might walk in newness of life."

Baptism is not the putting away of the filth of the flesh, but the interrogations of a good conscience toward God, through the resurrection of Jesus Christ (1 Pet. 3:21).

CHAPTER 34
OF CONFESSION

What is Confession?

Answer: Confession consists of two parts: the one is that we confess our sins; the other, that we receive absolution or forgiveness from the pastor as from God Himself, in no wise doubting, but firmly believing, that our sins are thereby forgiven before God in heaven.

What sins should we confess?

Answer: Before God we should acknowledge ourselves guilty of all manner of sins, even of these of which we are not aware, as we do in the Lord's Prayer. To the pastor we should confess only those sins which we know and feel in our hearts.

What are such sins?

Answer: Here examine yourself in the light of the Ten Commandments, whether as father or mother, son or daughter, master or servant, you have been disobedient, unfaithful, slothful, ill-tempered, unchaste, or quarrelsome, or whether you have injured any one by word or deed, stolen, neglected, or wasted aught, or done any other evil.

Father, I have sinned against heaven and in Thy sight (Luke 15:18).

Whose soever sins ye forgive, they are forgiven unto them (John 20:23).

CHAPTER 35
THE SACRAMENT OF THE ALTAR
I.

What is the Sacrament of the Altar?

Answer: It is the true body and blood of our Lord Jesus Christ, under the bread and wine, given unto us Christians to eat and to drink, as it was instituted by Christ Himself.

Where is it so written?

Answer: The holy evangelists, Matthew, Mark, and Luke, together with St. Paul, write thus:

"Our Lord Jesus Christ, in the night in which He was betrayed, took bread; and when He had given thanks, He brake it and gave it to His disciples, saying, Take, eat; this is My body, which is given for you; this do in remembrance of Me.

"After the same manner, also, He took the cup, when He had supped, and when He had given thanks, He gave it to them, saying, Drink ye all of it; this cup is the new testament in My blood, which is shed for you, and for many, for the remission of sins: this do, as oft as ye drink it, in remembrance of Me."

Jesus, let my soul be fed
With Thyself, the living bread,
For Thy flesh is meat indeed,
And Thy cleansing blood I need;
Let it cleanse from sin and shame,
That Thy death I may proclaim,
And forever bless Thy name.

CHAPTER 36

II.

What is the benefit of such eating and drinking?

Answer: It is pointed out in these words: "Given and shed for you for the remission of sins." Through these words the remission of sins, life and salvation are given unto us in the Sacrament; for where there is remission of sins, there is also life and salvation.

III.

How can the bodily eating and drinking produce such great benefits?

Answer: The eating and drinking, indeed, do not produce them, but the words: "Given and shed for you for the remission of sins." For besides the bodily eating and drinking, these words are the chief thing in the Sacrament; and he who believes them has what they say and declare, namely, the remission of sins.

IV.

Who, then, receives the Sacrament worthily?

Answer: Fasting and bodily preparation are indeed a good outward discipline, but he is truly worthy and well prepared who believes these words: "Given and shed for you for the remission of sins." But he who does not believe these words or who doubts them is unworthy and unprepared; for the words: "For you," require truly believing hearts.

Let a man prove himself, and so let him eat of the bread, and drink of the cup (1 Cor. 11:28).

This do in remembrance of Me (Luke 22:19).

Be thou faithful unto death, and I will give thee the crown of life (Rev. 2:10).

INTRODUCTION
Dale Lansing Asks Questions

DALE rubbed his eyes. Was it morning already? The sun was shining brightly into his room. He stretched his arms and sat up quickly. But then he noticed that Jim was still sound asleep, and that the house was very quiet. Oh yes, this was Sunday morning and he was supposed to be very quiet so everyone could sleep. He had better lie down again.

But as he lay down, he remembered last Sunday and wondered what this Sunday would be like. Just last Sunday, his church, his brand new church, had been dedicated. It had seemed as though everyone in town had crowded into his church, so that he had been afraid he would not be able to see or hear anything. He would never forget how he had felt when he had entered the church and had seen how beautiful it was. He had been sure the lump in his throat was going to choke him, and so he had swallowed hard several times.

It was interesting to be in a church that one had seen grow. All spring and summer, the new church that was being built had been the most interesting place in town. When the big hole had been dug, the scoop that was pulled by two horses had left piles of loose dirt into which he had jumped because it was fun to feel himself sink deeper and deeper into it. Soon his shoes had become heavy so that he could scarcely walk. Then he had taken them off and his stockings, too. And that was better yet! The dirt felt so cool and soft when his feet and toes sank into it.

Then had come the stones for the foundation, and hiding games had been more fun than ever. He remembered hiding one day behind a stone that wasn't smooth. His fingers had felt it first. Grooves! So he had followed the grooves with his fingers until suddenly he realized the grooves said something.

25

The A. D. on this stone had especially interested him. His father had explained it. He had said that B. C. and A. D. were letters to show whether time was before or after Christ. B. C. was easy to understand because anyone could see how B. C. could stand for *Before Christ*. But A. D. was different. It stood for the Latin words, *Anno Domini*, which meant "In the year of our Lord," or simply "After Christ."

This stone with the grooves, his father had told him, was a very important stone. All important buildings have such a stone— called a corner stone. By looking at the corner stone, one can tell how old a building is. Nowadays, his father had said, the corner stone almost always is in the foundation wall.

He remembered when the foundation was laid, how much fun it had been to squeeze through the openings where the windows were going to be.

And then a Sunday had come when the corner stone had been laid. It was lucky he had a dad who could arrange to get him close enough to see everything. He could still feel how quiet it had been and how the shivers had crept up and down his spine when into a shiny copper box had been placed a Bible, Sunday school papers, church records, a church history written by the pastor, and some other important looking papers. The box had been closed tightly with a lid. It had been lowered into the hollow of the corner stone, and the stone—box and all—had been sealed with cement.

After that Sunday, he had not been allowed to play in the church anymore. But there still had been interesting days, such as the day when the bricks had come. He had asked Dorothy and his friends to help him count them. They had counted over a thousand and they had hardly started. Then they had had to quit because they were all mixed up. Anyway, they knew there were thousands and thousands of bricks.

It was fun, too, to just stand around with his hands in his pockets and try to act like the grown-up men, to listen to them talk, and to look at what was happening.

Finally a very exciting day had come. That was the day a large truck had rumbled up to the church yard. Dale had run, too, when he had seen all the men leave their work, and run to balance a big box as it was unloaded from the truck. He had wondered what could be in the box when it had taken so long to take off the layers and layers of crating. Even when the crating was all off, he didn't know what was inside, because then there was paper—heavy paper that didn't tear easily. It was more exciting than any package he had ever seen because it took so long to open it. But finally—there it was! You couldn't guess what it was!

It was a bell! A bronze bell on which was written "In memory of James E. Lansing, 1836-1922."

All of a sudden, everyone had begun to talk about this James Lansing. Dale had had to walk away from the bell and the crowd and all of the interesting things that were being said, because he had felt a lump in his throat and his eyes had smarted. He thought it would have been interesting to know this James Lansing who had worked so hard to get a church started, and who had done so much for the people that now there was this beautiful bell being given to honor his memory.

He had waited and waited to hear the bell ring. But it hadn't been rung until last Sunday. Then it had rung in deep, strong tones, calling the people to church.

It was strange, thought Dale, that he couldn't sleep when everyone else was sleeping. Jim hadn't moved. Probably if he would be very quiet, he could just as well go outside and swing. There was a good view of the bell from the swing. It was fun to look at the bell, think about James Lansing, and pretend that he might be like him some day.

Dale dressed quickly, and went out on tip-toe past Jim's bed. Finally he reached the porch. But there was someone else there, ahead of him.

"Why Dale, couldn't you sleep on this beautiful September morning? Come, we shall leave a note for Mother and then you can go with me to make my morning calls."

About two hours later, Dr. Lansing and Dale were on their way home. From a high hill they saw their whole town.

"Dad!" burst from Dale's lips. "Dad, just look at all the church spires! And I can see our church spire. It points the highest of them all. It looks as though it could almost reach to heaven."

"I think," returned Dr. Lansing, "that those who first planned churches with spires had that hope in mind—that the spires would seem like fingers pointing to heaven—that they would help lift people's thoughts to heavenly things."

"But haven't there been churches with spires always?"

"No, there had been churches for over 1,200 years before church spires began to be used."

"What did churches look like then? Haven't church services been the same always either? How long have there been churches, anyway? Why—"

"Now, now, not so fast, Dale. One question at a time. I'll tell you what we'll do. Whenever possible, right after supper before I make calls, I'll take time to answer your questions. I'll tell you the story of the Christian Church from the beginning."

Finally supper was over. Everybody was waiting for Dad. Mother was in the rocker with three-year-old Joan on her lap. Dorothy, Dale's twin, was on the rug playing with the setter puppy. Jim was on the davenport reading the sports page. Dale lay sprawled out, his legs dangling over the arm of the big chair. He was munching apples, and watching Dad. He was hoping and hoping that Dad wouldn't have to go out. Suddenly up went Dale's legs and then in one motion, his legs reached the floor, his body turned and he sat up straight and tense.

"Hi Dad! Hurry now before the telephone rings again!"

"All right," said Dad sitting down beside Jim, "Tonight we shall start the story that we are going to call 'The March of Faith.' In other words, those Christians within the church who have permitted the Holy Spirit to lead them have been the men of faith. We shall see these men of faith marching down through the ages like Christian soldiers with the Christian creeds for their banner, with the Bible as their armor, and with Christ as their leader."

This book will tell you the stories which Dr. Lansing told about the men of faith and also some of the discussions that the Lansing family had about the Christian church.

Chapter 1

How the Christian Church Started

YOU know how disappointed you have been when someone hasn't kept a promise made to you. You never could be sure after that whether you could believe that person or not. I know someone who has kept every promise He ever made and He always will. Who is it? Of course. It's Jesus.

"Before Jesus ascended into heaven, He made two promises. He said: *'Lo, I am with you always, even unto the end of the world.'* This promise makes people say, 'Why, we can go through anything, when we know Christ is with us always.'

"The other promise was: 'I shall send the Holy Spirit who shall teach you concerning Me.' Jesus kept this promise by sending the Holy Spirit to work among His people."

"Work? I didn't know the Holy Spirit had work to do. That sounds like He was a person," interrupted Dorothy.

"Yes, the Holy Spirit is a person just as much as God the Father, and God the Son. His work is to enable you to believe in Jesus and to live according to His will. It is just as though the Holy Spirit holds a spot light and turns it on Jesus so that you may see Jesus more clearly, and so learn to love and trust Him. Those that believe in Jesus Christ, love Him, and are baptized, make up the true Christian church on earth."

"Dad," said Jim, "wait a minute. I don't understand."

"Well, Jim, I shall try to make it clear to you. The better you know Bible stories, the better you see Jesus. But that is not all.

29

At this time people worshipped in catacombs and forests
as well as in Solomon's porch, homes, and churches

The Bible tells you that you need Jesus as your Savior and that
you should follow Him as your Master. Whenever you read your
Bible or hear it read, the Holy Spirit works to help you see Jesus
as your Savior, and He also works to help you love Jesus enough to
do what He tells you. And then one thing more. When you love
and obey Jesus, you will little by little be changed so that you
become like Jesus. All of this is seeing Jesus, Jim.

"Now let's go on. The day the Holy Spirit came to earth is
called Pentecost Day and is the birthday of the Christian church.
Because there had been much prayer as preparation, it was an
eventful birthday. For Peter, through the power of the Holy
Spirit, preached a sermon that so stirred the hearts of the people
that 3,000 repented of their sins, believed in Jesus as their Savior,
and were baptized. You can read the sermon in Acts 2:14-36.

"Now that was how the church started. But God wasn't
satisfied to just start something. His church will grow until Jesus
comes again, for then the work here on earth will be finished.

"What happened this morning, Dale, when you threw rocks
into the river while I called on Mrs. Stewart? That's it! Each
rock made ripples that circled out farther and farther.

"That's exactly what happens to people. Let's take you for
example. Suppose you win a playmate to Christ by being obedient,
helpful, pure, and courageous, and by telling him about Christ.
Then there are two of you. And then the two of you win two
more. And so the circle of Christians widens about you like the
ripples in the river.

"So it was with those 3,000 Christians. Their hearts were so
filled with love for Christ that often they came together before
daylight to sing hymns of praise to God. Their love overflowed
into winning others. The Christian church started in Jerusalem
with Peter as the leader. In a few months, there were 5,000
believers. Soon the church was rippling out to take in Judæa and
Samaria. Still the ripples kept widening out farther and farther.

"Now a church couldn't grow like that without attracting
attention. Many of the Jews didn't like it that so many of their

Seven branched
candlestick of today is
a copy of the one taken
from the temple at the destruction of Jerusalem—70 A. D.

own people were becoming Christians. So they decided to use force. They beat the Christians, stoned them, wrecked their business places, took away their jobs, and made them suffer in many ways. This is what we call persecution. A person who would rather be killed than deny Jesus is called a martyr. Stephen was the first Christian martyr.

"Jesus had said, 'Lo, I am with you always.' He kept His promise. During the awful days of persecution, the Christians felt that Jesus was very close, giving them courage to endure suffering without denying Him or hating those who were cruel to them. Many unbelievers watching the courage and life of these Christians became believers themselves. I'll tell you about a bitter enemy of the Christians who became converted.

PAUL (?-67 A. D.?)

"His name was Saul. He probably was about six years younger than Jesus. He was born of Jewish parents. Young Saul was brought up under the strictest Jewish religious rules. He learned to fast twice a week and to look upon the eating of pork as sin. He never sat down to eat with anyone who was not a Jew. His parents taught him an intense love for the Jews. From the time he was a child, he always put his whole soul into whatever he did. Since Saul had a keen mind, his father sent him to the best Jewish teachers. Saul became one of the best educated and strictest of the Pharisees (strictest party of the Jews).

"When Saul heard about Jesus and His work, he hated Jesus and His followers with his whole heart. To him, Jesus was a false prophet. As a result, Saul did everything he could to destroy Christianity. He was present when Stephen was stoned. Saul was sure that Stephen 'got what was coming to him.'

"This is how Saul, the bitter enemy of Jesus, became Paul, the greatest witness for Jesus that has ever lived.

"He offered to go to Damascus to jail the Christians who lived there. On the road, Jesus came to him in a blinding light and said, *'Saul, Saul, why persecutest thou Me?'*

"Saul answered, *'Who art Thou, Lord?'*

"And then Jesus said, *'I am Jesus whom thou persecutest.'*

31

"The light had struck Saul with blindness. For three days, he was in the greatest misery of soul and mind. He realized the wrong he had done and the terrible sin he had committed in persecuting Christians. Then Jesus sent a believer to Saul with the message that he had been chosen to be a witness for Christ. So Saul was baptized, got back his sight, and became the apostle Paul.

"At first Paul was the leader of the church at Antioch. By the way, it was at Antioch that the name Christian was used for the first time. As Paul had given himself whole-heartedly to persecuting Christians, he now gave himself whole-heartedly to Christ and His service. The church at Antioch must have been fired with some of Paul's desire to serve Christ. It was this church that obeyed Christ's mission command and sent Paul out on his three missionary journeys.

"The enemies of Christ made Paul suffer far more than most Christians, but Christ gave Paul a joy and peace that nothing could take from him. When his back had been beaten into a bloody mass, and he had been locked up in a dark prison, Paul still sang songs of praise and thanksgiving to God. Jesus had saved him who had been a persecutor and a blasphemer and it made Paul so thankful and happy that he gladly gave himself as a witness to give the Gospel of Jesus Christ to those who did not know it. God used Paul to open the West for Christianity. With the help of such men as Luke, Barnabas, and Timothy, Paul organized congregations from Antioch to Rome. He went farther West—some think as far as Great Britain. Finally he was martyred during the persecutions of the cruellest emperor who ever lived—Nero.

"In a vision, John, the last of the apostles, saw Christ coming from victories over His enemies, and going on to further victories. He knew that what Christ had done for His church through persecutions and trials, and through the apostles, Paul, and individual Christians, He would continue to do as long as the world stands. He knew Christ would fulfill His promise: 'Lo, I am with you always.' His visions and his letters to the seven churches are in the last book of the Bible, the Book of Revelation."

BIBLE STUDY

1. Memorize Acts 1:8
2. Find two of Christ's promises—Matt. 28:19, 20; John 14:26
3. Read about the disciples' meetings—Acts 1:12-26
4. Read about Pentecost day—Acts 2:1-14
5. Read Peter's sermon—Acts 2:14-36
6. Read about Paul—Acts 7:55—8:3; 9:1-31; 11:29-30
7. Paul wrote letters called Epistles to his congregations. They are from Book 6 through 18 in the New Testament. Memorize the list
8. Find the following songs that early Christians sang: Isaiah 6:3; Luke 1:46; 1:68; 2:29

Oldest known Madonna
(St. Priscilla Holding Child),
found in catacombs

32

Chapter 2
I-H-S-V Changed Conditions for the Christian Church

YOU have heard that there were persecutions in the Christian Church before 100 A. D. But there were more to come. After the death of John in 98 A. D., the leadership of the church for about 70 years was entrusted to men who had received instruction from the apostles. In other words, just as Jesus had disciples or apostles whom he taught, so his apostles had disciples whom they taught. These disciples of the disciples worked faithfully, teaching and preaching about Christ. Some of these men, like Polycarp and Ignatius, who were disciples of John the apostle, became very old in the service of Christ. But when these men were old, a terrible thing happened. It is something that makes me ashamed of my white race. I have often wondered if the Chinese would have done it."

"Why Dad," exclaimed Dale, "what do the Chinese do better than we do?"

"The Chinese show a respect for old people that puts the whole world to shame.

"But to go on with our story.

SIMEON (13 B. C.-107 A. D.), BISHOP OF JERUSALEM

"Simeon stayed in Jerusalem even after the terrible destruction of the city in 70 A. D. He comforted and taught the people who were left. During the later persecutions, Simeon was tormented for many days, was cruelly scourged, and finally crucified even though he was 120 years old.

33

IGNATIUS (50?-115 A. D.), BISHOP OF ANTIOCH

"Ignatius, who was a staunch defender of the Christian faith and whose writings are still studied, was taken to Rome for execution. On his way he was permitted to visit his congregations at Smyrna. In Rome he was thrown before the lions in the arena and torn to pieces. His death came quickly as he prayed that it might.

POLYCARP (69-155 A. D.), BISHOP OF SMYRNA

"Polycarp had become a Christian when he was just a young boy. He had associated with John and some of the other disciples. Later, he became bishop of Smyrna. He loved to gather young people around him and tell them what he had learned from the apostles who had seen Christ. So dearly was Polycarp loved that when he became old, the members of his congregation tried to outdo each other in providing for his support, and when Christians of Smyrna began to be persecuted, they sent their aged bishop out into the country. When many Christians had been thrown to the beasts, and had been put to death, soldiers were sent to get Polycarp. As Polycarp entered the amphitheatre, a voice, which the excited feelings of the old man led him to regard as from heaven, spoke to him, 'Be strong, O Polycarp, and quit you like a man.' Polycarp was asked to deny Jesus, but he answered: 'Eighty-six years have I served Him, and He has never done me wrong. How then can I deny my King and my Savior?' When his executioners were about to nail him to the stake, Polycarp objected, saying: 'The God in whom I believe will certainly give me strength to stand in the midst of the flames as long as there is life in me.' He then offered a short, beautiful prayer, thanking God that he was soon to be given the martyr's crown. A fire was made under the pile of wood that the hate-filled people had gathered from the workshops in the town. But a high wind drove the flames to one side so they did not touch Polycarp's body. Then an executioner was ordered to kill Polycarp with a sword. So much blood flowed from the wounds that the flames were put out. A fire was again started. Polycarp's body was burned. Polycarp was the last of the disciples of the apostles."

"How awful!" said Dorothy, shuddering. "How long did the persecutions last?"

"There were ten persecutions in all, counting the three during the time of the apostles.

Bible completed by this time

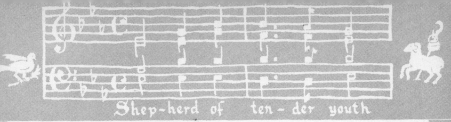

Shep-herd of ten-der youth

JUSTIN MARTYR (100-165 A. D.)

"Because of the cruelty of the persecutions, some of the Christian leaders wrote to the emperors in behalf of the Christians. These writings are called 'Apologies.' The greatest of these writers was Justin Martyr. Later he was asked to sacrifice to heathen gods. When he refused, he was beheaded.

"In spite of all the suffering during the persecutions, Christians were accomplishing things. You can get a picture of how fast Christianity was spreading when you know that in Rome alone, 40 churches were destroyed during one of the persecutions.

"Yes, Christianity was spreading. This made the Christians happy.

CLEMENT OF ALEXANDRIA (150-220 A. D.)

"Their joy expressed itself in hymns. The oldest known hymn was written during the time of persecution in 200 A. D. by Clement. It is called 'Shepherd of Tender Youth.'

"Their joy also showed itself in the way they lived. Because they realized that their lives were very short in comparison to eternity, they put their whole souls into winning others for Christ. As the Holy Spirit helped them to see Jesus, they became more like Jesus. They lived in such a way that people couldn't help but want to be like them. They were kind to their neighbors. If someone did mean things to them, they didn't do mean things in return. They treated women kindly and respectfully. A Christian man did not have more than one wife. Christians loved and cared for their children. When a fellow Christian was persecuted, they tried to give comfort and help. When Christians remained faithful to the end, they rejoiced.

"Finally, however, the physical suffering through persecutions by Jews and by Roman emperors ceased. The way it happened is an interesting story which could be called 'Sky Writing.' It was a different kind of sky writing from what you see today.

CONSTANTINE (274?-337 A. D.)

"One day, Constantine, who was one of the greatest of Roman emperors, was leading an army to an important battle when he saw something in the sky. It was shining and beautiful. It startled Constantine. It would have startled you, too. So Constantine stopped and then he saw the shining

35

THE APOSTLES' CREED

I BELIEVE IN GOD, the Father Almighty, Maker of heaven and earth. ¶And in Jesus Christ, His only Son, our Lord; Who was conceived by the Holy Ghost, Born of the Virgin Mary; Suffered under Pontius Pilate, Was crucified, dead, and buried; He descended into hell; The third day He rose again from the dead; He ascended into heaven, And sitteth on the right hand of God the Father Almighty; From thence He shall come to judge the quick and the dead. ¶I believe in the Holy Ghost; The holy Christian Church, the communion of saints; The forgiveness of sins; The resurrection of the body; And the life everlasting. Amen.

Apostles' Creed—authorship unknown
Time of appearance—1st or 2nd century

light become a blazing cross with the words: 'In Hoc Signo Vinces' around it. What language is that? Why, it's Latin. Constantine understood it because Latin was the language at that time. The Latin words meant, 'In this sign thou shalt conquer.' So now when you see the letters I H S V (don't confuse this with I H S), you know the letters stand for the Latin sentence Constantine saw in the sky.

"That very night, Constantine said, he had a dream in which he was told to put the cross upon his banners. Armies carry flags or banners, you know. Today in many churches you will see the Christian flag which has a red cross on a field of blue like the red cross in the blue sky that Constantine saw.

"Constantine won the battle. Then he became a Christian, at least in name. And then he sent out a decree—this was in 313—that there should be no more persecutions.

"That Constantine, an emperor, made Christianity the religion of his empire harmed the church. It resulted in the state-church. The church received the protection of the emperor, it is true. Christians now had freedom to worship, and security for their lives and property. But the church paid for this protection by submitting to the state's demands. Another result was that it became popular to become a Christian. Therefore, many became Christians but often only in name or for worldly gain.

"Within the large number of so-called Christians, there were those who stayed close to Christ and permitted the Holy Spirit to work through them. These made up the communion of true believers in Christ who were willing to obey Christ, their leader, and had as their banner of faith the Apostles' Creed. Through these believers, Christ worked out His purposes and fulfilled His promise: 'Lo, I am with you always.'"

BIBLE STUDY

1. Memorize Matthew 28:19, 20
2. Look up the following references to persecution: Matt. 5:11, 12; 23:34; Acts 5:41; 22:7; I Cor. 4:12; Phil. 3:6; Hebrews 10:34; Rev. 7:14

Chapter 3
Defenders of the Faith

IF you had lived in 325 A.D., near the highway leading into Nicea, you wouldn't have felt like sleeping. Such exciting things were happening. It was just like a parade. There were bishops galloping along on beautiful horses. These, you would have known, were coming from nearby towns. And yet how differently they dressed. Many bishops, dressed in bright-colored silks, satins, or velvets, came in wagons furnished by Constantine. Some came in large groups, from far away lands—those of brown skin probably from India or Persia, the black-skinned men from Africa, and the fair-skinned men from Great Britain. Many bishops had servants and young companions with them. Quite often, there were men with only one arm, or minus an eye, or with terrible scars. Then people would run to kiss the scars and you would know they were doing this to show honor to men who had endured persecution. Long afterward you would forget what these men looked like, but you would never forget how some of the men's faces glowed and that you had been told it was because they had lived close to Jesus."

"Why were all these bishops coming from such great distances along this highway?" asked Jim.

"Because Emperor Constantine had ordered all the bishops of his empire to a council at Nicea to draw up a creed and to settle the many disputes that were harming the Christians even more than the persecutions had.

"These disputes were between Christians and false prophets who did not let the Holy Spirit guide them in seeing Christ, but thought things out for themselves. Because they were often very brilliant, they fooled many people into believing things that were not true. One question about which there were many arguments was 'Who is Christ?' Some taught that Christ was only a man and not God. There are men who teach false things about Christ even today. Before you are very old, probably someone will tell you, 'Christ was the most perfect man who ever lived, but He wasn't God.' Then you will have to do what the defenders of the faith did at this time. You will have to ask the Holy Spirit to help you, while you study your Bible, to see Jesus clearly.

"Now to go back to Nicea. There were 318 bishops who came to Nicea. They had all their expenses, including traveling expenses, paid by Constantine, while for two months they discussed the various teachings about Christ, studied the Bible, and also the writings of the early Christians. Finally, the discussions, thinking, studying, reading, and praying resulted in a statement of belief called the Nicene Creed. In brief, the Nicene Creed states that Jesus Christ is true God as well as true man.

"Then Constantine invited all at the Council to a banquet. Probably the happiest person at that banquet was the man who had done the most in formulating the Creed. And he was not a bishop. He was just a small, radiant-faced, young attendant of the bishop from Alexandria. Many a bishop who had become shaken in his thinking by the seeming wisdom of the false teachers was strengthened by the clear testimony from God's Word that came from the lips of this young man whose name was Athanasius.

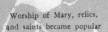

ATHANASIUS (293?-373 A. D.), BISHOP OF ALEXANDRIA

"Athanasius had been well-educated. He was a Bible student. Persecutions, and friendship with Anthony, a hermit, had had a great effect on his character. Soon after the Nicene Council, Athanasius was elected bishop of Alexandria. He won his people by his kindness, faithful work, and courage. Once while he was having services, a band of armed men burst into the church. Athanasius paid no attention. He asked the deacon to read the psalm. The people responded, 'For His mercy endureth forever.' Then with wild shouts, the soldiers rushed forward, but Athanasius made his escape in the crowd. Because of his teaching that Christ was God and man, he was exiled for 20 years out of the 45 years he was bishop. But as soon as anger against him died down, he returned. His people came in crowds to see him. The churches were full of rejoicing. Hardships, exile, and persecution didn't make Athanasius bitter. Once when he was to be exiled, he comforted his weeping parishioners by saying: 'Don't weep. It is just a cloud that will pass away.' There were times when the Nicene Creed was so unpopular with bishops and emperors that Athanasius seemed to stand alone against the world. Whether he stood alone or with the majority made no difference to him. Stormy as his life was, he died peacefully in his own house. To him more than any other, the church owes a debt of gratitude for defending the truth that Christ is God as well as man. Later, about the sixth century, a third Christian creed was formulated and called the Athanasian Creed in honor of Athanasius.

"Now we shall skip about 30 years, and go to two towns where small boys are growing up to become defenders of the faith like Athanasius.

CHRYSOSTOM (347-407 A. D.), BISHOP OF CONSTANTINOPLE

"At Antioch, Chrysostom was born of wealthy parents. Later while bishop of Constantinople, he used to assemble his congregation and march in midnight processions through the city, singing sacred songs. He was such an eloquent preacher that he was called the 'Golden Mouth' of his age. He thundered against the vices of his day,

Come Thou Savior of our race, Choicest gift of heavenly grace!

especially against the wickedness of Eudoxia, the empress. She angrily demanded his arrest, but the people besieged the palace until she told the emperor to recall Chrysostom.

"Later, when the emperor demanded that Chrysostom deny Christ, he stood firm for his faith. The emperor said, 'I will take away your money and property.'

" 'You cannot,' said Chrysostom. 'My treasure is in heaven.'

"The emperor became angry. 'You shall live alone on an island.'

" 'God is my friend. You cannot separate me from Him.'

"And then the emperor shouted, 'I shall take away your life.'

" 'My life is hid with Christ in God. I shall live forever,' quietly replied Chrysostom.

"Soldiers were then ordered to take Chrysostom into exile. They were so cruel that Chrysostom died on the way.

AUGUSTINE OF HIPPO (354-430 A. D.)

"Chrysostom was five years old when at Tagaste, Africa, Augustine was born. He, like Chrysostom, had a pious, praying mother. He also was brilliant. But while young, he began to associate with evil companions and live an impure life. Later, he taught at Milan. His mother, Monica, spoke to the great preacher, Ambrose, about her son. He comforted her, saying, 'It is impossible that the son of so many tears and prayers should perish.' His prediction came true. Augustine was persuaded by his mother to go to hear Ambrose, who succeeded in getting Augustine to study his Bible.

"One day Augustine and a friend were discussing how to find peace for their souls. Augustine was in agony because of his sins, and yet he was unwilling to give them up. During the conversation, Augustine became so affected by the truth about himself, that he burst into tears, left his friend, and went into another part of the garden. There he poured out his soul to God asking for mercy. Suddenly he seemed to hear a voice say, 'Take up and read.' He could see no one. He thought it a voice from heaven. He went back to his friend, took up the New Testament, and let the book open itself. What he read was Romans 13:13, 14. A new light shone into his soul. From that day, Augustine was a Christian.

"He was baptized by Ambrose, who, tradition says, composed the 'Te Deum' (Thee God We Praise) at his baptism. The remaining 43 years of his life, Augustine devoted his talents to service for Christ. He became bishop of Hippo. Luther said of Augustine: 'Next to the Bible, no teacher in the church is to be compared to Augustine.'

40

The Codex Sinaiticus, oldest known manuscript of N. T., was written about 350 A. D.

AMBROSE (340-397 A. D.), BISHOP OF MILAN

"One reason Ambrose was able to win Augustine was because of his hymns. Ambrose is called the Father of Latin hymnody. He recognized the value of church music and introduced congregational singing into his church. He wrote many beautiful hymns. His songs were simple enough to be learned by everyone and became very powerful in winning Christians. Augustine especially loved the hymn by Ambrose called: 'Come, Thou Savior of Our Race.'

"And so again we see that within the large membership of the Christian church, there was a communion of true believers being kept safe from false teaching and remaining true to the teachings of Christ. The instruments Christ used to carry out His promise: 'Lo, I am with you always,' were creeds such as the Apostles' Creed and the Nicene Creed, and defenders of the faith, such as Athanasius, Chrysostom, Ambrose, and Augustine."

BIBLE STUDY

1. Memorize Matthew 7:15
2. Find II Timothy 3:5 and Acts 20:29,30
3. Find a psalm that you think gave Athanasius comfort. Give reason
4. Find a psalm that you think gave Chrysostom comfort. Give reason
5. Find the words that Augustine read

THE NICENE CREED

I BELIEVE IN ONE GOD, the Father Almighty, Maker of heaven and earth, And of all things visible and invisible. ¶And in one Lord Jesus Christ, the only-begotten Son of God, Begotten of His Father before all worlds, God of God, Light of Light, Very God of Very God, Begotten, not made, Being of one substance with the Father; By whom all things were made; Who for us men, and for our salvation, came down from heaven, And was incarnate by the Holy Ghost of the Virgin Mary, And was made man; And was crucified also for us ,under Pontius Pilate. He suffered and was buried; And the third day He rose again, according to the Scriptures; And ascended into heaven, And sitteth on the right hand of the Father; and He shall come again with glory to judge both the quick and the dead; Whose kingdom shall have no end. ¶And I believe in the Holy Ghost, The Lord and Giver of life, Who proceedeth from the Father and the Son, Who with the Father and the Son together is worshipped and glorified, Who spake by the Prophets. And I believe in one holy Christian and Apostolic Church. I acknowledge one Baptism for the remission of sins; And I look for the Resurrection of the dead; And the Life of the world to come. Amen.

Nicene Creed—325 A. D.

Council of Carthage accepted 27 books of New Testament as inspired in 387, A. D.

Chapter 4

Some of My First Missionaries

DO you remember, Dorothy, when Dale and his playmates came in just as your cake started to bake? 'Mm! Smells good! What is it?' Dale asked as he went over to the oven to peek. Just then someone called outside. Bang, slammed the oven door. Out rushed the boys.

"The cake was a miserable failure. But when mother came home she said, 'Never mind. We shall make it good for something, anyway.'

"Something like that happened long ago. Athanasius' friend, Anthony, lived alone in the desert, in order to get away from the wickedness of the world. Others followed his example. Then monasteries were built. Soon monasteries spread to Asia and Europe.

"Now Christ had never intended that people should become hermits to lead holy lives. He wants people to live as the early Christians did and win others for Christ. Many monasteries were miserable failures and many monks fell into great sins. Still Christ carried out His promise: 'Lo, I am with you always,' by making the monasteries good for something anyway.

"Some of the monks became well educated. They studied, copied, and preserved the Bible and early church writings. It was in a monastery that the oldest manuscript of the New Testament was found. Many monks kept diaries that give us the history of those times. Often monks taught others, helped the poor, and used their monasteries for hospitals. Also some of the greatest early missionaries were monks who felt such a strong love for Christ that they were drawn out of the monasteries to give the Gospel to the heathen.

"Tonight, we are going to take an imaginary trip to see a few of these early missionaries. First we shall go to Ireland. There we see a weary, old monk resting by a stream.

PATRICK (378-461 A. D.), APOSTLE TO IRELAND

"'Why did you become a missionary to Ireland?' asks a young companion.

"'That's a long story,' replies the older. 'At the age of fifteen, I was grabbed by a pirate, and sold as a slave in Ireland. For six years I remained in hard slavery, tending cattle. Finally, protected by cliffs, I made my escape. I reached my father's house. I told him (he was a wealthy nobleman and a deacon in the church) that I wished to return to Ireland to preach the Gospel to those among whom I had been a slave. After studying in the monasteries of Gaul, I returned, in 440, to Ireland.'

"'And now, in 20 years, you have founded monasteries all over Ireland.'

"'Yes, but it was slow work at first. The heathen were hard to win.'

"'Why did you have bells made for all the monasteries?'

"'It was an easy way to call people to services. Bells always had a fascination for me. During persecutions, there were no bells to call people to worship. When the people no longer had to meet secretly, hand bells were used. Do you know when the first church bell was used? In 400, Paulinus, the bishop of Nola, Italy, thought of the plan of putting a large bell on the church roof to call people to services. It was much easier than having bell ringers run up and down streets. Because bells give me encouragement, I always announce my coming by ringing a bell that I carry with me.'

"Now we shall leave St. Patrick, the Apostle to Ireland. We shall cross the water from the east coast of Ireland and stop southwest of Scotland at a little island called Iona.

COLUMBA (521-597 A. D.), APOSTLE TO SCOTLAND

"There we see Columba, who left a home in which he had many advantages, since his parents were of royal blood, to found, with the help of twelve disciples, a monastery. Because of his enthusiastic leadership, the Gospel of Christ was given to the tribes in Scotland, in Northern England, and in Wales. His monastery at Iona became the mother monastery of many others, the greatest center of Christian learning for 200 years, and received the name 'Nursery of Saints.'

"Next we'll skip 137 years and go to England.

43

COLUMBA
378-961
A.D.

PATRICK
A.D. 378-461

AUGUSTINE
607

BONIFACE 652-755
A.D.

ST. ANSGAR
801-865 A.D.

AMBROSE
340-397
A.D.

ROME

In 400, Paulinus,
bishop of Nola, Italy,
placed a bell on the church roof.

AUGUSTINE OF H
354-43

Today from many a church tower
bells call the people to worship

Bells were used in connection with church services as long ago as the time of King David

After persecutions ceased, hand bells were used to call people to services

Soon bell towers were built—600 A. D.

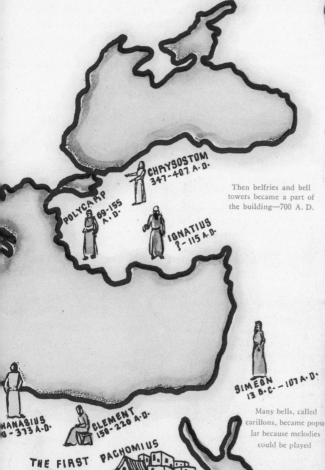

CHRYSOSTOM
347-407 A. D.

POLYCARP
69-155 A. D.

IGNATIUS
? - 115 A. D.

SIMEON
13 B. C. — 107 A. D.

Then belfries and bell towers became a part of the building—700 A. D.

ATHANASIUS
0 - 373 A. D.

CLEMENT
150-220 A. D.

THE FIRST MONASTERY 335 A. D.

PACHOMIUS

Many bells, called carillons, became popular because melodies could be played

Monastery   Monk preaching   Round church

AUGUSTINE, FIRST ARCHBISHOP OF CANTERBURY

(Arrived in England in 607)

"We arrive to hear bells ringing in celebration of the baptism of the King of Kent by Augustine (a different Augustine from the one in your last story). How happy the king's Christian wife looks. How thankful Augustine is, for now he knows England is open to Christianity.

"There is a story back of this baptism.

"One day, Gregory, a priest, went into the Roman market place and saw three boys being sold as slaves. 'Who are they?' he asked.

" 'They are Angles.'

" 'They should be called angels, not Angles,' said Gregory. 'Their fair skin, blue eyes, and golden hair are beautiful.'

"After that, Gregory wanted to go to England to tell the Angles about Jesus. But the pope would not give permission. It looked as though God had closed the way for Christianizing England. Later Gregory saw that God's way is best. Gregory became pope. Then he sent Augustine with 40 missionaries to England. How much better that was than one man. Augustine became the first bishop of Canterbury and began building the Canterbury Cathedral.

"Germany next! A hundred years later!

BONIFACE (680?-755 A. D.), APOSTLE TO THE GERMANS

"There we see Boniface kneeling. 'These heathen with their many gods are so slow to win. Even the oak tree is sacred to them. Help me to win them,' he prayed.

"God gave him an idea. He hurried to ring the bell, which called people to services. A large group gathered. Boniface said, 'My God would like us to have a suitable place in which to worship Him. If He protects me against your gods as I cut down your sacred oak tree, will you help me build a church?'

" 'Yes,' answered the people.

"Breathlessly they watched Boniface raise his axe. Chips flew. Nothing happened to Boniface. 'But wait till he reaches the spirit,' they thought.

"Down went the tree, and there stood Boniface.

46

Octagonal building

By 6th century, the Athanasian Creed was in use
Exact date unknown
Author unknown

Monks teaching

"Then startling things happened. The fallen oak furnished material for a Christian church. Within a year, the people of that region had accepted Christianity, at least in name. Then this 'Apostle to the Germans' went farther into Germany, organizing schools, churches, and monasteries, until a band of heathen killed him. He died with a Bible in his hands.

"Now on to Denmark! A hundred years later!"

ANSGAR (801-865 A. D.), APOSTLE TO THE NORTH

"The first bell is ringing in this North country. We see St. Ansgar, the Apostle to the North, with tears of joy in his eyes.

" 'Why are you so happy?' we ask.

" 'Because the sound takes me back many years to peaceful Corwey. The bells of eve-ning were sounding across the valley. A little procession of monks, led by the oldest, was forming in the courtyard. I was the last in line. As we moved slowly to the chapel, I wished there were some way to serve Christ besides this monotonous life. All the while, my feet moved to the soft chant. I went in and knelt with the rest.

" 'After services, the old priest raised his hands and said: "Listen, broth-ers. News has come that the Christian king of Denmark wishes someone to go with him to give the Gospel to his people."

" 'We monks shivered and huddled together. We knew that King Harold had fled from his country to save his life. At Corwey, life was easy. Too easy, I thought, as I jumped to my feet and said: "Send me."

" ' "Do you know the dangers? Remember they are savages. You are so young," the old priest began.

" ' "I am not afraid," I begged.

" 'Here in Denmark, I began to preach right away. I saw need around me everywhere. So one day when I saw some slaves being sold, I bought twelve bright-looking boys, and began to teach them. Before many years, they were ready to go out to teach. They made fine missionaries.

" 'Four times I was driven out of Denmark. But as soon as I could, I went back. The ringing of this bell today makes me grateful that I was able to leave Corwey and work in this land. Strange, is it not, that bells have seemed to move with Christianity into heathen lands the world over? More than any other instrument, bells seem to belong with churches.' "

BIBLE STUDY

1. Memorize Isaiah 6:8
2. Find the following mission verses: Romans 1:16; Acts 11:18; John 1:12; I Cor. 3:11; Mark 16:15; Matt. 9:37, 38

St. Peter's Cathedral

Gregory the great—last bishop and first pope (590-604)

Gregorian Chant

Organs were used at given dates

Chapter 5

The Christian Church Is Threatened

T HIS story will be about three different kinds of storms that threatened the church at this time," said Dr. Lansing.

"The first was like a storm at sea with one wave after another dashing against the shore. Soon after the year 400, tribes of heathen people began moving into civilized lands. Several tribes of Goths pushed down into Italy. Then followed the Lombards, and then the Huns.

"Strange names, aren't they? But they were strange, ignorant, wild tribes that loved to fight more than anything else.

"The same thing happened in Gaul. Vandals swept over Gaul and Spain and down into Africa, destroying everything as they went. That is why, if you tear your books, or scratch your name on buildings or furniture, you, too, are a Vandal. Then the Franks, the strongest tribe in Europe, conquered Gaul. From them, Gaul got the name France.

"Then, from Africa, came the Vandals, who conquered Rome in 476. As a result, the western half of the Roman empire broke into pieces, each ruled over by a different tribe. Only the eastern part, of which Constantinople was the capital, went on for nearly a thousand years more, until—. You'll have to wait for that story.

"People speak of the date 476 as the end of Ancient History, and the time from 476 to 1000 as the Dark Ages, because during those 500 years, the wild heathen tribes that were unable to read or write ruled over those who had once been educated Christian rulers.

48

"It seemed as though the heathen tribes were going to completely destroy the church. But the church still stood. No matter how many tribes of heathens conquered the Christians, there were some Christians who remained true to Christ, and He used them to fulfill His promise. It was because of these Christians that the first thing that the heathen tribes learned was not reading and writing, but the Christian religion.

ULFILAS (311-383 A. D.), APOSTLE TO THE GOTHS

"The Goths were conquered by the Christianity of the Romans that they conquered. When Ulfilas became a Christian, he invented a Gothic alphabet and translated the Bible into Gothic. Therefore, he is called the 'Apostle to the Goths.'

CLOVIS (465-511 A. D.) AND CLOTILDA, THE CHRISTIAN RULERS OF THE FRANKS

"In France, Christianity won its place through Clovis, king of the Franks. His wife, Clotilda, became a Christian. Clovis was just then going to war. To please his wife, he promised her that if he won the battle, he would become a Christian, too. He was victorious. He kept his word. With about 3,000 of his soldiers, he was baptized.

"You have already heard how England, Ireland, Scotland, Germany, and Denmark became Christian. There are interesting stories about the Christianizing of many more countries. I'll just briefly mention two a little later in this story. There were other things that happened first.

FIVE CENTERS OF CHRISTIANITY

Bell towers become a part
of church architecture

Mohammedan mosques, Northern Romanesque and Spanish
Romanesque were new styles in church architecture

Mohammedan mosque

Renaissance ornament

"Even before the many dashing waves of this first storm subsided, another storm started. It was like a wind storm sweeping along at a terrific speed.

"It started with one man, an Arabian camel driver. He lived in Mecca, in far-off Arabia. His name was Mohammed. One day  he told his wife about a vision he had had of a new religion he should start. Ten years later, in 632, Mohammed died. But his new religion didn't stop. His wife's father became the leader, and went out to conquer the world. 'Money, or your life, or be a Mohammedan,' these Arabian conquerors said.

"Jerusalem, Alexandria, and Antioch fell. Twice they tried to conquer Constantinople, but were driven back by red hot tar and burning oil that was poured from the walls.

"Then they tried the opposite direction. They conquered the northern coast of Africa, took boats across the sea, conquered Spain and marched into France. It really seemed that they would conquer the world.

"But, finally, they were stopped at Tours by a Frenchman whose name was Charles the Hammer, because he could strike such terrific blows. This was in 732, just 100 years after Mohammed's death. And yet in those 100 years, Mohammedanism won so many followers that even now 250,000,000 people—that is 11% of all the people in the world—are Mohammedans. We can be thankful that in spite of Mohammedanism, the Christian church still stood with the strong light of true Christians within it.

Rome and Constantinople only two centers of Christianity left

EUROPE

MOHAMMEDAN DOMINIONS - 732 A.D.

ASIA

CHARLEMAGNE (742-814 A. D.)

"Soon after this last storm, came some bright, sunny days. In 800, Charlemagne, the king of France and grandson of Charles the Hammer, was so powerful that he conquered many countries. Because he helped Italy conquer some troublesome tribes, the pope crowned him as emperor of the whole Roman empire. Charlemagne wanted all the people in his empire to be Christian and be educated. He gathered his family together for family devotion. One of the books he liked best for devotion was the 'City of God' written by Augustine, bishop of Hippo. After Charlemagne died, there was no one strong enough to hold the Roman empire together, so once again it broke into pieces.

"Then because it had been light for awhile, it seemed darker than ever. If it's dark in a room, you get used to it. But if you turn on a light and then turn it off, the room seems darker, doesn't it?

"However even in these dark years, a ray of light appeared whenever a heathen tribe became Christian. I said I would tell you about two other groups of people who became Christian. Now we have come to the time in history where these stories fit in.

VLADIMIR THE GREAT (956-1015 A. D.)

"Russia became Christian in 988 during the reign of Vladimir the Great. When he was baptized, he ordered that all idols should be destroyed, and that the large image of the favorite Russian god should be tied to a horse's tail, dragged through the streets, broken with clubs, and thrown into the river. Then while thousands of his people were baptized in the river, he knelt on the bank, thanking God that his country was becoming Christian.

Battle of Stiklestad

SAINT OLAV (995-1030 A. D.)

"Early one morning in Norway, the heathen farmers of Gudbrandsdal stood with bowed heads as a huge image of Thor, beaming with gold and silver, was carried before them. Then King Olav said, 'Your god is both blind and deaf. He can save neither himself nor others. He can go nowhere unless carried. Look toward the east. There is our God, moving with great light.' As the farmers looked to the east, one of the king's men struck the god so that it broke. Out of it ran rats, lizards and snakes. The farmers were very frightened. Then Gudbrand said, 'Since our god could not protect himself and therefore cannot help us, we are willing to believe in your God.' All of them accepted Christianity, at least in name, and were baptized.

"In 1030, King Olav spent another night in prayer. Then the war trumpets sounded. King Olav's men shouted, 'Forward, Forward, Christmen, Cross-men, King's-men!' and advanced toward the enemy to begin the most notable battle of Norwegian history. King Olav was killed in this battle of Stiklestad. After his death, he was called St. Olav and all his people united to make Norway a Christian land because they knew that was what King Olav had tried so hard to accomplish.

"Ever since Constantine's mother went to Palestine, it has been popular for Christians to travel there. In 1000 A. D., Jerusalem belonged to the Mohammedan Turks. They didn't like to have Christians coming to see Christ's  tomb. Some of the returning Christians told frightful stories about the way the Turks treated them.

52

"So another storm started in 1095. It was like a thunder and lightning storm. The Turks thundered while for almost 200 years the Christians formed crusades to flash like lightning against them. Thousands of Christians joined the eight crusades and were called crusaders (crossbearers). They got this name because they sewed red cloth in the form of a cross on their coats as a sign that they were soldiers of the cross.

RICHARD THE LION-HEARTED (1157-1199 A. D.)

"Probably the most famous of all the crusaders was Richard the Lion-Hearted of England. He was one of the leaders of the Third Crusade. He was hard on wrongdoers but fair and square. So people loved him. Even his enemies admired him. Saladin, who was the Mohammedan King of Jerusalem at the time of the Third Crusade, even though he was attacked by Richard, admired him and became his friend. Then Saladin, instead of fighting Richard, made a friendly agreement with him to treat Christ's tomb and Christians who came to Jerusalem properly. So Richard went home to England again.

"But the agreement between Richard and Saladin didn't last. Five more crusades were formed. But the crusaders did not succeed in driving the Turks out of Palestine. They almost drained the life-blood out of the church. Still the church stood. Still Christ fulfilled His promise by making the crusades good for something. For the crusades were like schools. They revived interest in languages and other studies. This revival of learning Christ used to make the lives of true Christians shine still more brightly as you will see in the next story."

BIBLE STUDY

1. Memorize Matt. 5:16
2. Look up the following about false prophets: II Tim. 3:5; Matt 7:15; Acts 20:29, 30
3. Look up the following and tell how they fit the lesson: John 1:12; Mark 16:15; Matt. 9:37, 38

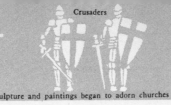

Sculpture and paintings began to adorn churches

Chapter 6

Preparations for a Church Reformation

"BOOM! Boom! Boom! sounded the cannon," said Dr. Lansing. Sleepy Dale sat up wide awake. "Boom! Boom!" continued Dr. Lansing. "And down went the walls of Constantinople. Because of the invention of gunpowder, the Mohammedan Turks, in 1453, at last conquered Constantinople, a thousand years after the fall of Rome.

"Out on the seas, there was a lapping, churning, and breaking of water against the sides of many ships. Explorers needed no longer fear if clouds hid the stars or sun. A magnetic needle had been invented. In all weather, the compass could be a guide.

"In Germany, a printer exclaimed, 'At last, I've invented a printing press. I shall print the most important book first of all.' That's how the Latin Bible came to be the first book printed.

"But not powder, the compass, nor the press was the people's chief interest. Their chief interest during and after the crusades was their church. That is why at this time, there were more beautiful cathedrals built than at any time before or since."

"What is a cathedral, Dad?" interrupted Dale.

"It is a large church in charge of a bishop and gets its name from the bishop's special chair called a 'cathedra.' The people spent much money and time in building cathedrals which were often more splendid than palaces of kings. The Cathedral of Cologne was started in 1248 and it took 632 years to complete it.

"Many cathedrals were built in a new style, called Gothic—not because the Goths had anything to do with them, however. Ever since the wild tribes of Goths conquered Italy, people called everything wild by the name Gothic. People thought the new Gothic churches with their pointed, arched roofs wouldn't stand—that they were wild. But they did stand. They were beautiful. They were always built in the shape of a cross with the altar to the east because that is the direction of Jerusalem. They had doors and

54

windows with pointed tops, like hands placed together in prayer. They had high steeples, like fingers pointing to heaven.

"Inside the cathedrals was art work done by great artists such as Raphael who painted so many madonnas, Da Vinci who painted 'The Last Supper,' and Michelangelo who spent four years painting the ceiling of the Sistine Chapel. These artists painted Bible pictures and so made the Bible clearer. Their religious art therefore pointed people's thoughts heavenward.

"Inventions that performed miracles, Gothic cathedrals and great religious art that pointed heavenward,—these seemed to be preparing the world for a change. And they were. Something was just about ready to happen. But that comes in the next story.

"First there had to be still more pointing heavenward.

"The lives of most of the members of the church, and even of popes and priests, were scandalously immoral at this time. And yet, there were still those who longed for peace with God, found it in a life of devotion to Christ, and stood out above the rest like fingers pointing to heaven. Through them, Christ fulfilled His promise: 'Lo, I am with you always.'

BERNARD OF CLAIRVAUX (1091-1153)

"In France, a finger pointed heavenward in the life of Bernard. He started a monastery in a wild region that was the haunt of robbers. He called it Clairvaux, or Beautiful Valley. He thought it was a loss of time to sleep, and never ate more than barely enough to keep him alive. So he looked like a living skeleton. He had such great influence over people that when he became a monk, his uncle and four of his five brothers went with him. He was the most famous hymn writer of his age. His 'O Sacred Head Now Wounded' is the greatest of Good Friday hymns. He also wrote 'Jesus, the Very Thought is Sweet,' 'O Jesus, King Most Wonderful,' 'O What Precious Balm and Healing,' and 'Jesus, Thou Joy of Living Hearts.' When he preached in favor of the second crusade, whole cities joined. When the crusade failed, Bernard was blamed. His sorrow over the failure hastened his death. Luther said, 'If ever there was a pious monk, it was St. Bernard.'

55

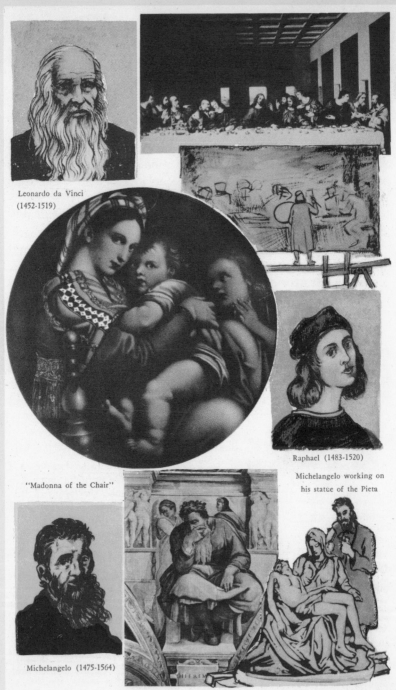

Leonardo da Vinci
(1452-1519)

"Madonna of the Chair"

Raphael (1483-1520)

Michelangelo working on
his statue of the Pieta

Michelangelo (1475-1564)

"Jeremiah" in Sistine Chapel of Vatican

Rheims Cathedral (France)

Compass

Gunpowder destroys
walls of Constantinople

Cologne Cathedral (Germany)

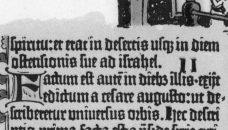

spiritu: et erat in deſertis uſqȝ in diem
oſtenſionis ſue ad iſrahel. II
Factum eſt autē in diebȝ illis·exiſt
ēdictum a ceſare auguſto:ut de-
ſcriberetur uniuerſus orbis. Hec deſcri
ptio prima facta eſt a pſide ſyrie cyri
no. et ibāt omnes ut pfiterenᵗ:ſinguli

Section from Gutenberg Bible

Gutenberg in his press room

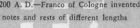

FRANCIS OF ASSISI (1182-1226)

"Nearly one hundred years later, in a monastery courtyard in Assisi, Italy, a young, barefoot monk dressed in a coarse, brown gown, called the birds by name as he fed them crumbs. He looked so boyish, kind and gentle that you would hardly have thought he was like a finger pointing high to heaven. But he was. His simple life of poverty and his preaching won many followers. Because Francis was so passionately fond of all living things and spoke to the birds, the sheep, bees, and rabbits as his brothers and sisters, he is called the sweetest character of the Middle Ages.

JOHN WYCLIFF (1320-1384)

"Nearly 150 years later, a finger again pointed heavenward, this time in England. Wycliff was an educated, fearless preacher. He loved and studied the Bible. He said: 'To be ignorant of the Bible is to be ignorant of Christ,' and 'The Bible must decide all questions of faith and morals.' He preached against the sins of his time. He realized that the common people needed to be taught. So he did two things for them. He translated the Bible into English, and he organized some college graduates into traveling preachers who went all over England, speaking to the people in their own language and trying to turn them from wicked living. Because of what he did for the English people, Wycliff is called the 'Morning Star of the Reformation.'

JOHN HUSS (1369-1415)

"Ten years before Wycliff died, a boy was born in Bohemia, who was to become Wycliff's greatest disciple. John Huss became a preacher at Prague, established a school for singers, and also taught at the university. The moral conditions in Prague were very low. In the midst of this sunken community, Huss preached against the immorality of the clergy, against indulgences, and pilgrimages. He was like a finger pointing heavenward. But because of his preaching, the emperor summoned him to appear before a council, and promised him safe conduct.

"However, when Huss arrived, the emperor went back on his word. Huss was thrown into a monastery cell filled with poisonous sewer odors. Later he was taken out of the cell and led to the stake. He was asked to recant, but he replied: 'God is my witness that the great purpose of my preaching and writing was to convert men from sin. In the truth of that Gospel which I hitherto have written, taught, and preached, I now joyfully die.' He clasped his hands and prayed until he was stifled in the smoke. His ashes and the soil on which they lay were removed and thrown into the Rhine. A year later, his disciple, Jerome of Prague, was also burned.

THOMAS A KEMPIS (1380-1471)

"When Huss was seven years old, Thomas á Kempis was born in Germany. He liked books and became a monk in a monastery that was so poor that he had to earn a living by copying manuscripts. He spent so much time writing that he became stoop-shouldered and so bent that when the other monks bent over in prayer, he could stand. He had soft brown eyes and a shy manner. It was this shy man who wrote several hymns, one of which is 'Light's Abode, Celestial Salem,' and also a book called the 'Imitation of Christ.' This book is one of the sweetest, tenderest devotion books in Christian literature, has been translated into many languages, and has pointed many lives heavenward.

GIROLAMO SAVONAROLA (1452-1498)

"Before Thomas á Kempis died, most of the Florentines were listening to a monk with a stern, gaunt face, a bold, hooked nose, and piercing black eyes, who denounced in flaming words the evil practices into which the people had fallen. The audience listened wide-eyed, month after month, until there resulted a spiritual and moral revival of that pleasure-loving city. Savonarola also wrote hymns, one of which is 'Jesus, Refuge of the Weary.' For five years, Savonarola, the monk, was ruler of Florence. Finally the people turned against him. He and two followers were hanged on the gallows and then burned.

"God used these men to point the thoughts of people heavenward, to keep alive their faith in Christ, and to prepare their hearts for the light of the Gospel that again was to be given a chance to shine because of the Reformation."

BIBLE STUDY

1. Memorize Matthew 5:6
2. How do the following apply to your lesson: Rev. 2:10; II Tim. 4:18; Matt. 5:16; Psalms 109:5
3. Find one reference to "Jerusalem the Golden" in Revelation
4. Find a reference to Bernard of Clairvaux' Good Friday hymn in Isaiah 53:3-5

59

The Wartburg Castle

Chapter 7
Why My Church Is Called the Lutheran Church

IN Germany, in 1483, a day-old baby had been baptized and given the name, Martin. Upon beginning school he showed a brilliant mind. But no one paid any attention. Everyone was too busy talking about Columbus.

"One day at the University of Erfurt, as Luther was searching through the different books, he came upon a large, old volume—a Latin Bible. It was the first time he had seen a Bible. No one paid attention to him as he sat down to read. No one noticed how delighted he was with the Bible. No one realized that the desire that came to Luther that day to own such a Bible, that he might read through and through, would one day lead him to translate the Bible so that the German people could have the Bible in their own language.

"In 1508, no one paid attention to a pale and emaciated monk of 25 years who walked into Wittenberg over the wooden bridge that crossed the Elbe. They were too busy talking about Tetzel, an indulgence-seller.

"Tetzel, dressed in gorgeous robes, entered a city amid the beating of drums, the blaze of torches, and the peal of bells.

Luther discovering Bible

A long procession followed him. Setting up a great red cross, and putting down beside it a huge money box, Tetzel pictured purgatory and hell. Men cried for mercy. Women screamed. 'Indulgences,' he would say, 'are God's precious gifts. When your money rattles in the chest, your sins are forgiven. Pay for the sins of loved ones who are dead, and they will escape from purgatory to heaven.'

Wittenberg

"And the poor people bought. They didn't know better. Women took off their jewelry to give to Tetzel. Tetzel had secretaries in purple robes make out receipts that were printed in red and gold and had a ribbon and the big seal of the pope attached. These receipts were called indulgences. They were supposed to give full pardon for all sins.

Luther's Seal

Tetzel

61

"Now Luther, who had gone through deep soul struggles, knew that God's forgiveness could not be purchased for money. He preached against indulgences. When Tetzel came near Wittenberg, Luther could stand it no longer. On October 31, 1517, he nailed 95 Theses (statements) to the church door. One of the Theses was: 'Pardon for sin is from Christ and is free.'

"Tetzel raged and cursed. The pope paid no attention. He thought it was just a quarrel between the monks and said: 'To tell the truth, a pretty good head rests on Brother Martin's broad shoulders.'

"The small blaze started by the nailing of the Theses spread to light up Germany and then all of Christendom. Then the pope began to take notice. He sent out a decree that Luther's writings should be burned and that Luther was an outlaw unless he would recant (take back what he had said). As a result, all over Christendom there were bonfires of Luther's books.

"At Wittenberg there was another kind of bonfire. At the head of a procession of students and professors, Luther passed out of the university gates and went on to the market square. There a professor lit the fire. Then Luther put into the flames the paper in which the pope condemned him. By this act, Luther, who had been outlawed from the church, showed that he rejected the authority of the pope in all matters of Christian faith.

"Then the emperor Charles V arranged a Diet (meeting) at Worms. From every part of Germany came nobles and princes. A representative of the pope spoke to the Diet for three hours demanding that Luther be burned without a hearing. However, the emperor summoned Luther to the Diet and promised him safe conduct. Remembering what had happened to Huss, Luther's friends were worried. But Luther said, 'Though there should be as many devils in Worms as there are tiles on the roofs, I would go.'

"After 14 days of travel, Luther reached Worms. The watchman on the cathedral tower blew his horn to announce Luther's arrival. Then it seemed as if all the townsfolk rushed to see Luther.

"The next afternoon a herald was sent to get Luther. The crowds were so thick in the main streets that he went through the gardens from house to house and so gained the place of the Diet. Luther was asked to recant what he had written. He asked for time to prepare his answer.

"After a night of prayer, he appeared before the Diet again, and gave his courageous answer concluding with these words: 'Unless I am convinced, by Scripture or by right reason, for I trust neither in popes nor in councils since they have often erred and contradicted themselves—unless I am thus convinced, I am bound by the texts of the Bible. My conscience is captive to the Word of God. I neither can nor will recant anything, since it is neither right nor safe to act against conscience. God help me. Amen.'

"The next morning, Luther, with a few friends, left Worms. Suddenly in a narrow forest road, his carriage was stopped by horsemen wearing masks and carrying weapons. Luther was seized, placed on a horse, and hurried away at break-neck speed to the Wartburg Castle. He had been seized by friends who were going to keep him in hiding.

"It was while he was at the Wartburg that he translated the New Testament from Greek into German. In less than a year, at the risk of his life, he returned to Wittenberg to preach against those who began to misuse the liberty brought by the Reformation. Later he wrote his hymns, the Catechism, and translated the Old Testament from Hebrew to German.

"After the Diet of Worms, the emperor planned to get rid of Luther and his followers. But Christ was fulfilling His promise: 'Lo, I am with you always.' For all at once, the emperor became so busy in other parts of his kingdom that he did not return to Germany for nine years.

"During those nine years, the blaze, started at Wittenberg by Luther, had spread, blazing higher and higher to bring on the great light of day which is called the Modern Age. It was too late to stop the fire now. But Charles didn't know that. So he ordered Luther's followers to attend the Diet of Augsburg to give an account of their faith. Since Luther had been declared an outlaw, he was taken secretly to a castle where he was safe from enemies and yet near enough to consult.

"Melanchthon prepared the articles of faith based on articles written by Luther. When Luther read the articles, he fully approved of them.

"The arrival of Charles in Augsburg was spectacular and colorful with a parade of kings, princes, and ambassadors. On June 25, 1530, they met at the palace of the bishop. The room was filled to capacity. Many even stood outside the windows. All were eager to hear the Confession of the Lutherans. (A name given to Luther's followers.)

"There were impressive opening services. Then Dr. Beyer, a man with a penetrating voice, read slowly and loudly, in German, the articles of the Confession. He was heard plainly by the crowds outside.

"The reading of the Augsburg Confession caused different reactions. Some gloried in the light caused by this Lutheran group, and joined their ranks. Some were sorry or angry that they had paid no attention to the blaze until it was too late to put it out.

"With the close of the Diet of Augsburg, Lutherans, like the first Christians, had the Bible in their own language, and a banner of faith which included the Apostle's Creed, the Nicene Creed, the Athanasian Creed, Luther's Catechism, and the Augsburg Confession.

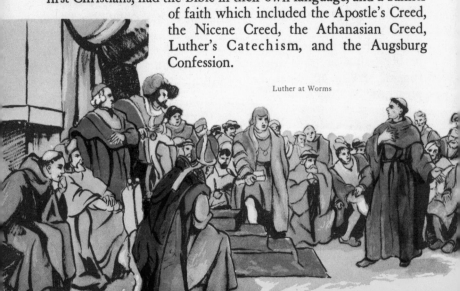

Luther at Worms

Reading the Augsburg Confession

"With the Bible and their Banner of Faith, Lutherans felt able to withstand the Catholics who, after the Diet of Augsburg, threatened them with open warfare. The Lutheran princes in 1531 formed a Schmalkald League for defensive purposes. The League was so strong that in 1532, the emperor granted freedom of worship to Lutherans. This religious peace actually lasted until 1546. During this time, Lutheranism spread to other countries.

"Luther died in 1546, while he was at Eisleben settling a dispute between two counts. As Luther's body was taken back to Wittenberg, bells were rung in every town. Common people and nobility, rich and poor, gathered to meet the funeral procession. Luther's body was buried in a grave beneath the floor at the foot of the pulpit of the Cathedral Church after a very impressive funeral service at which both Bugenhagen and Melanchthon preached."

BIBLE STUDY

1. Memorize Joshua 1:9
2. Find and read Psalm 46. This Psalm was the inspiration for Luther's "A Mighty Fortress"
3. Memorize Rom. 3:28, which made Luther realize he couldn't be saved by good works
4. Look up following references to faith: Luke 7:50; Eph. 6:16; I Tim. 6:12; Rom. 3:28, 5:1; Gal. 2:16

Chapter 8

The Singing Church

I N your last story, you heard that many were joining the ranks of the Lutherans. Do you know why? Do you know what made Luther begin writing hymns, and when he wrote his first hymn?"

Dr. Lansing's eyes twinkled as his family watched him.

"Now I'm going to answer all these questions as well as some more that I'll ask you later, by means of a story.

"The story takes place in Wittenberg during a June morning of 1531. There are three characters: Margaret, her older brother Carl, and her mother. And here's the story:

"Margaret was bubbling over with a secret. It was to be a surprise for Carl who had just returned from several years of schooling at Hanover. But it was so hard to keep this secret that Margaret clapped her hands tightly over her mouth and ran to join some friends who also were on their way to church.

"Later when Margaret was seated next to Carl in the church, she drew out of her skirt pocket a hymn book and glanced at Carl to see if he looked surprised. But he evidently hadn't noticed.

"The services began. Margaret and her mother joined in the opening hymn. To their astonishment, Carl, too, sang as well as they.

"'Oh, Carl,' said disappointed Margaret, after the services. 'We thought it would be a big surprise for you today that our congregation had begun to sing at services. And instead, you surprised us. We had a secret, and you had a secret. How funny!'

"Margaret laughed and was going to join her friends, when her mother's question made her decide she'd rather stay to listen.

"'But, Carl,' Mother was saying, 'how does it happen you have a hymn book, too, when you've been so far away?'

"'These hymn books, Mother, have already spread all over Germany and into many parts of the world. It wasn't preachers that introduced Lutheranism into Hanover. It wasn't the German Bible or religious tracts. It was Luther's hymn book which introduced congregational singing again and made us feel we were taking an active part in the services. No longer did we just sit through a service and have Gregorian chants sung by a trained choir. Congregational singing made our church warm with a new life and power. How we loved to sing! But it isn't only in Wittenberg and Hanover that there are singing churches. Everywhere Lutheranism is singing itself into the hearts of the people. Therefore the Lutheran church is being called the "Singing Church." And Luther's hymn, "A Mighty Fortress," is called the "Battle Hymn of Protestantism" or "Luther in Song" because it is full of his courage and faith.

" 'Have you heard how Luther began writing hymns?' Carl continued. 'No? Melanchthon said last night that Luther, who has always loved music, had often expressed the wish that someone would write Christian songs of such spiritual value that they could be used during church worship. And then something happened that opened the gift of song writing in Luther's own soul.

" 'In Antwerp in 1523, a prior of a monastery was choked to death in his prison cell. Two youths of the same monastery were burned to death. News came to Luther that before the smoke smothered their voices, both had sung in praise of God.

" 'This news fanned into a flame the poetic spark in Luther's soul. Immediately, he sat down and wrote a festival hymn commemorating the death of these first Lutheran martyrs.

" 'In 1524, the first Lutheran hymn book was published, containing 8 hymns, 4 of which were by Luther. I was happy when Melanchthon gave me a copy last night. That same year, a larger hymn book was published containing 25 hymns, 18 of which were Luther's. These hymn books spread as though angels were the carriers. I treasure mine highly.'

" 'I treasure mine, too,' added Mother, 'because I received it from Katherine Luther one evening after I had spent a day helping her with guests. It makes me think of the many times I have seen Conrad Rupf and Johann Walther sitting at the table, busily writing music that Luther composed as he paced the large room, trying the tunes, singing them, or playing them on his flute.'

" 'I'm sure,' said Carl, 'that in years to come the hymn book will be considered one of Luther's greatest contributions.'

" 'Of course,' corrected Mother, 'his hymns cannot be compared to his giving us the Bible in our own language.'

" 'And yet, through hymns, the most precious truths of Scripture can be sung into the hearts of Christian people. Furthermore, Mother, think how these beautiful Lutheran chorales have enriched music already, and how congregational singing has won followers for Christ. I'm positive that Luther's hymn book will do great things for music and the world.'

"Margaret wondered what these 'great things' would be. But even Carl didn't know. He was merely predicting something which was more true than he realized. For if Margaret and he could have lived just 200 years

longer, they would have seen the singing church produce the greatest music ever written.

"I have time to mention only a few great Lutheran musicians.

"Just fifty years after Luther died, *Phillip Nicolai* (1556-1608) sat looking out of his parsonage window. 'That's 170 victims that have been buried this week,' he said. 'How dreadful this plague is. I may be next.'

"And then this sad pastor sat down to study his Bible and write a series of meditations that he called the 'Mirror of Joy.' He planned to leave these meditations as comforting messages to those of his congregation who would be left in case he too should die of the plague. But Nicolai did not die. God had further use for him.

"Nicolai became a Lutheran pastor in Hamburg, and was called a second Chrysostom. But his greatest contribution was his hymns, many of which were first written in his 'Mirror of Joy.' Nicolai was a musical genius because he not only wrote the poems but also the music for his hymns. His 'Wake, Awake, for Night Is Flying' is called the King of Chorales, and 'The Morning Star Upon Us Gleams,' the Queen of Chorales.

"A year before Nicolai died, another musical genius by the name of *Paul Gerhardt* (1607-1676) was born in Germany. His ability blossomed at a wedding when he wrote a poem to a bridal couple. Paul Gerhardt also became a Lutheran pastor. Because of his faith, he was persecuted and put out of office. He was cheerful in spite of his many trials and wrote hymns that have been a comfort to many. A hymn he wrote at this time was 'Thy Way and All Thy Sorrows.' There were 123 of his hymns published. He is called the preacher-poet and the greatest hymn writer of his day.

"Ten years after Gerhardt's death, in March 1685, two boys were born in Germany. Both showed they were musical geniuses from the time they were small.

68

"For six months, ten-year-old Bach crept out of bed when every one was asleep and tiptoed along the cold stone floor to a cabinet in which a book of masterpieces was locked. He'd stick his hand through the grating of the cabinet door, roll the book, and jerk it free. Then he'd go back to his room to copy the masterpieces by moonlight. How happy he was until his brother learned what he'd done and to punish him took away the book he'd worked so hard to copy. Once he walked 200 miles to go to a choir school. Later, he wrote much beautiful music, including 226 cantatas, many chorales and motets, and a great deal of organ music. *Johann Sebastian Bach* (1685-1750) is the master of musicians and the greatest of organists.

"The father of *George Handel* (1685-1759) forbade his practicing. So Handel, who was less than ten, stole out of bed night after night and in bare feet and nightgown practiced by candlelight on a clavichord hidden in the

attic. When his father heard the music one night and discovered George in the attic, he decided his son should be given an opportunity to study music. 'The Messiah' was written by Handel when he was 56 years old. The first time it was performed in London, the audience was so inspired by the 'Hallelujah Chorus' that everyone, even the king who was present, rose and remained standing until the chorus ended. Ever since then it is the custom to stand during the performance of this chorus.

"Through the contributions of men who used their great talent to glorify God in their chorales, cantatas, oratorios, organ music, and hymns, Christ has been able to win many followers. Therefore, even through music, Christ has been able to fulfill His promise: 'Lo, I am with you always.'"

BIBLE STUDY

1. Memorize Ephesians 5:19
2. Following are references to music. Be able to tell in your own words
   Rev. 5:8; Gen. 4:21; I Sam. 16:16; II Chr. 29:25; Daniel 3:5
3. Find following references to singing: Psalms 100:2; 126:2; 68:25

69

Luther's parsonage becomes a model Christian home

Chapter 9

The Reformation Produces Results

HOW surprised the Lansing family was the night that Dr. Lansing, loaded down with paste, scissors, pictures, clippings, and notebook, came into the living room.

"Tonight," he said, "I'm not going to tell you the story. We're going to work it out together. We are going to pretend that we are living during and after the time of Luther, and that we are making a scrap book of just the most important news items of that time. Joan can be in charge of the paste and scissors, Dorothy can cut the news items, Mother can paste, and the boys and I will try to choose the most important news."

The following is a result of their work:

THE REFORMATION IN OTHER COUNTRIES

While Luther was preaching in Germany against the false teachings of the church, and the wicked and ungodly living of the priests, rulers and people, men were also preaching against these same evils in other countries.

Ulrich Zwingli (1484-1531) who was seven weeks younger than Luther, followed in Luther's footsteps and became the reformer in Switzerland. He fearlessly preached against the worship of saints and the sale of indulgences from his pulpit at Zurich. He thought it was wrong to have anything in churches unless commanded by the Bible, and so he preached against the use of pictures, organs, and bells. Because he disagreed with Luther on the Sacrament of the Altar, there was a division in the Protestant church. It wasn't long before there were many different Protestant churches.

About the same time that Luther was at the head of the Reformation in Germany, and Zwingli in Switzerland, *Thomas Cranmer* (1489-1556) was introducing the Reformation into England. With Cranmer's influential help, Henry VIII made the church of England independent from the Catholic church. Then the State church of England became the Episcopal church.

John Calvin (1509-1564), a Frenchman, had to flee to Switzerland because of a speech in which he denounced the immorality of the clergy in France. While in Switzerland, he became a pastor and an author, and made the work of Zwingli of world-wide importance. He became the great organizer, theologian, and disciplinarian of the Calvinistic church.

John Knox (1505?-1572) fled to Geneva, Switzerland, during the persecutions in England. He became a disciple of Calvin. Later he became a pastor in Scotland, and won the country to Calvinism (the Presbyterian church).

CO-WORKERS OF LUTHER

Well-educated professors of Universities helped Luther in the work of the Reformation.

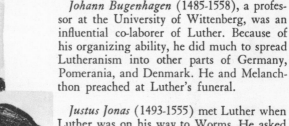

Johann Bugenhagen (1485-1558), a professor at the University of Wittenberg, was an influential co-laborer of Luther. Because of his organizing ability, he did much to spread Lutheranism into other parts of Germany, Pomerania, and Denmark. He and Melanchthon preached at Luther's funeral.

Justus Jonas (1493-1555) met Luther when Luther was on his way to Worms. He asked Luther's permission to accompany him. From then on, the two men were friends. Later he translated the writings of Luther and Melanchthon into other languages. Since he was a brilliant student of languages, he was well-fitted for this work. Jonas gave all his talents to cooperate with Luther in the work of the Reformation. He was called the "Orator of the Reformation." Jonas was one of the men with Luther at his death bed.

Philip Melanchthon (1497-1560) was small of stature but great in knowledge. He was a child in simplicity and sweetness of temper but a master in theology. He was Luther's faithful friend and co-laborer in the Reformation Movement. Among other things, he will always be remembered as the author of the Augsburg Confession.

Three great artists became friends of Luther and used their talent to help spread the Reformation. (The Chicago Art Institute has originals of these three artists.)

Albrecht Durer (1471-1528) made drawings and wood cuts of Reformation leaders. He also made many illustrations of Bible stories. His drawing of "Praying Hands" has the following interesting story:

Durer and his friend decided that while one studied art, the other would work. His friend insisted that he be the first one to work. He labored cheerfully, looking forward to the time when it would be his turn to study art.

One day, Durer came home with enough money from selling a woodcut to pay rent for a long time.

So his friend too began to use his brush. But he found that the hard menial work had twisted his fingers so that he could no longer hold the brush with skill.

Durer was broken-hearted. When he came home one day to see his friend in prayer, he thought: "I can never give back the skill of those hands. But I can paint his hands like they are now while he is praying, and immortalize the hands which have done so much for me."

Luther" by Cranach

Lucas Cranach (1472-1553) became a Lutheran while he lived in Wittenberg as the court painter of Frederick, the elector of Saxony. He illustrated Bible stories, religious books, and painted many pictures of Luther, Melanchthon, and Luther's wife.

Hans Holbein (1497-1543) made the illustrations for certain Lutheran pamphlets, painted portraits of Reformation leaders, and fearlessly showed in his drawings the evils of his time. His portrait of Melanchthon has received much praise.

Woodcut by Durer

"Melanchthon" by Holbein

Illustration by Holbein

LUTHERANISM IN DENMARK, NORWAY, SWEDEN, ICELAND, FINLAND, AND THE BALTIC PROVINCES

Denmark

In *1536,* Christian III called a diet in Copenhagen which formally adopted the Evangelical Lutheran faith as the official religion of the country.

Hans Tausen (1494-1561) was called the Danish Luther.

Later *Thomas Kingo* (1634-1703) became Denmark's first great Lutheran hymnist. He never failed to make a personal appeal in his hymns, among which are: "On My Heart Imprint Thine Image," "Praise to Thee and Adoration," and "He that Believes and Is Baptized."

Hans Adolph Brorson (1694-1764) began to write hymns in Danish because his congregation was singing from German hymn books. Following are hymns of his: "Behold a Host," "Thy Little Ones, Dear Lord, Are We," and "Life's Day Is Ended."

Norway

In *1537,* Lutheranism became the established religion in Norway, but it was not until the reign of Christian IV (1577-1648) that the Lutheran church became the church of all parts of Norway. Bishop Jörgen Eriksen of Stavanger was called the Luther of Norway.

Iceland

Iceland became Lutheran through missionaries sent from Norway.

Sweden

In *1593,* the general council of the Swedish church in Upsala declared its unshaken faith in the teachings of the Augsburg Confession.

Finland, Lapland, and the Baltic Provinces

Finland became Lutheran through the influence of Sweden; Lapland through the influence of Sweden and Norway; and the Baltic Provinces through German influence.

THE BOOK OF CONCORD

The Book of Concord, the last of Lutheran confessions, was published on the fiftieth anniversary of the presentation of the Augsburg Confession to the Diet of Augsburg—June 25, 1580.

The Book of Concord includes the Apostles' Creed, Nicene Creed, Athanasian Creed, Augsburg Confession, the Apology, the Schmalkald Articles, Luther's two Catechisms and the Formula of Concord. It was signed by 51 princes, 35 cities, and 9,000 theologians.

GUSTAVUS ADOLPHUS, THE LION OF THE NORTH

Even though Gustavus Adolphus fell in the Battle of Lutzen, he saved Lutheranism for Germany.

Ever since Luther's time when the emperor after conquering his enemies had returned to Germany to crush Lutheranism, and had found Lutheranism to be so strong that he couldn't crush it, there had been struggles between the Catholics and Lutherans. Finally, these struggles developed into the Thirty Years' War. For a while, it seemed as if the Lutheran princes and their armies were going to be destroyed, and that Lutheranism would be crushed in Germany. But Christ fulfilled His promise by arousing an interest in the heart of the Lutheran king of Sweden for the suffering Lutherans of Germany.

The mother of *Gustavus Adolphus* (1594-1632) had been a strict disciplinarian. "For who would command must first learn to obey," she had said.

When King Gustavus of Sweden felt called of God to help the Lutherans in Germany who were going through the horrors of the Thirty Years' War, he obeyed.

When he landed in Germany, he told his men: "The more you pray, the more victories you will gain. Incessant prayer is half the victory."

His army went from victory to victory.

Before the Battle of Lutzen, the entire Lutheran army sang, "A Mighty Fortress." Wallenstein, the leader of the enemy, heard it and sneered. Then the Swedish section of the army sang the song written by Adolphus: "Fear Not, O Little Flock, the Foe."

When Adolphus was shot, he said: "This day I seal with my blood the liberty and religion of the German nation."

BIBLE TRANSLATIONS

Luther's translation of the Bible into German inspired many others to make translations. There were two important English translations.

William Tyndale (1484-1536), a brilliant Greek and Hebrew scholar, hoped, by translating the Bible into English, to do what Luther had done for the German people through his translation of the Bible into German. Tyndale's first attempt at translating the Bible was a failure. He then decided to go to live a year at Worms where he might confer with Luther. His translation is remarkably perfect.

Thousands of Tyndale's translations were smuggled into England by being packed in sacks of flour and in bales of clothing. Spies reported the smuggling to Catholic Archbishop Wolsey whose anger caused Tyndale to be burned at the stake for translating the Bible into English.

King James (1566-1625), a man of considerable learning, was interested in theological affairs. In 1604, when King James was president of a conference of clergy, a discussion arose about the imperfect translation of the Bible then in use.

King James authorized a new edition. 47 translators were hired. Men were even sent to the Holy Land to get accurate information.

For seven years, the translators worked. In 1611, the first edition was ready. The King James Authorized Bible is used a great deal even today.

John Bunyan (1628-1688) of England, though he did not translate the Bible, wrote a book that was used by God to influence many people to become Christians. He was a Puritan, and was put into Bedford county jail for twelve years because he did not preach in agreement with the state church. There he wrote "Pilgrim's Progress" which still is a favorite story of Christian people and has been translated into many languages.

BIBLE STUDY

1. Memorize Psalm 145:13 and 18
2. Christ wants you to make good use of your talents: Matt. 25:20
3. The Word of God shall be given to all people: Acts 2:5-8; Rev. 14:6
4. Gustavus Adolphus' mother was right in teaching him to obey: Eph. 6:1-3; Prov. 22:6; Ex. 19:5

Gustavus Adolphus before
Battle of Lutzen

Scene from "Pilgrim's Progress"

John Bunyan

Hans Nielsen Hauge

Music by Thomas Kingo

Praise to Thee and ad - o - ra - tion, Blessed Jesus,

Christ is borne.   Chap.ij.

out of the citie of Nazareth, into Ju-
John 7.42   dea, vnto the citie of Dauid, which is
called Bethlehem, (because he was of
the house and linage of Dauid,)

5 To be taxed with Mary his e-
spoused wife, being great with child.

6 And so it was, that while they
were there, the dayes were accomplished that she should be deliuered.

7 And she brought foorth her first
borne sonne, and wrapped him in swad-
ling clothes, and laid him in a manger,
because there was no roome for them in
the Inne.

8 And there were in the same coun-
trey shepheards abiding in ye field, keeping watch ouer their flocke by night.

Portion from King James Bible

Da Vinci was 31 years when Luther was born
Durer was 12 years when Luther was born
Cranach was 11 years when Luther was born
Michelangelo was 8 years when Luther was born
Raphael was born the same year as Luther
Luther was:
    1 year when Zwingli was born
    5 years when Del Sarto was born
    9 years when Columbus discovered America
    11 years when Correggio was born
    14 years when Holbein was born
    14 years when Melanchthon was born
    15 years when Savonarola was burned
    15 years when da Gama sailed around Cape of Good Hope
    17 years when Cellini was born
    39 years when Magellan sailed around the world

Kaiserwerth

August H. Francke

University of Halle

Chapter 10

The Pietistic Movement

IN order to make clear the teachings of the Bible, many discussions were necessary between theologians (Bible students). This resulted in a one-sided emphasis on pure doctrine (teaching) and in an intellectual understanding of Christianity. But often, that was as far as it went. People did not *live* their Christianity as the early Christians had. And yet, though the situation was serious, Christ kept His promise. He raised a man to start a movement toward more godly, Christian living.

"We will continue our scrap book now with a chapter on this movement called the Pietistic Movement," said Dr. Lansing.

PIETISM SPREADS AMONG LUTHERANS IN GERMANY

Philip J. Spener (1635-1705), pastor in Berlin, was the founder of the Pietistic movement.

August H. Francke (1663-1727) brought the Pietistic movement to its great climax in Germany. His life work was done in connection with the University of Halle. He added Inner Missions as an important phase of Lutheran work. His Orphan's Home and Bible Institute became very famous. The University of Halle supplied Europe and America with Lutheran teachers, pastors, missionaries, and influential laymen.

Theodore Fliedner (1800-1864) founded in 1836, at Kaiserwerth, the first deaconess house which trained nurses for hospitals and care of the poor. (One of the nurses trained here was Florence Nightingale.)

PIETISM SPREADS TO SCANDINAVIAN COUNTRIES

Norway

Hauge (1771-1824) cheers his friends from his prison window.

Hauge became a Christian when he was 25 years old. For one year, he preached in his home community. Then for 6 years, he traveled through Norway preaching sometimes four times a day. He led many to Christ. He was a "practical Christian." As he traveled and preached, he also showed farmers how to run their farms better, started mills, and business places. Because lay preaching was forbidden in Norway, *Hans Nielsen Hauge* was put into prison for seven years.

One day while Hauge was in his prison cell, he sat watching a little candle burn. His heart was sad as he thought of his two friends who, though they had walked from Bergen to Christiania to see him, hadn't been permitted to see or speak to him. Then he heard far off chimes of Christmas bells. He fell to his knees in prayer and song.

Outside, far under the prison window, stood his two friends, thinking about what Hauge had done to spiritually awaken the people of Norway.

Suddenly the men's thoughts were interrupted by hearing Hauge's song. When he finished, they startled Hauge by continuing the song.

Then these two friends of Hauge, as they looked up at the little window in the gray wall, saw a light shine from it.

"Look," cried the men, "Hauge is holding his candle to his window to preach the victory of light over darkness. Let us take Hauge's message from farm to farm all over our land."

Denmark

Pontoppidan (1698-1764) writes for Lutheran youth.

Erick Pontoppidan, who was bishop of Bergen, Norway, and then became a teacher at the University of Copenhagen until his death, has made a worthwhile contribution to the education of Lutheran youth through his explanation to Luther's Catechism.

Sweden

Rosenius (1816-1868) occupies important place in Pietistic Movement in Sweden.

Carl Olaf Rosenius was a lay preacher in Sweden. He edited two publications—"The Missionary Times" and "The Pietist"—through which he was able to stir the hearts of people all over his land. By his writings and preaching, he brought light, joy, and comfort to numberless souls even beyond the borders of Sweden. He led people to peace with Christ through assurance of the forgiveness of their sins.

One of the books compiled from his writings in "The Pietist" is the devotion book, "A Faithful Guide to Peace with God."

PIETISM SPREADS TO ENGLAND

The Methodist church started in England as a reaction against immorality and lack of spiritual interest. *John Wesley* (1703-1791) was the organizer. He was ably assisted by *George Whitefield* (1714-1770), a great pulpit orator, and *Charles Wesley* (1708-1788), a great hymn writer. The three men had studied at Oxford University and had been ordained as Episcopal ministers. The Wesley brothers served as missionaries in Georgia. Later in London, John was brought to the knowledge of the truth by reading Luther's preface to "Romans," and Charles, by Luther's preface to "Galatians." No doubt the growth of the Wesleyan Methodist Church was to a great extent due to the beautiful hymns written by Charles. Among his well-loved hymns are: "Jesus, Lover of My Soul," "Hark! the Herald Angels Sing," and "Love, Divine, All Love Excelling."

PIETISM RESULTS IN MISSIONARIES
Bartholomew Ziegenbalg (1683-1753) goes to India.

When Francke was asked to send a promising student to the Danish colonies in India, he sent Ziegenbalg who quickly learned the Tamil dialect. In less than a year, he had translated Luther's Catechism into Tamil. Later, he translated the New Testament, 38 books, many tracts, and also the Old Testament. The faith of Ziegenbalg, the first Lutheran foreign missionary, triumphed over disappointments, suffering, and persecution.

Hans Egede (1685-1758) becomes first missionary to Greenland.
"But they are not there any more! They all died 800 years ago."

"How do we know they all died? They might have had children and grandchildren whose descendants are still living there with nobody to tell them about God," said Hans Egede, who had been reading a book.

The book told how Eric the Red, the Norse sea-rover, had discovered Greenland, and that a colony from Norway had gone there and settled.

Hans could never get these people off his mind. Finally, in 1721, fifteen years after the above conversation, he went to Greenland, where he found that all the Norsemen had died. Later, his son Paul translated the Bible and other books into the Eskimo language, trained native pastors, and worked faithfully for many years.

PIETISM RESULTS IN GREAT HYMNISTS
Two pastors who were sons of pastors became great hymn writers.

Grundtvig Church in Copenhagen

Nikolai F. S. Grundtvig (1783-1872) was a Dane. Among his hymns are: "Built on the Rock, the Church Doth Stand," "The Happy Christmas Comes Once More," and "Peace to Soothe Our Bitter Woes."

Magnus B. Landstad (1802-1880), of Norway, bought a package of books for four cents. In it was a German book of Nicolai's songs and a Danish book of hymns. These books inspired him to write hymns, among which are: "I Know a Sleep in Jesus' Name," "There Many Shall Come from the East and the West," and "Before Thee God, Who Knowest All." Later, he edited a hymn book for the Church of Norway.

The greatest Scandinavian organist and composer was:

Ludvig M. Lindeman (1812-1887), who together with the greatest organists of Europe dedicated the giant organ of the new Albert Hall in London. Lindeman's melodies—"Koralbok"—were adopted by the Church of Norway as the melodies for Landstad's hymn book.

BIBLE STUDY
1. Memorize James 1:22
2. Christ wants us to do deeds of mercy: James 2:18; 1:27
3. The Pietists thought that Christianity had become worldly and that worship was largely lip service: II Tim. 3:5
4. Note Christ's commands: Matt. 9:38; 24:14; 28:19; Mark 13:10

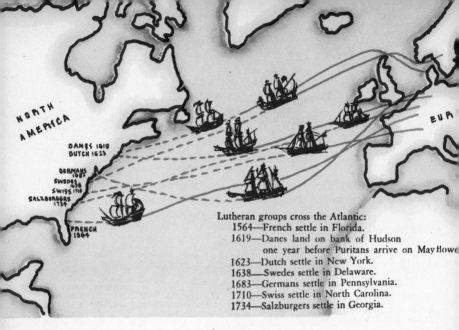

Lutheran groups cross the Atlantic:
1564—French settle in Florida.
1619—Danes land on bank of Hudson
        one year before Puritans arrive on MayHowe
1623—Dutch settle in New York.
1638—Swedes settle in Delaware.
1683—Germans settle in Pennsylvania.
1710—Swiss settle in North Carolina.
1734—Salzburgers settle in Georgia.

Chapter 11

Lutheranism Crosses the Ocean

WHAT would you like to know about the first Lutherans in our country?" asked Dr. Lansing.

"I'd like to know when the first Lutherans came here, and where they lived. I'd like to know who the first pastor was, what the first churches were like, whether the Lutherans did anything for America, who the first—," said Jim.

"He doesn't give anybody else a chance," interrupted Dale.

"We're all going to have a chance now," said Dr. Lansing. "Let's see what we can find about Lutheranism crossing the ocean."

The following pages are what they found:

1564
FRENCH LUTHERANS SETTLED IN FLORIDA

The French Huguenot, Admiral Coligny, established a colony of Lutherans near St. Augustine, Florida. These were the first Lutherans in North America. They were beheaded in 1565 by the Spanish whose placard on a cross near their graves said: "We slew them not as Frenchmen, but as Lutherans."

1619
ONE YEAR BEFORE ARRIVAL OF PURITANS IN MAYFLOWER DANISH LUTHERANS REACHED HUDSON BAY

The first Lutheran cemetery was dedicated in America, when the crew of two Danish vessels seeking the N. W. passage to India, buried 40 of their dead on the Hudson Bay. In 1620, their pastor, the Lutheran *Rasmus Jensen,* the first Protestant pastor to have lived and labored in North America, was buried. Just two months before his death, he had conducted the first Lutheran Christmas service in North America and had been presented by the Danish sailors with white fox skins to line his gown.

1623
DUTCH LUTHERANS LEFT NETHERLANDS BECAUSE OF POLITICAL COMMOTIONS

The Dutch with a few Swedes and Germans settled at Manhattan Island and Fort Orange (Albany).

In *1626, Peter Minuit,* a German, purchased Manhattan Island for the Dutch from the Indians for $24.00 in ribbons and beads.

The Dutch Lutherans had no more than settled, however, before they realized they had bitter enemies in the Calvinists who were determined either to win them into the Calvinistic church or to crush them. It was not long before the Lutherans were fined if they even listened to a Lutheran sermon. In spite of the bitter persecution by the Calvinists, the Lutherans continued strong in their faith. Among the Lutherans of this first Dutch Lutheran colony was:

Jonas Bronck (?-1643) a Dane, who had studied in the Netherlands and had come to America with the Dutch. His library, the earliest of which any record survives in New York, contained books on theology, medicine, history, law, and science, in Danish, Dutch, Latin, and German languages, and also Luther's German Bible and Catechism. The name of Bronck is perpetuated in the Bronx River, Bronx Borough, and Bronx Park.

Finally, in *1657,* the Lutherans won the sympathy and help of the West India Company which made it possible for them to call their first pastor. But when *Rev. John Ernest Goetwater* came, the Calvinists increased their persecution and were so cruel to Rev. Goetwater that the Lutherans hid him in a barn. Finally, however, Peter Stuyvesant, the Calvinistic governor, got his way and Rev. Goetwater was sent back to Amsterdam.

Peter Stuyvesant

Rev. Goetwater

Stocks
Form of Persecution

There were six more long years of persecution for the Lutherans, and then the West India Company realized that the actions of the Calvinists were proving harmful to the growth and prosperity of the colony at New Amsterdam and ordered Peter Stuyvesant to treat the Lutherans better.

The next year, in *1664*, persecutions of Dutch Lutherans ceased because then the English conquered New Amsterdam (they named it New York).

In *1668*, *Jacob Fabricius*, the first permanent pastor to Dutch Lutherans, arrived. Later he served the Swedes in a conscientious, upright manner.

In *1671*, Fabricius installed *Arensius*, who served as pastor of the Lutheran church in New York until about 1700. During this time, a Lutheran church was built near Bowling Green.

1638
SWEDES CAME TO DELAWARE WITH A MISSIONARY PURPOSE

The "Key of Calmar," a war vessel, and the "Griffin," a small vessel, laden with Swedish people, supplies, articles for trading with the Indians, and devotional books, landed on the banks of the Delaware to found a New Sweden. These were the first Protestants to settle in America whose chief reason for coming was a missionary purpose.

Peter Minuit, in their behalf, purchased the west bank of the Delaware from the Indians for a brass kettle and some trinkets. Later more land was bought so that they owned Delaware and Southern Pennsylvania.

In *1639*, *Reorus Torkillus*, the first Lutheran pastor to settle permanently in North America, came. In 1643, he was buried where the "Old Swedes Church" of Philadelphia now stands. Before his death, three vessels brought Swedish immigrants and additional clergymen. Among them were:

Lieutenant Colonel John Printz (1592-1663), Governor of New Sweden. Under his strict rule, the colony increased in influence. Delaware was dotted with pleasant hamlets. Gov. Printz built himself a palace of brick on the Island of Tinicum. He erected forts, mills, and trading posts. He made the religious training of children and grown-ups compulsory.

Johan Campanius (1601-1683), who had served as chaplain in Russia, and taught and preached in Sweden, was sent to New Sweden where he worked for more than five years. While here, he became interested in the Delaware Indians, learned their language, prepared the first known Indian vocabulary, and finished translating Luther's Catechism into the Indian language in 1648. Also the first church erected in Pennsylvania was built while he was here. It was consecrated in 1646 as the Old Swedes Church.

In *1655*, the Dutch Calvinists conquered New Sweden. Then followed a long period of trials. The Dutch Governor's haughty wife sold Tinicum and the church. There is no record of the way in which the Swedes got back their church. But it is known that the Swedes reaped two days in harvest time, for the Dutch, in order to get back their church bell.

Minuit buying Delaware

Old Swedes Chur

In *1664*, the English conquered the Dutch and were more tolerant.

In *1682*, William Penn with many Quakers arrived in Delaware. The Swedes were good to the Quakers.

When an English ship stopped at Delaware, the Swedish people were able to win the sympathy of a Swedish man on board who, when he returned to Stockholm, won the notice of King Charles XI to the Lutherans in New Sweden who had been without a pastor over 30 years. King Charles sent a letter of inquiry. Charles Springer was chosen to write the letter of reply telling about conditions and asking for Bibles, Catechisms, and devotion books. The letter was circulated in Sweden.

Andrew Rudman, Erick Björk and *Jonas Auren* were chosen to go to New Sweden. They were ready to sail when it was discovered that no Indian Catechisms were among the books for America. The King sent 500 Indian Catechisms with his initials printed in gilt as his gift.

In *1697*, Rudman and his associates landed in New Sweden. Rudman chose as his field the Wicaco Church where the Gloria Dei Church was completed and consecrated on July 2, 1700. About the same time Björk built the Holy Trinity Church.

Three principles distinguished this Swedish colony—first, religious tolerance; second, the honorable treatment and Christianizing of the Indian; and third, the prohibition of slavery. (There was a commemorative stamp issued in 1938 to celebrate the coming of the Swedes and Finns in 1638.)

1683
GERMAN LUTHERANS CAME TO PENNSYLVANIA FOR RELIGIOUS FREEDOM

The first Germans who came to America were those who came with Penn's Quakers. *Rev. Heinrich Koester* conducted the first German Lutheran service in America in 1694 in Germantown. The first German Lutheran congregation in America was that of Falckner's Swamp (New Hanover) in Pennsylvania about 1700. Its first pastor was:

Justus Falckner (1672-1723), the real estate agent who turned preacher. Falckner was trained in the University of Halle for the ministry but he decided he'd make a better real estate agent. He came to America and surveyed and promoted a section of land that is still known as Falckner's Swamp. He became acquainted with Rudman and Björk who influenced the gifted, learned man to give his talents to the ministry. He, a German, was ordained in 1703 in the Swedish Gloria Dei Church to serve a Dutch congregation in New York. His pastorate was 200 miles long. His diary and well-kept records still exist and are a fine source of information. It is interesting that his diary includes a prayer for each entry. He wrote and published the first Lutheran text book in America. His hymn, "Rise, Ye Children of Salvation" is still being sung in Lutheran churches.

Rise, ye children of sal – va – tion

Heinrich Christiansen
builds first house

First Lutheran cemetery

Slavery forbidden by
Swedish colony

Old Swedes Church

Reorus Torkillus

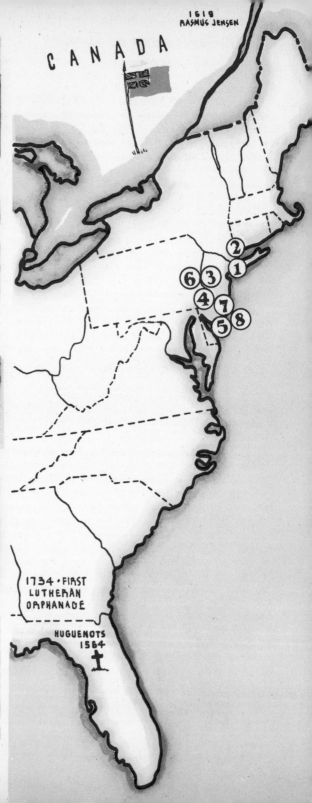

CANADA

1618
RASMUS JENSEN

1734 · FIRST
LUTHERAN
ORPHANADE

HUGUENOTS
1564

LUTHERAN FIRSTS IN AMERICA

Johan Campanius

1564—The first Lutheran colony settled by French near St. Augustine, Florida.

1613—Heinrich Christiansen built the first American house on Manhattan Island.

1619—The first Lutheran services of worship held on North American soil were conducted on Hudson Bay between August, 1619, and February, 1620, by Rev. Rasmus Jensen who had accompanied Captain Jens Munck and his 66 men from Denmark on their exploring expedition to the New World. Especially important was the Christmas Day service, 1619.

1619—The first Lutheran cemetery was dedicated when 40 Danish dead were buried on shore of Hudson Bay.

1620—The first Lutheran pastor buried in North America was the Rev. Rasmus Jensen who died at the Hudson Bay settlement on February 20, 1620, and was buried there.

1637—The first American colony to forbid slavery was that of New Sweden, on the Delaware River, settled by Finnish and Swedish Lutherans.

1638—The first Lutheran church was erected in connection with Fort Christina, in Wilmington, Delaware.

1639—The first Lutheran pastor in America—Reorus Torkillus of Sweden.

1642—The first Protestant missionary to the American Indians was the Rev. Johan Campanius, a Lutheran pastor in the Swedish-Finnish colony on the Delaware River.

Luther's Small Catechism in Indian dialect

1646—The first book translated into an American Indian dialect was Luther's Small Catechism, done by the Rev. Johan Campanius, pastor of the Swedish-Finnish colony on the Delaware River.

1646—Erection of first Lutheran Church in America by Johan Campanius—Swedish Lutheran Church on Tinicum Island.

1700—First German Lutheran Church was built at Falckner's Swamp near New Hanover, Pennsylvania.

1703—The first Lutheran minister ordained in North America was the Rev. Justus Falckner, in the (then) Lutheran Gloria Dei Church, Philadelphia.

1708—The first Lutheran theological book issued in America was written in Dutch by Justus Falckner and printed in New York. It was "Fundamental Instruction in the Christian Doctrine."

1713—The first pastor to attend to the spiritual welfare of negro slaves on the Western Hemisphere was the Rev. Christian Fischer, pastor of the Danish Lutheran Church on St. Thomas Island, West Indies. In 1713 he baptized the first slave.

Justus Falckner

1715—Rev. J. M. Magens translated the Bible into the Creole language. He also translated into English, 40 Danish sermons, setting forth the Lutheran faith. These sermons were printed as the first English Lutheran book (of any size) in America.

1715—First American-born Lutheran pastor at Swedesboro, New Jersey —John Abraham Lidenius.

1734-35—The first test case of the freedom of the press in America centered around John Peter Zenger of New York, a printer, who was one of the Lutheran Palatinates.

1735—The first conference of Lutheran pastors in America was held at Zion Church, Oldwick, N. J.

1737—The first Protestant orphanage in the American colonies was at Ebenezer, Georgia, built by the Salzburg Lutherans who had settled there.

1740—Old Hebron church built in Madison County, Virginia. Part of the present building is in regular use as the oldest (owned) Lutheran church in America.

First Lutheran Synod meeting held at St. Michael's Church, Philadelphia

1743—First service conducted in the Old Augustus church, Trappe, Pennsylvania. The church still remains unaltered and is used occasionally.

1748—The first Lutheran synod in America was organized August 15, 1748, in St. Michael's Church, Philadelphia, under the leadership of Henry Melchior Muhlenberg.

1763—The first charitable society in America was organized by the Germans at Philadelphia.

1795—The first English Lutheran hymnbook was published by the Rev. Dr. John Christopher Kunze of New York. Incidentally, Dr. Kunze in 1784 became a professor of Oriental languages and German. He was also a regent of King's College which later became Columbia University.

Hymn Book published by Dr. Kunze

In *1710*, 4,000 Palatinates landed in New York. They were the first Lutherans driven to these shores by religious persecution. During the time of Louis XIV of France, Germany was overrun by barbarous soldiers who knew no pity for old men, women, or children. Soon the roads which then lay deep in snow, were blackened by large multitudes of men, women, and children fleeing from the soldiers. Many died of cold. Enough survived to fill the streets of Europe with men who had been thriving farmers and shop keepers and now were beggars. Under stress of misery, thousands of inhabitants, in many cases entire villages, were forced by their sufferings to snap every bond that held them to their native land and flee to England and America. Most of them settled in Pennsylvania, Virginia, and the Carolinas. One of the Palatinates who came to New York was:

John Conrad Weiser, Jr. (1696-1760). His father had an Indian visitor one day who took a great fancy to the seventeen year old boy. The Indian asked permission to take the boy to his tribal home. This was granted. John spent eight months with the chief's tribe during which time he learned the language and customs and was adopted by the tribe. In 1732, John became the official Indian interpreter of Pennsylvania. From the day of his adoption to the day of his death, he signed every treaty with the Indians in the Pennsylvania territory. He cast the deciding vote in the Iroquois powwow that decided that the Iroquois should fight with the English and not with the French. When the Revolution came, his influence swung the tribe away from the English and toward the Americans. Because of Weiser, our nation became English instead of French, and then American instead of English, and so Protestant instead of Catholic. When he died, the Indians came to mourn over his grave for years, saying: "We are at a great loss. We sit in great darkness by the death of Conrad Weiser. Since his death we cannot so well understand each other." He was a sincere and earnest Christian, respected by both white and red men. He became a faithful lay-helper of the Patriarch Muhlenberg. One of his daughters became the wife of Muhlenberg.

1710

SWISS SETTLED IN NORTH CAROLINA

A great many Swiss settled at New Berne, North Carolina, with two shiploads of Palatinates. A year later, a terrible Indian massacre nearly exterminated the colony. Those who were left suffered many hardships. They were without a pastor and without a church. Finally they fled to Virginia because of fear of Indians. Rev. J. C. Stoever organized a congregation in Virginia of which he was the first pastor.

In *1735*, Swiss who settled in Orangeburg, North Carolina, organized a Lutheran congregation.

In *1737*, still more Swiss came and also a pastor, J. U. Giesendanner, who had taught at Halle. He served the Swiss in Carolina for ten years. About *1743*, a house of worship of wood and clay was built.

1734
PERSECUTED SALZBURGERS CAME TO GEORGIA

It took courage and faith to be a Salzburg Lutheran.

In *1684*, the Catholic archbishop issued an edict driving out of the country in mid-winter all Protestants refusing to be converted and requiring all children under fourteen years to remain and become Catholic. (How would you have felt if you had been a mother or father who had to leave your little children? How would you have felt if you had been a child and had seen your parents leave you?)

In *1727*, began several years of the most horrible persecutions by the Catholics upon Salzburg Lutherans. Therefore, in *1731*, on a Sunday, 100 men walked over rocky mountain paths to a market village where they seated themselves around a table on which was placed a vessel of salt. Each man, with earnest prayer, dipped the wet fingers of his right hand into the salt, and then lifting his fingers, took a solemn oath to the Triune God never to desert the Lutheran faith. Then he swallowed the salt.

Two months later, Lutherans were ordered to be out of the country within a week. Christ used these persecuted Salzburgers to quicken the faith of those whom they met. Their march out of their country to other lands was like a triumphal procession in behalf of their faith. The Salzburgers found homes in many countries.

A company of 91 Salzburgers landed in America in *1734*. They were accompanied by two pastors, *J. M. Bolzius* and *I. C. Gronau,* both of whom had been pupils at Francke's Orphan House at Halle and had been chosen by Francke to go with the Salzburgers.

In *1735*, three more groups of Salzburgers arrived in Georgia. With one of these groups, the two Wesley brothers had crossed the ocean. A deep impression was made upon John Wesley by the calmness, the child-like confidence, the heroic spirit, and the joyful singing of these Lutherans during a storm when every other heart was quaking with terror. Wesley's religious experiences had not yet reached a stage of deep faith or joy. The courageous, joyous faith of the Salzburgers was a revelation which blessed Wesley's spiritual life and the Methodist church he founded.

BIBLE STUDY
1. Memorize I Cor. 10:13
2. Other Bible passages which bring out somewhat the same idea are: Rom. 8:35; Luke 21:12; II Tim. 3:12

ECCLESIA PLANTANDA

The Signing of the Constitution

Heinrich Melchior Muhlenberg

George Washington

Chapter 12

The Lutheran Church During the Time of Washington

S O FAR, we have traced the Lutheran groups up to the settlement of the Salzburgers in Georgia in 1734," said Dr. Lansing. "Tonight, we are going to find out what Lutherans did during the time of Washington.

"One night in September, 1741, a young man who was deep in thought strolled through the Halle University grounds. He thought of his parents who had baptized him the same day he was born. He remembered how he had studied every spare minute while he had helped to earn the family living, so that when he had been able to enter school, he had easily taken first place in his studies. He remembered his joy when he was told that because of his rapid progress, he was going to be given the financial aid necessary for him to complete his University studies. There through the friends he had chosen, he had come into contact with the Pietistic Move-

Three Muhlenberg Sons

Frederick Augustus Conrad

John Peter Gabriel

Gotthilf Henry Ernestus

F. A. Muhlenberg—First Speaker
of the House

Sara Austin making
the first flag

ment and had received an appointment to teach in the Orphan House at
Halle. Later he had been told that because of his Christian life, aptness
in teaching, and love for missions, the Halle leaders had decided to send
him as a missionary to India. But circumstances had prevented his going.
Christopher Schwartz had been sent instead.

" 'I wonder why God didn't let me go,' he thought.

"Just then he reached the home of Dr. Gotthelf Francke (son of the
Francke who founded Halle). He had been invited for supper.

"They had no more than seated themselves at the table when
Dr. Francke said:

" 'Some time ago, a few men came from America to plead
for pastors. They told us that for over fifty years, many of the
Germans had had no pastors; that in many places where there
had been pastors, they had been inefficient impostors and had
done the church more harm than good; that from the hearts of
the American Germans had gone many prayers to God to awaken
the hearts of European Lutherans to their needs; and that since
their repeated letters had been unsuccessful, they had decided to
send men to plead the needs of their people, arouse sympathy,

Election of John Hanson as first president
of "United States in Congress Assembled"

Sexton ringing
Liberty Bell

Muhlenberg on way to America
from Germany

He carried on his "care of all the churches"
from Georgia to New York

collect money for building schools and churches, and to seek a capable man to teach the young and to gather all the isolated Lutheran groups into churches again.

" 'And now after careful investigation and much prayer, we feel that, as God sent Moses to His people groaning in Egypt and raised Luther with the light of His Word for those who were eager for enlightenment, so now He is calling you to go to America to gather the scattered Lutherans together and found the Lutheran church in America.'

"For a short while, there was silence at that table.

"Then with tears in his eyes, *Heinrich Melchior Muhlenberg* (1711-1787) stood and said, 'The church must be planted. Dr. Francke, I will go.'

"Mrs. Francke was so happy that she said, 'Heinrich, I will make you a warm coat to take with you.' (Mothers are the same the world over, aren't they? I'm sure Muhlenberg often thought of Mrs. Francke's motherliness with gratitude.)

"In December, Muhlenberg preached his farewell sermon. He stayed awhile in England, and then set sail for America. It took him 110 days to cross the ocean. He suffered from seasickness. The ship was overloaded. People were afraid. In the midst of suffering and fear, he heard a Salzburg mother sing, 'A Mighty Fortress.'

" 'That is better protection than the ten iron cannon with which this vessel is provided,' said Muhlenberg.

"He taught the children. The Negro slaves became his mission field. The ship became a church and all on board were his congregation.

"Muhlenberg visited the Salzburgers in Georgia, and some of the Lutherans in the Carolinas before he took another boat for Pennsylvania. He arrived there in November, 1742, almost a year after leaving Germany.

"It would take several books to tell all of the interesting things that Muhlenberg did. Briefly, we might say that he planted the church in America by 'bringing order out of confusion.' At first he was the only Lutheran pastor in the middle colonies, and there were only a few weak congregations. He kept in touch with Halle, from which came other Lutheran pastors to help him. Forty-five years later, when Muhlenberg died, there were 25 pastors and 5,000 Lutheran members in these same states. He organized congregations under constitutions that are patterns for church constitutions today. He was the author of the first Lutheran liturgy in this country. He instructed Jacob van Buskirk, the first all-American Lutheran pastor, born, educated, and ordained here. He gave three of his sons to the ministry and two daughters to be pastors' wives. He organized, in 1748, the first Lutheran Synod, the Ministerium of Penn-

90

The Indians named him "Gachswungarorachs"

His son, Peter, laid aside his clergy gown to show his uniform under it

sylvania; founded schools; purchased ground for a theological seminary in 1749; worked for the establishment of an Orphans' Home near Philadelphia, and wrote the preface and assisted in the hymn selection of the hymn-book of 1786. He carried on his 'care of all the churches' from Georgia to New York where he supplied churches for months at a time. There are accounts of his journeys through deep snows and swamps where it took five hours to go ten miles on horseback. Sometimes in administering to different nationalities, he preached in three different languages on a Sunday. He did considerable work with the Indians who named him 'Gachswungarorachs' which means 'The Preacher — whose — words — should — go — through — hard — hearts — of — men — like — a — saw — through — a — gnarled — tree.'

"In 1800, because of Dr. Muhlenberg's leadership and supervision, there were Lutheran congregations along the whole East coast and to the very summit of the Alleghenies. No other church could, at the time, boast of a ministry that surpassed the Lutheran in intellectual culture, in pastoral ability and faithfulness, and in pulpit eloquence. Such men, guided by the Holy Spirit, were used by Christ to carry out His promise here in America.

"Dr. Muhlenberg had eleven children. He supervised the education of his children carefully. Three of his boys he sent to Halle to receive their higher education.

"The oldest son of Dr. Muhlenberg was *John Peter Gabriel* (1746-1807).

"In 1776, *Peter* preached from Ecclesiastes 3:1-8, which ends: 'A time for war and a time for peace.' After the benediction, he laid aside his black gown, showing the Continental uniform under it, for he had been made Colonel of the 8th Virginia Regiment at the request of Washington. Then while the drums beat outside the church door, he enrolled 300 men of his own charge, and marched away to save the day at Brandywine, to penetrate farthest of our four columns into the British line at Germantown, to starve and shiver at Valley Forge, and finally to lead the victorious charge at Yorktown which ended the war. Later, he was a United States senator in the first, third, and sixth Congresses of the United States, and Supervisor of Internal Revenue and Collector of the Port of Philadelphia. He never lost interest in the church, however. He was the leader in founding Old St. John's in 1806, the first entirely English Lutheran church in the world. There are statues of Peter in the City Hall, Philadelphia, and in Statuary Hall in the Washington Capitol.

"When Peter first became a pastor, he was sent to the Germans in Virginia, a colony that had a state church. Therefore, Peter had to cross the ocean and go through the form of a second ordination in England in order

91

to perform legal marriage ceremonies. Through Peter's influence, the Virginia legislature, in 1785, passed a bill establishing religious freedom. This caused enough interest so that soon afterwards the nation passed the first amendment to the Constitution which made our nation a place where church and state are to be separate, and where religious freedom is granted to all people.

> ARTICLE I (adopted 1791)
> Freedom of Religion, Speech, Press, Assembly, and Petition
> CONGRESS shall make no law respecting an establishment of religion, or prohibiting the free exercise thereof; or abridging the freedom of speech, or of the press; or the right of the people peaceably to assemble, and to petition the government for a redress of grievances.

"The second son was *Frederick Augustus Conrad* (1750-1801). He became pastor in New York and Pennsylvania. He was present at the reading of the Declaration of Independence. He became Speaker of the Pennsylvania Assembly. From 1789-1797, he served in the congresses elected under the Constitution. He was the first Speaker of the House as well as of the third United States Congress. As Speaker of the House, he and John Adams, Vice President of the United States and President of the Senate, signed the first ten amendments to the Constitution, commonly known as the Bill of Rights, which were introduced in Congress by James Madison. Their final ratification by three-fourths of the states was committed to Congress by the President, George Washington, December 30, 1791.

"The third son was *Gotthilf Henry Ernestus* (1753-1815) who became a pastor to Trinity Church, Lancaster, Pennsylvania, in 1780, where he labored until his death. His special interest, outside of pastoral duties, was in education. He wrote a German dictionary, and discovered and described 100 new species of plants and grasses. He was considered the greatest botanist of his day in both America and Europe. His name has been given to many plants he discovered.

"The Germans of Pennsylvania were all on the side of Liberty.

"Besides the Muhlenbergs, another Lutheran leader was *Baron von Steuben* who, as inspector, saved the United States Treasury over $600,000. Historians rank him next to Washington and Greene for valuable services. His 'Rules of Discipline' created our national army and still forms the basis of our military tactics. (There was a Commemorative Steuben Stamp in 1930.)

"At the same time that the Germans were active in the affairs of our country, the Swedish people were doing their part, too.

Stiegel Glass   Wertmuller's Washington   William Muhlenberg's composition

"In the Gloria Dei Lutheran Church in Philadelphia, *Sara Austin* (1754-1831), and other members of the Ladies' Aid made the first American flag. It was presented to John Paul Jones. This flag, which had only 12 stars, received the first salute granted the Star Spangled Banner in Europe. This flag is now preserved in the National Museum in Washington. Later, Congress asked Betsy Ross to make a national flag. This flag contained 13 stars.

"*John Morton* (1723-1777), a signer of the Declaration of Independence, was the speaker of the Pennsylvania Assembly. Six states voted in favor of and six against secession. Pennsylvania was divided. John Morton arose from a sick bed, journeyed to Philadelphia on horseback, and cast the deciding vote for independence.

"The first election of a president, after the ratification of the Articles of the Confederation, took place in 1781 when *John Hanson* (1721-1783) was chosen first 'President of the United States in Congress Assembled.' His election was made by delegates of 13 states, and he served for one year.

"So far, I've mentioned those who contributed to religious and political advancement in our country. Lutherans were active in other fields too.

"The Swedish *Adolf Ulrich Wertmüller* (1751-1811) was a famous painter during Colonial times not only in America but also in Europe. His portrait of Washington has been much praised and was reproduced in the centennial edition of Washington Irving's 'Life of George Washington.'

"*Baron Henry William Stiegel* (1729-1785), when he came to America, laid out the town of Mannheim, Pennsylvania, to house his employees. He became the first manufacturer of iron and glass. In his chapel, he conducted divine services for those in his employ. He gave to Zion Lutheran Church in Mannheim the land on which it stands. When he lost his wealth, he earned a living as a teacher and lay-preacher among his neighbors and former employees. Stiegel glass is considered the greatest of early glass. Some of it is colored a rich, deep blue. Fine collections of Stiegel glass are in the Metropolitan Museum and in the Chicago Art Institute.

"*William Augustus Muhlenberg* (1796-1877) was baptized and died a Lutheran, although because he did not understand German, he belonged to the English Episcopal Church for awhile. He organized the first Bible society in America; helped to secure the first public school law in Pennsylvania; and composed many hymns of which 'Savior, Like a Shepherd Lead Us' is the best known."

BIBLE STUDY

1. Memorize Acts 16:5
2. The following verses give various phases of a pastor's work:
   II Cor. 11:28; Acts 14:23; Eph. 5:25-27

Chapter 13

The Lutheran Church Moves Westward

I T'S good to have a home, and to be able to sit down with one's family and relax," said Dr. Lansing wearily. "Now let's see. Where were we? That's right. We had got as far as the Colonial period with Lutherans taking an active part in the spiritual, political, and cultural upbuilding of our country. Now we come to a fascinating story in the growth of our Lutheran church—the period from 1800 to 1900.

"In the early 1800's, there wasn't much progress because America was suffering the after-effects of the Revolutionary War. Many of the churches had been burned, or converted into hospitals, prisons, or even stables, and were unfit for worship when war ceased. Because pastors had been drawn to the defense of their country and into politics, congregations were left without spiritual leadership just when such guidance was needed to fight against the immorality and unbelief that swept the country after the war.

"Yet Christ was fulfilling His promise: 'Lo, I am with you always.' There were yet good, worthy, and able men who worked faithfully. With their help, the congregations that had suffered from the war gradually were rebuilt, and also new congregations were organized.

 "As early as 1797, *Hartwick Seminary*, the oldest Lutheran Seminary in the United States, was started with *Dr. J. C. Kunze* as the theological professor. In 1815, the Hartwick Seminary building was built in New York by means of an estate left by *Pastor J. C. Hartwig*.

"Most of the early settlers—the Dutch, Swedes, Germans, Swiss, and Salzburgers—remained in the East because there they had established homes and built churches.

"Because they realized that in order to have pastors they would need a Seminary to train pastors in America, *Gettysburg Seminary*, the first Lutheran Seminary in this country under church control, was built in 1826. It opened with ten students and one professor, *Pastor S. S. Schmucker*.

Later *Pastors E. L. Hazelius* and *Charles P. Krauth* became professors. In 1832, Pennsylvania College was also founded at Gettysburg in order that the young men would have a proper education before studying theology.

"You will remember that it was at Gettysburg, Pennsylvania, that the Battle of Gettysburg was fought and that it was near the campus of the Gettysburg Seminary that Lincoln gave his famous Gettysburg Address.

GETTYSBURG SEMINARY

PENNSYLVANIA

GETTYSBURG ●

S. S. Schmucker

"Some of the younger people, and those who were interested in settling on cheaper lands, traveled West. With them, the church moved Westward

"Where was this West? At first, it was just beyond the early settlements along the Atlantic coast. Gradually, the cheap lands beyond the Alleghenies became the West.

1818—LUTHERAN WORK ORGANIZED IN OHIO

"When the people began to move down the western slopes of the Alleghenies and across into Ohio, there were among them many Lutherans seeking homes in the West. Lutheran missionaries of the Pennsylvania Ministerium followed the Lutheran families. On the west side of the mountains, they were cut off from the pastors of the East. These missionary pastors, among whom were *John Stauch, William G. Foerster,* and *Paul Henkel,* organized in 1818, at Somerset, Ohio, the oldest Lutheran organization West of the Alleghenies, called the Joint Synod of Ohio.

"The first pioneer Lutheran pastor in Ohio was John Stauch. Pastor Paul Henkel and his five sons, who were pastors, made the name Henkel well-loved from Virginia to Ohio.

"Lutheran work in Ohio made steady progress, however. From the beginning, special interest was taken in education. The Theological Seminary at Columbus was established in 1830. Capital University, also at Columbus, was founded in 1850.

"Later, other Lutheran schools were built, among which were the Lutheran Theological Seminary at Columbia, South Carolina, in 1831, and Roanoke College in Salem, Virginia, in 1853.

John Stauch

WITTENBERG COLLEGE
SPRINGFIELD, OHIO

CANTON

CRADLE OF EVANGELICAL LUTHERAN
SEMINARY, CANTON

CAPITAL UNIVERSITY,
COLUMBUS

OHIO

Paul Henkel

96

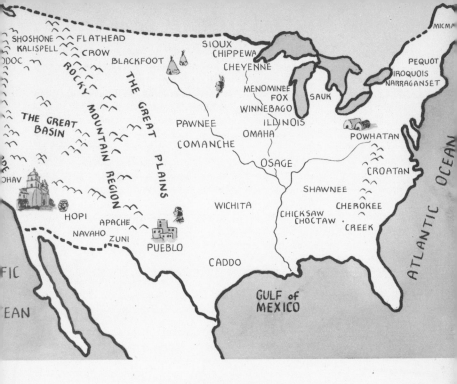

A map of America, showing the Indian tribes
during the great migration—Westward

1825-1870—THE GREAT LUTHERAN IMMIGRATION FROM EUROPE AND THE MIGRATION—WESTWARD

"Can you imagine your family selling most of its possessions and then starting out in a small boat on a long journey across thousands of miles of water, and finally arriving in a new world? Can you imagine finding yourself among strange people who speak different languages, live and dress differently, and have different customs?

"That's what many were doing from 1800 A. D. and on. Thousands of people came each year to America from Europe. After the long ocean trip, many went on by boat, by train, on horseback, in ox carts, in covered wagons, and on foot, to settle in the West.

"Some crossed the Alleghenies and settled in the Mississippi Valley. Some went on to cross the Rockies and build along the Pacific coast.

"Among these pioneers were Puritans, Quakers, Baptists, Presbyterians, Episcopalians, Methodists, Lutherans, and Catholics. They were French, Dutch, Spanish, German, English, Scotch, Irish, Bohemian, Russian, Icelandic, and Scandinavian. These and many more had an interesting part in building the West.

1825—NORSE CAME TO AMERICA

"In 1825, the first of a large number of people from Norway came to our country. There were 54 Norwegians, including a baby girl born to Mr. and Mrs. Larson while on the ocean, who came to America in the sloop *Restoration*. (A commemorative stamp was issued in 1925 which shows the sloop *Restoration*). It had taken them three months to cross the Atlantic. These people settled in New York. But, it was not long before the cheap land of the west appealed to them.

"In 1834, six families moved to Illinois to what became known as the Fox River Settlement. Among these early pioneers were pastors, school-teachers, and lay-preachers who established churches and schools. The early Norwegian pioneers taught their children the Catechism, hymns, and Bible stories. *Elling Eielsen,* a lay-preacher who lived in the Fox River settlement, organized the first Lutheran congregation in Fox River. In 1842, he walked all the way to New York City and back to get an edition of the Catechism printed for use in instructing the children. That was the first Norwegian book printed in America. The cane he used on this and other journeys is now in the Luther College Museum in Decorah.

98

MINNESOTA

CONCORDIA COLLEGE
1891

● MOORHEAD

ST. OLAF COLLEGE
DEDICATED IN 1875
BEGAN WITH 2 TEACHERS
AND 36 STUDENTS
T. MOHN - 1st PRESIDENT
NORTHFIELD

AUGUSTANA COLLEGE
1860

UX
LS ●

BELOIT
1861

ST. ANSGAR
1853

MAHA
●
1871

ASKA

LUTHER COLLEGE
BEGAN IN PARSONAGE LACROSSE CO. WIS. 1861
LUTHER COLLEGE BUILDING DEDICATED OCT. 1865
DR. LAUR. LARSON - FIRST PRESIDENT

SUGAR CREEK 1843

MICHIGAN

WISCONSIN

LUTHER THEOLOGICAL SEMINARY
ST. PAUL, MINN.

MINNEAPOLIS
● ST. PAUL

NORTHFIELD
RED WING
1863

ELSTAD 1854

DECORAH
1851

IOWA

MUSKEGO-1843

HAUGES SYNOD 1846
JEFFERSON
● PRAIRIE 1844
EAST
KOSHKONONG 1846-NORWEGIAN 1st
WEST 1844 LUTHERAN SYNOD CLINTON
KOSHKONONG ● 1844
1844

ROCK
PRAIRIE
● 1844

CHICAGO
1848

ILLINOIS
FOX RIVER
● 1836

Elling Eielsen   C. L. Clausen   J. W. C. Dietrichson

"In 1839, a group of Norwegians settled in Wisconsin. Then it wasn't so long before there were Norwegian settlements in Iowa, Minnesota, the Dakotas, and even in Texas where Lutherans had settled as early as 1821.

"In every settlement, lay-preachers faithfully tried to give the Gospel to the Norwegian people and to organize church work among them. Lay-preachers in Norway also were interested in their countrymen who were going to America. One of these Christian lay-preachers offered to take care of the expenses if an ordained pastor would go to America to help organize Lutheran churches. That was how it happened that *Pastor J. W. C. Dietrichson* came to Wisconsin in 1844, and held his first service in a granary at East Koshkonong and the following day under a large oak tree at West Koshkonong. Other ordained pastors from Norway came to continue the work in America.

99

"The Muskego settlement is one of the most noted Norwegian settlements in America because it was the 'mother colony' to numerous other settlements and because it witnessed some important beginnings. *Even Heg* of Muskego, because of his character and wealth, became the leader. His farm, purchased in 1839, became the stopping place for hundreds of Norwegians in search of homes in Wisconsin and the West. Since the small log cabins of the settlers could not accommodate the great numbers of immigrants who passed through Muskego, Heg's large barn was used. This barn had many uses during those early days. It was used as a social and religious center for the community. In 1843, cholera swept Muskego, missing only one family. Then the Heg barn was used as a hospital. Heg was a lay-preacher and conducted services in his barn. Sunday school classes were conducted there. When *C. L. Clausen* arrived in Muskego in 1843, he preached in the Heg barn and organized a congregation. The Muskego church was started in 1843, but before it was finished, Pastor Clausen confirmed his first class and also performed an interesting double wedding in the Heg barn.

"The Muskego congregation was organized in 1843, and the Muskego church was built by members of the congregation on ground donated by Even Heg. It was dedicated in 1845. When later, a larger church was built, the first church was sold to a farmer who used it as a granary and later as a stable. It was secured by President Hoyme and Pastor Gerhard Rasmussen and was moved in 1904 to the campus of Luther Seminary in St. Paul where it still stands. The furniture in it now is an exact copy of the original.

1839—GERMANS SETTLED IN MISSOURI

"In 1839, 700 Saxons from Germany settled in Missouri. These Saxons had sold their possessions and had put their money into a common treasury. Out of this fund, five ships were chartered.

"Four ships arrived safely in New Orleans, but the last ship to leave Bremen harbor, the *Amalia,* with 30 on board never arrived. Pastor Carl Ferdinand Walther was to have been the clergyman of this group, but owing to last minute arrangements, he boarded another ship instead. (God works in a mysterious way His wonders to perform.)

"From New Orleans, the Saxons continued their journey up the Mississippi to St. Louis. Some of the Saxons went on to found homes in the wilderness, away from the city. Others settled in St. Louis and founded Trinity Church, the mother of Missouri Synod Lutheranism in America. Christ Episcopal Church graciously allowed the congregation to use their church until Trinity Church could be built. The Saxon immigrants built churches and schools just as soon as they built their homes. Several of their oldest buildings are very interesting in that they were a combination parsonage, church and school.

"When O. H. Walther, pastor of Trinity congregation died, his brother *Carl Ferdinand Wilhelm Walther* (1811-1887) was called. It was he who became the great leader, editor and theologian of the Missouri Synod.

First
President
of
Missouri
Synod
1847

C. F. W. Walther

First
Editor
and
Founder
of
"Lutheraner"

MISSOURI

NEBRASKA

ST. LOUIS

SOUTH WING - 1850   CENTRAL SECTION - 1858   NORTH WING - 1852

CONCORDIA SEMINARY AT ST. LOUIS - 1850 - 83

LOG-CABIN COLLEGE - 1839

A COMBINATION BUILDING
USED FOR PARSONAGE
CHURCH AND SCHOOL AT
ALTENBURG, MO.

KANSAS

ARKANSAS

39 - A GROUP OF 700 SAXONS
NARTERED 5 SHIPS TO TAKE
HEM TO AMERICA.
NE SHIP NEVER ARRIVED.

THESE LUTHERAN PILGRIMS
CAME UP THE MISSISSIPPI RIVER
TO ST. LOUIS.

101

1839—PRUSSIANS SETTLED AT BUFFALO

"Also in 1839, Prussian Lutherans from Germany came to America. *Pastor Grabau* and *Heinrich von Rohr* were tired of being imprisoned for holding fast to the teachings of the Gospel. With a company of courageous people, they hired two boats and came to America. When they arrived in New York City after a long voyage, the majority of the group left at once for Buffalo to found their first church and parochial school. Under the leadership of Pastor Grabau, the congregation was soon flourishing.

"Pastor Kindermann also brought a group of Prussians to Lebanon, Wisconsin, in 1843.

Von Rohr

Pastor Grabau

1839—POMERANIANS SETTLED IN WISCONSIN

"*Von Rohr* took forty of the most robust families—most of them Pomeranians—and set out for Wisconsin where they penetrated the deeply-wooded country sixteen miles northwest of Milwaukee. They called their settlement Freistadt. Pastor Grabau encouraged Von Rohr to prepare himself for the ministry. Von Rohr went to the East to study and at the age of 47, he was ordained as pastor. Later, Heinrich von Rohr's son, Philip, became ordained as a pastor, too, and was very active in the Wisconsin Synod.

1839—DANES CAME TO WISCONSIN

"From 1839 to 1890, people from the farming districts of Denmark arrived in this country. More than half a million Danes settled in large cities from New York to San Francisco. Large Danish rural settlements are found in the Central states. The Danes were mostly a group of scattered people, however. They often settled in Norwegian or Swedish communities and worshiped in the Norwegian or Swedish churches.

"Claus L. Clausen, the second Lutheran pastor among the Norwegians in America, was a Danish lay-preacher. Although Clausen's work was principally among the Norwegians in Wisconsin, Iowa, and Minnesota, he organized several Danish congregations, too.

"In 1851, the first congregation at Racine, Wisconsin, was organized in the home of the layman, John Lawson. The first pastor, *Ole Andrewson,* was a Norwegian. The services were conducted in Norwegian and Danish until 1863. After that time, Danish only was used. In 1886, Trinity Seminary and Dana College were founded at Blair, Nebraska.

WISCONSIN

SWEDES USUALLY TRAVELLED WESTWARD BY AN INDIRECT WATER ROUTE—NEW YORK TO ALBANY ON THE HUDSON, THEN TO BUFFALO VIA THE ERIE CANAL, TO CHICAGO ON THE GREAT LAKES—FROM THERE THEY WENT INLAND TO ILLINOIS, IOWA AND MINNESOTA—

MICHIGAN

AUGUSTANA COLLEGE AND THEOLOGICAL SEMINARY AT ROCK ISLAND

CHICAGO

INDIANA

ROCK ISLAND

IMMANUEL CHURCH CHICAGO—1848

EARLY CHURCH AT ANDOVER 1851

ILLINOIS

Lars P. Esbjorn   T. N. Hasselquist   Erland Carlsson

1850—SWEDES CAME TO ANDOVER, ILLINOIS

"Many Swedish people came to our country from 1845 and on. Their usual route was from New York up the Hudson to Albany, then on the Erie Canal to Buffalo, then by way of the Great Lakes to Chicago, and then inland to Illinois, Iowa, and Minnesota. Many of these Swedish immigrants were loyal Lutherans who came to America with the Bible, hymn book, and Catechism. These books they studied faithfully. Lay-preachers conducted services in the homes until pastors arrived from the homeland.

"Among the pastors in Sweden who had watched with anxious eyes the departure of their people for America was *Lars P. Esbjorn.* In 1849, he left his native church and came to America. He followed his countrymen West. His first work was at Andover, Illinois, where with ten members he started the first Swedish Lutheran Church of Andover in 1850. Esbjorn is considered by the Swedes much the same as Muhlenberg is by the Germans. He traveled all over the Central states organizing and encouraging Swedish Lutheran work. In Boston, he was introduced to the famous Swedish Lutheran singer, *Jenny Lind,* who gave him $1,500 for this work. He was the founder of the Augustana Synod.

"Among the earliest Swedish Lutheran congregations are Immanuel in Chicago and New Sweden in Iowa, both founded in 1848.

"Three years after Esbjorn began his work in America, *T. N. Hasselquist* came to Galesburg and the next year *Erland Carlsson* arrived at Chicago. These two men undertook the work of teaching younger men and thus built up a native ministry. With Esbjorn, they did much to establish the Swedish Lutheran Church in America.

103

FAMOUS SWEDISH PEOPLE OF THAT TIME

"*Alfred Bernard Nobel* (1830-1896), the Swedish engineer who studied mechanical engineering in the United States, produced the formula for dynamite in 1867. His will provided $9,000,000 to establish the Nobel Foundation which awards yearly prizes for merit in physics, chemistry, literature, medicine, and world peace. The Foundation is managed by a board of directors, all residents of Stockholm.

"*John Ericsson* (1803-1889), the inventor of the screw propeller, constructed the little Monitor, which destroyed the dread Merrimac of the South and turned the scale in favor of the Northern army. (A commemorative Ericsson stamp was issued in 1926.)

1850—FINNS SETTLED IN MICHIGAN

"By 1850, other groups of immigrants were coming to our shores. They were the Finnish Lutherans who settled in Northern Michigan and from there spread to other states of the Union. In 1876, *Pastor A. E. Backman,* the pioneer minister among the Finns, came from Finland to Calumet, Michigan, to organize work among the Finnish Lutherans there. *Pastor Nikander* did much to organize their synod, which is called the Suomi Synod. He became the first president. The question of getting pastors for the thousands of unchurched Finns was the first problem taken up by the Synod with the result that in 1896 the Suomi College and Theological Seminary, for the training of a native ministry, was founded in Hancock, Michigan.

"One of the very first Lutheran churches in Wyoming was erected by the coal-mining Finns of Carbon in eastern Wyoming. A strong congregation is in Astoria, Oregon. A great many of the salmon fisheries and canneries of Washington are run by Finnish Lutherans. But the main center of Finnish Lutheran work is in northern Michigan.

1870—ICELANDERS SETTLED NEAR WINNIPEG

"In 1870, Icelanders came to America and settled on Washington Island, Wisconsin. By 1875, Icelanders were coming to America in large numbers. *Pastor Jon Biárnason* and *Pastor Pall Thorlacksson* organized congregations in 1877 and 1878. Icelandic Lutheran congregations were organized in Nebraska, Minnesota, and Nova Scotia. The largest groups of Icelanders are in North Dakota, and in New Iceland near Winnipeg. The Lutheran church, painted a bright blue, which is in Winnipeg, is quite a landmark. In 1885, two pastors, Jon Bjärnason and *H. B. Thorgrimsen,* organized the Icelandic Evangelical Lutheran Synod of North America.

LUTHERAN IMMIGRANTS OF OTHER COUNTRIES

"At this time, there were Lutherans from other countries who also came to America to establish homes and build Lutheran churches. Among these were Lutherans from Poland, Russia, and Latvia.

ENGLISH LUTHERAN CONGREGATIONS ESTABLISHED

"Another very interesting story in the movement of the Lutheran Church Westward was that of organizing English Lutheran Churches. *William A. Passavant* (1821-1894) of Pittsburgh, Pennsylvania, was very interested in keeping Lutheran young people in the Lutheran Church. He realized that in order to do so, English Lutheran congregations would have to be established. Among the men who continued this work of organizing English Lutheran congregations were Pastors *Trabert, Haupt,* and *G. H. Gerberding* (1847-1927).

W. A. Passavant

"The first English Lutheran congregation in America, which has had an uninterrupted existence, was founded in Philadelphia in 1806 and called St. John's Lutheran Church.

VALUE OF HYMNS REALIZED

"As the church moved westward, Christian people realized as never before, the value of hymns in spreading the Gospel. The years from 1800 to 1900 produced many great hymnists among whom are:

August Toplady—(1740-1778)—Rock of Ages.
Reginald Heber—(1783-1825)—Holy, Holy, Holy; From Greenland's Icy Mountains.
Charlotte Elliot—(1789-1871)—Just As I Am.
John Bowring—(1792-1872)—In the Cross of Christ I Glory.
Sarah Adams—(1805-1848)—Nearer My God to Thee.
Ray Palmer—(1808-1887)—My Faith Looks up to Thee.
Edward Hopper—(1818-1888)—Jesus, Savior, Pilot Me.
Phillips Brooks—(1835-1893)—O Little Town of Bethlehem.

Rock of Ages, cleft for me, Let me hide myself in Thee

"The glorious way in which Christ fulfills His promise: 'Lo, I am with you always' can be seen in the results of the Lutheran church moving westward. For now, on this great continent of America are many thousand Lutheran church spires pointing heavenward and representing congregations of countless nationalities who have kept their faith in spite of the obstacles and difficulties of building our country—Westward."

BIBLE STUDY

1. Memorize Acts 9:31
2. Look up following verses which speak of growth in church membership: Acts 2:47; 1:8; 10:41

The words, "In God We Trust" were first used in 1864 on a two cent coin. The idea originated with a pastor. The exact wording was proposed by Secretary Chase.

The Lutheran Church Moves Westward

★The first Lutheran congregations in each state, the year the congregation was organized, the synod or former nationality of the group responsible for the organization of the congregation.

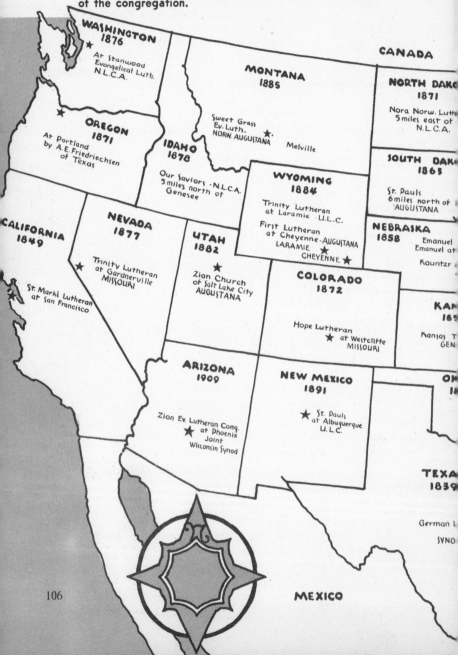

WASHINGTON 1876
At Stanwood
Evangelical Luth.
N.L.C.A.

MONTANA 1885
Sweet Grass
Ev. Luth.
NORW. AUGUSTANA
Melville

CANADA

**NORTH DAKO
1871**
Nora Norw. Luth.
5 miles east of
N.L.C.A.

OREGON 1871
At Portland
by A.E. Friedriechsen
of Texas

IDAHO 1878
Our Saviors - N.L.C.A.
5 miles north of
Genesee

WYOMING 1884
Trinity Lutheran
at Laramie · U.L.C.
First Lutheran
at Cheyenne - AUGUSTANA
LARAMIE
CHEYENNE ★

**SOUTH DAK
1865**
St. Pauls
6 miles north of
AUGUSTANA

NEBRASKA 1858
Emanuel
Emanuel at
Kountzr

CALIFORNIA 1849
St. Marks Lutheran
at San Francisco

NEVADA 1877
Trinity Lutheran
at Gardnerville
MISSOURI

UTAH 1882
Zion Church
of Salt Lake City
AUGUSTANA

COLORADO 1872
Hope Lutheran
at Westcliffe
MISSOURI

**KAN
18

Kansas T
GEN

ARIZONA 1909
Zion Ev. Lutheran Cong.
at Phoenix
Joint
Wisconsin Synod

NEW MEXICO 1891
St. Pauls
at Albuquerque
U.L.C.

**OK
18

**TEXA
1839

German L
SYNO

MEXICO

106

First Lutheran of St. Paul - AUGUSTANA (Feb. 25, 1854)

Immanuel - 8 miles east of Racine - MISSOURI

Elstad Norw. Luth. - 8 miles S.E. of Lanesboro - N.L.C.
Highland Prairie - 8 miles south of Rushford - N.L.C.

North Prairie at Filmore County - AUGUSTANA
Root Prairie of Filmore County - AUGUSTANA
Chisago Lake - AUGUSTANA

VERMONT
1873

West
Rutland
N.L.C.A.

At Berlin Mills
N.L.C.A.

1881
NEW
HAMPSHIRE

MASSACHUSETTS
1857
Zion Lutheran at
Boston - MISSOURI

CONNECTICUT
1865
Trinity Lutheran
at New Haven
U.L.C.

R.
I.

MAINE
1740

Waldeboro
GERMAN

NESOTA
1854

WISCONSIN
1839

Am. Luth. Church
at Freistadt
BUFFALO SYNOD

MICHIGAN
1833

Zion Lutheran at
Washtenaw Co.
GERMAN

VER-
MONT
1873

NEW
YORK
1642-44

Lutheran Church
at Albany

NEW
HAMP-
SHIRE

MASSA-
CHUSETTS

CONN.

R.I.

OWA
846

e Lutheran
Brighton
UTH. CHURCH

ILLINOIS
1827

Union County

MISSOURI
1839

Trinity Luth.
at St. Louis
MISSOURI

INDIANA
1810

Mt. Solomon
7 miles west
of Corydon
SYNOD.
of WEST

N. CAR.

OHIO
1800

Jefferson County
GERMAN

U.L.C.
Hopeful Luth.
Church at Florence

KENTUCKY
1606

PENNSYLVANIA
New Göteburg - SWEDES
Gloria Dei - PHILADELPHIA
1677

N.J.

St. Peter's
Luth. at
Shepherdstown

W.VIRGINIA
1750
U.L.C.

Madison
Hebron Lutheran
U.L.C.

VIRGINIA
1717

NEW
JERSEY
1643

Fort Nya
Elfsborg
SWEDES

MD.

DE.

Trin-
ity
at
Wilming-
ton.
SWEDES
1638
DELA-
WARE

ARKANSAS
1868
Fort Smith
MISSOURI

TENNESSEE
1793

MISSIS-
SIPPI
1846

New Hope
Church at
Sallis
U.L.C.

ALABAMA
1834
SO. CAR. SYNOD

Flatt Creek

Boque-Chitto
Creek

Monroeville

GEORGIA
1734

Jerusalem Church
at Ebenezer
U.L.C.

NORTH CAROLINA
Organ at Salisbury
1745
GERMAN
St. Johns at Concord
Friedens at
Gibbonville

SOUTH
CAROLINA
1562?
Huguenot Luth.
Church
FRENCH

MARYLAND
1649
Cecil County

SWEDES

LOUISIANA
1840

St. Pauls
at New Orleans
MISSOURI

Bethlehem

near
Lake City
U.L.C.

D. OF C. 1769
Ev. Luth. Church
at Georgetown

FLORIDA
French
Lutheran
Congregation
1564

107

1700—7 ministers, 20 congregations in United States and Canada

1800—50 pastors, 300 congregations in United States and Canada

Chapter 14

Lutheran Beginnings Become Organized

YOU remember in the beginning of your last story, I showed you a map of America as it looked in 1800," said Dr. Lansing. "Indian tribes were scattered all over America. Few people were living beyond the Eastern settlements. (See P. 97.) By 1900, our country looked very different. (See Pp. 106 and 107.) So many people had come from Norway, Germany, Denmark, Sweden, Finland, Iceland, and other countries that there were large cities in every one of our forty-eight states. In these cities were built sky scrapers, beautiful buildings, schools, libraries, hospitals, and many homes. Small towns and farms also were scattered all over the United States. Distant parts of our country were connected by good roads and railways.

"As our country changed, so Lutheran Church work changed. In 1700, the problem in our church was to get the church planted. By 1800, the church was growing—Westward, and at the same time building churches, colleges, seminaries, orphans' homes, and hospitals, as well as sending out missionaries to foreign lands.

"It wasn't long before the Lutheran people realized that in order to keep the many Lutherans, who were coming to America, within the Lutheran Church, it would have to organize further. At first, different congregations banded together into synods for various reasons: because of nationality, doctrine, church customs, and location. By 1900, there were about 60 Lutheran synods in our country.

"But there had to be further organization. As early as 1872, the Missouri Synod and several other synods organized the Evangelical Lutheran Synodical Conference.

"Since 1900, such organizing has continued further.

"In 1917, three Norwegian Synods joined as the Norwegian Lutheran Church of America (N. L. C. A.). Even though it was the Norwegians who started the work of these synods, some of the Norwegian Lutheran Churches, in cities, have more than twenty different nationalities belonging to their congregations, and use only the English language in carrying on the work.

"In 1918, during Armistice Week, 45 synods joined to form the United Lutheran Church of America (U. L. C.).

"In 1930, the middle west synods of German background formed the American Lutheran Church.

"Also in 1930, the American Lutheran Church, the Norwegian Lutheran Church of America, the Lutheran Free Church, the United Danish Lutheran Church, and the Swedish Augustana Synod formed the American Lutheran Conference.

"So, instead of thinking of Lutherans in this country as being divided into over 60 different synods, you can now think of about 97 per cent of Lutherans as belonging to one of three groups. (To which one do you belong?):

the Synodical Conference

the United Lutheran Church of America

the American Lutheran Conference

These three Lutheran groups total some four million worshipers, all believing, teaching, and preaching the Open Bible.

"In 1918, the National Lutheran Council, comprised of representatives elected from various Lutheran Synods, was organized. It represents the Lutheran church as a whole in America. It has a fine statistical and reference library.

"However, the Lutheran church, realizing that there were Lutherans all over the world (Pp. 110-111—map showing Lutheranism in the world), felt it must go one step further. In 1923, the first Lutheran World Convention met at Eisenach, where long years ago Luther played and sang for coins in its quaint streets, and where, by his beautiful singing, he won the interest of Ursula Cotta. Twenty-two nations were represented at this Lutheran World Convention, and opened the meeting with the singing of 'A Mighty Fortress.' In memory, they again saw Luther standing alone at Worms with the Bible in his hand as he exclaimed, 'God help me. Amen.' In gratitude, they thanked God that through these more than 400 years since Luther's time, there have been followers of Luther who have gone out with surrendered lives and with Open Bibles to win the world for Christ.

In 1933, Germany issued coins in commemoration of the 450th anniversary of Martin Luther's birth.

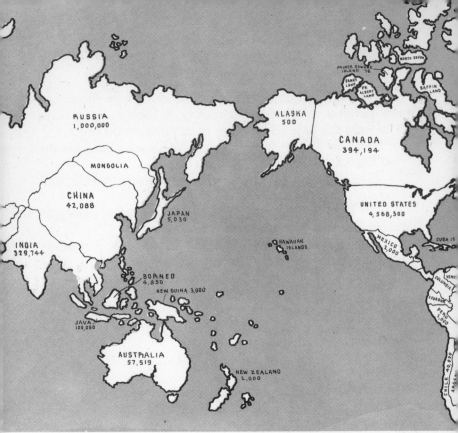

LUTHERANS IN THE WORLD*

Africa	376,977
Asia	432,893
Europe	56,662,429
North America	4,983,134
Oceania	348,704
South America	304,705
	63,108,842

Per cent: 3.8

NORTH AMERICA		SOUTH AMERICA	
Canada	394,194	British Guiana	505
New Foundland	12	Dutch Guiana	3,200
Prince Edward Island	76	Brazil	220,000
Greenland	14,355	Argentina	30,000
Mexico	2,000	Chile	40,000
United States	4,568,300	Paraguay	4,000
Alaska	500	Peru	2,000
Porto Rico	1,492	Uruguay	4,000
Virgin Islands	2,047	Venezuela	1,000
Cuba	158		
	4,983,134		304,705

*Lutheran World Almanac, 1934-1937

Java and Mandura	100,000
Sumatra	176,117
Other Dutch Islands	3,718
Hawaii	1,500
	348,704

ASIA

British Possessions	
India	329,744
Mesopotamia	159
Palestine	354
China	42,088
French Possessions	
French India	158
Syria	180
Japan	5,030
Persia	1,000
Siberia	54,000
Turkey (Asia)	180
	432,893

EUROPE

Austria	248,078
Belgium	25,000
England	250,000
Scotland	20,000
Irish Free State	500
North Ireland	500
Bulgaria	2,000
Czechoslovakia	642,073
Denmark	3,200,372
Faroes Is.	19,617
Iceland	94,227
Danzig	200,000
Estonia	895,232
Finland	3,614,625
France	300,000
Germany 33,774,754
Greece	3,500
Holland	100,000
Hungary	525,515
Italy	20,000
Jugoslavia	250,000
Latvia	1,055,067
Lithuania	68,800
Luxemburg	500
Norway	2,741,877
Svalbard Is.	4,000
Poland	1,000,000
Portugal	1,000
Rumania	405,668
Russia	1,000,000
Spain	4,000
Sweden	6,105,330
Switzerland	90,094
Turkey (Europe)	100
	56,662,429

AFRICA

British Possessions	
Tanganyika	6,584
Sudan	200
Basutoland	400
S. W. Africa.............	62,924
N. Nigeria	970
S. Africa Union	179,688
Egypt	3,410
French Possessions	
Tunis	40
Madagascar	116,297
Italian Possessions	
Ethiopia	3,000
It. Somaliland	2,679
Libya	210
Liberia	575
	376,977

OCEANIA

Australia	57,519
New Guinea Is.	3,000
New Zealand Is.	2,000
Borneo Island	4,850

"Besides the banding together of individual members into congregations; of various congregations into synods; of several synods into conferences; and of all Lutherans into a World Conference, there are other organizations, some of which are Women's Missionary Societies, Lutheran Brotherhoods, Leagues of young people, Lutheran Daughters, Dorcas Societies, and Willing Helpers.

"What do all these organizations do?

"They carry on the great work of the church which is to give the Gospel to all people and win others for Christ.

"In order to fulfill this mission, the various organizations engage in many activities. There is scarcely anything more interesting than a study of the many activities of the church. For it takes one not only into churches, offices, board rooms, convention halls, but also into schools, printing and publishing houses, and hospitals. It takes one into nearby homes where there is sorrow and into foreign lands where there is ignorance of salvation. It takes one around the corner to a Jewish tailor, an Italian grocer, a Chinese laundry man, and into the jungles of Africa to souls groping for light and help. It takes one into large and modern colleges, and into miserable leper huts in China and India. It is a fascinating study.

"The Christian church has not won the whole world for Christ, nor has it won even all members of Christian churches. Though much has been done, there still remains much to be done. How much remains to be done you can see by this chart."

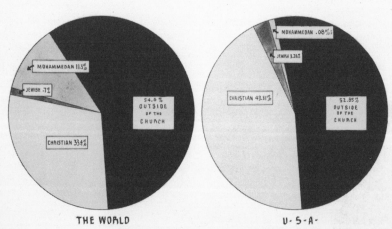

THE WORLD   U-S-A-

Based on 1937 Lutheran World Almanac Figures

112

"Why, Dad," burst from Jim, "I didn't have any idea there were so many heathens now."

"No, most people don't give much thought to anybody except themselves. This chart proves it. If every Christian would win another person for Christ, think how fast this black section could be made smaller. You need not go across the water to win souls for Christ either. There's probably someone in your class room, in the neighborhood, or among your friends that you can win.

"The best way to be a soul winner is to know about the past and understand the present needs. That is why, so far, I have tried to have people come out of the pages of the New Testament, and out of history books to meet you so that you could see them overcoming difficulties, fighting wrong and winning others for Christ. I hope you have seen the heroes of faith as they've marched by in our stories. They have blazed a trail of courageous living with Christ. But the trail is not finished as you see by the chart. Others must join the march so there will be a continuous line of heroes of faith. You too will want to join the ranks of heroes. It is not easy. It takes men and women, boys and girls, who are willing to trust in Jesus Christ their Savior, and His promise: 'Lo, I am with you always.'

"Now we will leave the heroes of the past and see what men and women, boys and girls are doing and can do today so that they can be a part of the March of Faith. There are of course heroes from all Christian Churches joining this March of Faith, but we shall limit ourselves to the work being done by Lutherans."

BIBLE STUDY

1. Memorize Matt. 8:11
2. Other Bible verses that speak of Christians in many lands are: Acts 10:34, 35; Rev. 5:9
3. Bible verses that tell Christians to work together in love are: Phil. 1:27-30; 2:1-4

TO BE FILLED IN BY THE STUDENT

The President of our Synod is ....

There are .... pastors in our Synod.

There are .... congregations in our Synod.

The baptized membership in our Synod is .... souls.

Chapter 15

The House of God

SIXTEEN hours and ten minutes from coast to coast! See America by plane," read Jim. "Just think what you'd see in a few hours!"

"Yes," said Dr. Lansing, "you'd see interesting and changing pictures—forests and prairies, mountains and plains, cities, towns, and farms, tall skyscrapers, and squatty huts. But there is one thing that seldom would be missing in these changing pictures."

"What is that?" asked Dorothy and Dale together.

"Churches! Everywhere there would be churches. If you took a trip in some other direction, you'd find churches along that route, too.

"From the time of the tabernacle up to the present, there have been buildings used for worship. They have had different names —tabernacle, temple, sanctuary, basilica, cathedral, and church. But no matter what the church building has been called, it has always been a holy place used for worship of God, for the teaching and preaching of the Word of God, and for the administering of the Sacraments. Because the church exists to win souls for Christ, it should suggest spiritual truths and create spiritual feelings. A church building should never look like a bank, a theatre, or a lecture hall. A church should always leave the impression— *this is the House of God*.

"In order to set a church building apart as a *House of God,* there is scarcely a church in the world, however humble or plain, that has not employed art of some kind in its building. There was more art used in churches of the Middle Ages than there has been since then. Because most of the people then were uneducated, pictures and symbols were the people's books. The beautiful cathedrals, filled with pictures and symbols, were like Bibles in stone. They were like substitutes for the Bible. However, even though art included the finest in painting and sculpture, it couldn't give what the Bible gives; and so it was that the Dark Ages didn't disappear until Luther came to give the Open Bible.

"Since, as Jim read, it only takes 16 hours to cross the continent, you will see many churches during your life time. In order that when you enter a House of God, no matter how humble or magnificent, you may enter it with an attitude of devotion and praise because you understand the meaning of the different parts of the church, I am not going to tell you a story tonight. Instead, I am going to pretend that I'm your guide, and that we're taking a trip through—any Lutheran church.

"I won't need to say anything further about the church exterior. You have seen pictures of churches used during the time of each of the stories I've told you. You have already heard that the Gothic church became the best loved. It is especially a favorite among Lutherans. Even some of the simplest country churches have been made beautiful with Gothic steeples, colored windows, and high, arched ceilings.

"Now let's go inside. In Gothic churches, the floor plan looks like this drawing. As you've heard before, it is in the shape of a cross. Most churches have the same plan except that they have no transepts.

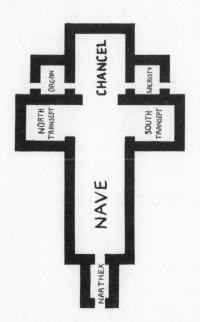

"The *narthex* or *vestibule* is the entrance room of the church. Since it is a part of the church, it is not the place for visiting or talking.

"The *nave* is the part of the church building where the pews are, and where the congregation (Christ's church on earth) is seated. Since the church is God's ship of salvation over the waters of life, the sign for the church is a ship. That is why this part of the church building is called the nave.

"Pews were not used in the nave until the time of the Reformation. Before the Reformation, people stood during the service.

"The *chancel* is elevated above the nave. Sometimes, the chancel is three steps higher than the nave. There were two meanings for the three steps being used. They are symbolic of the trinity and also of the three Christian characteristics—faith, hope, and love.

"The chancel corresponds to the Holy Place of the tabernacle and temple. It is the part of the building where the baptismal font, the pulpit, and the altar are placed.

115

"The *pulpit* is the place from which the sermon is given. There have not always been pulpits. The 'cathedra' was used by the bishop when he preached. In Italy, a preaching platform in the nave was used. The Reformation made the sermon an important part of the service and brought back the use of the pulpit.

"The *baptismal font* is where the Sacrament of baptism is administered. Children as well as adults have been baptized ever since the time of Christ. In the Cathedral church at Syracuse, in Sicily, there is a baptismal font from the third century. It holds about two gallons of water. It has a dedication stating that a certain Xosimus dedicated the font to God to be used for baptism.

"The *altar* is at the center back of the chancel. It is the symbol of the presence of God. It suggests the sacrifice of Jesus.

"During the time of the apostles, the altar was a table. In the catacombs, the altar was a stone slab. Later, the altar enclosed the relics of saints. Now it is the place from which the Lord's Supper is administered.

"From the time that churches were first built after the time of Christ, the altar has often been placed in the east end of the church. There are several reasons for this: Christ arose with the rising sun; out of the East came the glory of the Gospel to the West; and to the East is Jerusalem which is symbolic of the New Jerusalem."

"What is this called?" asked Dorothy pointing to the cloth on the pulpit.

"That is called a *pulpit fall.* It always hangs over the edge of the pulpit. The altar has an *altar cover* corresponding in color to the pulpit fall. It hangs over the front edge of the altar, and is covered with a white linen cloth the size of the altar top."

"Are the pulpit fall and altar cover always red?" asked Dorothy.

"No, there are five colors, called liturgical colors, that may be used in churches.

"*White* is the color of perfection and of the purity of God. It represents perfect glory, beauty, holiness, and joy and so is used as a festival color.

"*Red* is the color of fire and blood. It represents the lives of martyrs, saints, and heroes of the church. It is also the color used to represent the Holy Spirit.

"*Green* is the color of life and victory. It represents growth in Christian life.

"*Violet* is the color of repentance and preparation.

"*Black* is the color of great sorrow and death.

"Besides these five colors, two other colors are used in stained windows.

"*Blue* is the color of wisdom, loyalty, hope, and thought.

"*Yellow* is the color representing the goodness of God, treasures in heaven, and the achievements of the faithful.

"During the celebrating of the Sacrament of the Altar, the sacramental vessels are placed on the altar. They are the:

paten, the plate to hold wafers (unleavened bread);

chalice, which holds the wine (often individual communion cups in trays are used). The lighted candles are a reminder that it was evening when Jesus instituted the Lord's Supper, and that He is the light of the world."

"What are the letters on the altar cloth for?" interrupted Jim.

"That's a symbol. There are many symbols in the church—in the furniture, altar cloth, and stained windows."

"I've heard the word 'symbolism.' It sounds hard and uninteresting," said Dale, looking bored.

"But it isn't hard at all, and it's very interesting," corrected Dr. Lansing. "Everyone—everywhere—since earliest times has used symbols. Of course, symbolism has its dangers. The symbol may be taken as the thing itself and thus cause idolatry. But symbolism is more common than you think. Red and green lights which direct traffic are symbols telling you when to stop or go. The hand-clasp is the symbol of friendship. The raised hat is the symbol of respect. The national flag is the symbol of your country and commands your respect because of what it means. The words I am using now are symbols of my thoughts—they are not the thoughts themselves. A large shoe outside a shop is the sign of the shoemaker. A revolving striped pole in red, white, and blue is the sign of the barber. Symbols are outward signs which suggest a deeper truth and meaning.

"And so it is not at all surprising that the church has employed symbols in its devotional life. You can find many symbols in the Bible both in the Old Testament and New Testament. God gave directions for the use of symbols in the tabernacle. At the Passover feast, the Jews ate a bit of unleavened bread—a reminder of their fathers' hasty flight from Egypt. God wanted symbols to teach or inspire, reminding people of some important fact, some outstanding event, some great truth, and His promise: 'Lo, I am with you always.'

"In Jesus' life and teaching, you will find the richest symbolism in the Bible. His parables are symbols, for Jesus did not exactly define what His kingdom is. He merely stated it is *like* a net cast into the sea, or *like* a sower who went out to sow. When Jesus spoke of Himself, He used these statements: 'I am the Good Shepherd,' 'I am the Door,' 'I am the Vine,' and 'I am the Light.' The Book of Revelation is full of symbols. Artists have labored to express these symbols of Christian faith in stone, wood, glass, and metals.

"No doubt the first Christian symbol which will come to your mind is the Holy Cross of which there are over 400 forms. Christians have always held the cross in reverence because it stands for the suffering and death of Jesus.

"But the Holy Cross is not the only symbol Christians use. There are hundreds of interesting symbols that you will find in churches. After you know their meaning, churches will not only be beautiful, inspiring buildings, but they will have a wealth of meaning for you, and will inspire you to think of Jesus. As you understand the meaning of the 'House of God' and the message of the symbols, you will have an increased reverence and desire to take an active part in the worship.

"I hope you will want to make a further study of symbolism when you get older. Now I have time to tell you only about those symbols that you will see most often:

LATIN CROSS—This is the favorite of all crosses.

GREEK CROSS—Often you will see 5 Greek crosses on altar cloths, representing the 5 wounds of Christ.

TAU CROSS—This is called the Old Testament Cross because it was the form raised up by Moses in the wilderness. It is called the *Cross of Prophecy*.

MALTESE CROSS—This cross represents the eight Beatitudes, each point representing a Beatitude.

 ALPHA AND OMEGA—The first and last letters of the Greek alphabet, telling us that Christ is the beginning and end of all things. Rev. 1:8.

 CHI RHO (XP)—The first two letters of the Greek word for Christ. Therefore, it is the monogram or abbreviation for the word, Christ.

 IHC or IHS—The monogram or abbreviation of the Greek word for Jesus. It is the first three letters of the Greek word for Jesus.

  INRI—The inscription over the cross of our Lord. John 19:19. It means: Jesus of Nazareth, the King of the Jews.

 CIRCLE—Eternity (since it is an endless figure)
Unity of the Godhead.

 BUTTERFLY—Resurrection. This is used as a symbol because of the butterfly's emergence from the cocoon.

 CROSS and CROWN—Victory over death.

 CROWN OF THORNS—Passion of Jesus.

 THREE NAILS—Passion (suffering) of Jesus.

 ANCHOR—Christian hope. Hebrews 6:19.

NET (Drag Net)—The kingdom of heaven; the Church. Matt. 13:47.

 SHIP—The Church. In many Danish Lutheran churches, a ship model is hung from the ceiling at the head of the center aisle. I Peter 3:18-21.

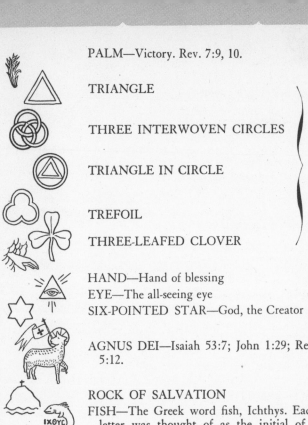

PALM—Victory. Rev. 7:9, 10.

TRIANGLE

THREE INTERWOVEN CIRCLES

TRIANGLE IN CIRCLE   } Trinity

TREFOIL

THREE-LEAFED CLOVER

HAND—Hand of blessing
EYE—The all-seeing eye   } God, the Father
SIX-POINTED STAR—God, the Creator

AGNUS DEI—Isaiah 53:7; John 1:29; Rev. 5:12.

ROCK OF SALVATION

FISH—The Greek word fish, Ichthys. Each letter was thought of as the initial of a word in the sentence: 'Jesus Christ, Son of God, Savior.' Became a symbol of early Christians.

VINE—'I am the true vine'—John 15:1.

THE GOOD SHEPHERD—'I am the good shepherd'—John 10:11.

} God, the Son

CANDLES—Jesus Christ the light of the world (should be *real* candles).

7 LAMPS } 7 Gifts of the
          Holy Spirit
7 FLAMES }   } God, the
                             Holy Spirit

DESCENDING DOVE

CHALICE, with host rising from it ⎫
⎬ Sacrament of
⎭ Lord's Supper

GRAPES

OPEN BIBLE—God's Holy Word

FONT—Sacrament of Baptism

LUTHER'S SEAL—The emblem commonly known as Luther's Seal has become the symbol of the Lutheran church. (See p. 61.) Luther describes it as follows:

'There should be a black cross in the naturally red heart; for from the heart, we must believe in the Crucified One in order to be saved. The cross, indeed, causes pain, yet it does not kill, but rather promotes the vital energy of the heart. Such a heart should stand in a white rose, to show that faith gives joy, comfort, and peace, and it should be white, because that is the color of spirits and of angels, and the joy not of the world. The rose, finally, should be placed in a sky-blue field, as this joy is already the beginning of the heavenly, and is comprehended in the hope of heaven, and that field should be encircled by a golden ring, because heavenly salvation endures forever and is valuable above all other possessions.'

THE EVANGELISTS

 S. Matthew: winged man, for his Gospel begins with the human ancestry of Christ.

 S. Mark: winged lion, for his Gospel opens with a description of the 'voice of one crying in the wilderness.'

 S. Luke: winged ox, for this Gospel gives the most complete account of the sacrificial death of Christ.

 S. John: eagle, for his Gospel soars heavenward."

121

"That was interesting, Dad," exclaimed Dale. "I didn't know that was what was meant by symbolism. I can hardly wait to see which of these symbols are used in our church. Couldn't you take us over there and explain the symbols we have in our church?"

"Yes, I think that can be arranged. Now there's one thing more you should know. In many Lutheran churches, altar paintings are used, or a sculptured reproduction of Thorwaldsen's 'Christ.'

"Religious art is another interesting subject that I hope you can study later. You have already heard about the great religious artists, Michelangelo, da Vinci, Raphael, Holbein, Durer, and Cranach. There have been many other great religious artists. In our Lutheran churches in America, reproductions of the art of two German Lutheran painters and of one great Danish Lutheran sculptor are the most commonly used.

"Johann Heinrich Hofmann (1824-1902) is especially well known for his paintings portraying the life of Christ. Paintings that have been used a great deal for altar paintings are his *Christ in Gethsemane, The Rich Young Ruler, Jesus Preaching from a Boat,* and *The Sermon on the Mount.*

"Bernard Plockhorst (1825-1907) is well known for his *Christ Blessing the Children, The Triumphal Entry into Jerusalem,* and *The Good Shepherd.*

"Bertel Thorwaldsen (1770-1844) was the son of a wood-carver from Iceland who had settled in Denmark. For the Lutheran *Cathedral Church of Our Lady* at Copenhagen, Denmark, Thorwaldsen made statues of Christ and the twelve apostles as well as an angel baptismal font. It is this statue of Christ which has been reproduced for many Lutheran altars in our country."

BIBLE STUDY

1. The lofty spire points to the true home above: Col. 3:2, Phil. 3:20. Memorize one of these
2. The tower speaks of strength: Psalm 46
3. The main door opens wide and inviting: Luke 14:17; Matt. 25:10
4. God commands services to be devotional: Ex. 3:5
5. The wide aisle to the altar is a type of the way of grace, which leads to the mercy of God, through the merits of Christ: Prov. 15:24; Heb. 10:19-25

Chapter 16

My Congregation at Sunday Morning Services

"RIGHT now, Dale, would be a good time to answer the question you asked last fall about church services," decided Dr. Lansing. "Heroes of faith have met together for worship since earliest times. But forms of worship have varied from time to time, as you have already heard.

"Lutheran worship of today can be traced back to the early Christian church. There are some things, too, that are similar in Lutheran worship to that of the Roman Catholic church. For even when a Reformation was necessary, everything was not wrong with the Catholic church. That would be to say that for 1500 years, Christ had forsaken His church, and forgotten His promise. You know that wasn't true. Luther was used by God to purify and harmonize worship with the teachings of the Bible, and to make the service such that everyone could take part. Before the time of Luther, the emphasis was on the altar service, and the sermon was often left out. Luther made the Word of God and the preaching of it the center of the service. Lutheran worship for the whole church year centers about Christ."

"What do you mean by church year? Is the church year different from an ordinary year?" asked Jim.

"Yes, you know that the calendar year is determined by the movement of the earth around the sun. It has its special days and seasons. The church year, too, has its special days and seasons to which you can look forward year by year. It also has its Sun, the Sun of Righteousness, Jesus Christ. Its special days celebrate Him, the events of His life, and His church.

"Advent begins the church year, which is not divided into months, but into two halves, like semesters in school. The first semester (from Advent to Trinity) tells about what Jesus does for you. The second tells what Jesus can do in you if you permit Him, and what He is doing for the church. The church year has three important festivals—Easter, Pentecost, and Christmas.

"This is a chart of the Christian church year."

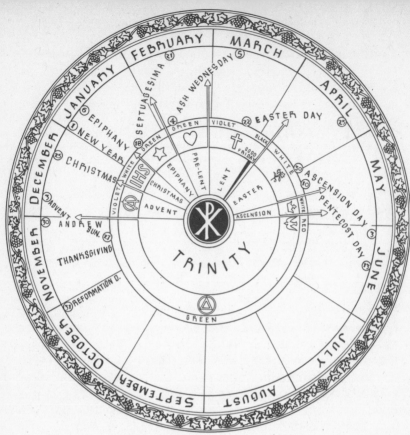

NOTE: The symbols represent the messages emphasized during the church seasons. The liturgical colors for each season are also given. The dates for movable days of the church year are indicated by curved lines.

FIXED DAYS OF THE CHURCH YEAR

Christmas Day ....December 25   Epiphany ....January 6
New Year's Day ....January 1   Reformation Day ....October 31

MOVABLE DAYS OF THE CHURCH YEAR

Advent Sunday is always the nearest Sunday to November 30.
Septuagesima Sunday is approximately 70 days before Easter.
Sexagesima Sunday is approximately 60 days before Easter.
Quinquagesima Sunday is approximately 50 days before Easter.
Easter celebrations were definitely decided by the Council of Nicea as follows: "The first Sunday after the full moon of the spring equinox shall be celebrated as the Day of Resurrection."
Ascension Day is 40 days after Easter.
Pentecost is 7 weeks or 50 days after Easter.
Trinity Sunday is 8 weeks after Easter.

"Tell us about our Sunday morning service," said Jim.
"All right. Imagine yourself in church on a Sunday morning.

You have come early enough to bow your head in silent prayer before the service begins. Probably you pray the prayer Dale and Dorothy learned in Sunday school. What was it?"

Dorothy and Dale folded their hands and in unison prayed:

> "In silent prayer, my head, I bow;
> Come to Thy temple, O Lord, and bless me now.
> Bless all Thy people who call upon Thy name;
> Bless Thou the pastor who doth Thy Word proclaim;
> Bless Thou our service, our prayer, and our praise;
> Bless all Thy church on earth through endless days. Amen."

"We'll all learn that prayer," said Mrs. Lansing. "Grown-ups, as well as children, need to pray when they enter church. Mothers, especially, need to forget Sunday dinners, Ladies' Aid suppers, and other problems, so their hearts can truly worship God."

"Then," continued Dr. Lansing, "as you listen to the organ, you study the symbols in the pulpit, the baptismal font, the altar, and the windows so as to get their message about Christ.

"The pastor comes in quietly. He stands before the altar which is now no longer a place of sacrifice because the last great sacrifice has been offered—that of Jesus on the cross. However, the altar is symbolic of that sacrifice and therefore of the presence of God."

"Oh yes, Dad," interrupted Dale, "why does the pastor turn toward the altar sometimes and toward us at other times?"

"When the pastor prays, he turns to the altar, symbolizing that he turns to God. The pastor does not do the praying for the congregation. He is the congregation's mouthpiece. Therefore, as he kneels and leads you in prayer, you should bow your head and pray with him. When the pastor turns toward you, it symbolizes that he brings a message from God.

"Now imagine that the service is ready to begin.

The Opening Prayer

"In the *opening prayer,* you pray with the pastor asking God to bless the service, to open your heart to receive the Word, and to send the Holy Spirit to help you believe in Jesus and live according to His will.

The Confession

"After the opening hymn, many congregations confess their sins. The pastor facing the altar leads you in *confession of your sins.*

The Kyrie

"This is followed by congregational singing of the *Kyrie* which stands for Greek words meaning, 'Lord have mercy.' These words were used often during the time of Jesus by the sick and sinful who came to Him. The Kyrie is repeated three times, once to each person in the Godhead.

The Absolution

"God always pardons the sins of a penitent heart that comes to Him in Jesus' name. Therefore in the *absolution*, the pastor turns as Christ's messenger to announce the glorious news of forgiveness of sins through Christ.

The Gloria

"How fitting it is that after the absolution the pastor joyously sings or speaks the *Gloria*, and that you chime in thankfully to finish the song that was first sung by heavenly hosts above the fields of Bethlehem—*And on earth, peace, good will toward men.*

The Collect

"The *collect* begins with the beautiful greeting Christ used on Easter morning, and that early Christians also used, *The Lord be with you.* You answer, *And with thy spirit.* The collects are short prayers (one for each Sunday) that go back so far that no one knows who first worded them. They are sung or spoken by the pastor. Since they are your prayers, you sing Amen at the close.

The Epistle   The Gospel

"Next, a portion of the Word of God is read. It is called the *Epistle* if it is taken from one of the epistles. It is called the *Lesson* if it is taken from one of the other books of the Bible. It is never taken from one of the Gospels, however. In most churches, a *Gospel lesson* is also read. This is always taken from one of the four Gospels.

"Through the Epistle lesson and the Gospel lesson, God speaks to you. What He says to you is more important than anything that you may sing or say to or about Him, so you should listen when the pastor reads these portions. If you give in to the temptation that comes to you to allow your mind to wander to school lessons or tests or your next hike, then there won't be any blessing in this part of the service for you.

The Creed

"Many congregations confess the *Apostles' Creed*. It is the shortest and oldest confession of faith and doctrine that the Christian church possesses. In the early days of the church, the creeds were considered so sacred that before they were recited, all who were not confessing Christians were dismissed. Think of this every time you confess the Apostles' Creed. Give your confession clearly, thoughtfully, and honestly.

The Sermon

"The *sermon* is based on the Bible and is the high peak of a Lutheran service. Sermons follow the church year in presenting the life of Jesus. Texts have been carefully chosen to give you step by step a connected, progressive understanding of Christian faith and life, and the way of salvation. Therefore, if you miss a Sunday, it's just like missing a chapter of an interesting, important story.

The Apostolic Benediction

"After the sermon, many pastors pronounce the *Apostolic benediction* (II Cor. 13:14).

The Hymns

"In between these different parts of the service are hymns of prayer, confession, joy, and hope. The Lutheran church has a rich hymnody which has an interesting history that I hope you can study some time. Lutheran hymn books contain a wide variety of hymns. The pastor carefully chooses hymns to further explain truths presented in lesson texts and sermons.

The Offering

"The *offering* is not a minor thing. Throughout the service, God continually gives—gives forgiveness, promise of life, grace, wisdom, and guidance. In the offering, the congregation is given an opportunity to give to the Lord's work. If rightly understood, and rightly given, offerings would take care of all church expenses.

The Aaronic Benediction

"The *Aaronic benediction* was first used by the high priest, Aaron:
The Lord bless thee, and keep thee.
The Lord make His face shine upon thee, and be gracious unto thee.
The Lord lift up His countenance upon thee and give thee peace.

The Closing Prayer

"In the *closing prayer,* you pray with the pastor that you may make right use of the Word so that you may have life and salvation.

"All Lutheran churches don't include all these parts in their Sunday morning services. Some have more; some less. Some churches use what is called the 'common service.' Your salvation does not depend upon the form of service but upon whether you receive the saving truth of God's Word into your heart as God speaks to you through His Word in every service.

"The more you understand the Lutheran service, the more you will appreciate and love it. Every Sunday from the opening prayer to the benediction, your heart will experience over and over again a joy and gratitude that Jesus came to save you from your sins. You will gradually be led to exclaim with the Psalmist —'My heart longeth, yea even fainteth for the courts of the Lord, for a day in Thy courts is better than a thousand.'"

BIBLE STUDY

1. Memorize I Cor. 14:40
2. Find the following and tell what they command or promise about church services: Heb. 10:24-25; I Cor. 14:26; Matt. 18:20; Psalm 100; 122:1; II Chron. 6:19-31; Lev. 19:30
3. Find Jesus' attitude toward the church of His day: Luke 4:16

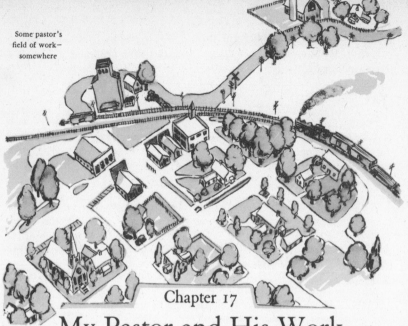

Some pastor's
field of work—
somewhere

Chapter 17

My Pastor and His Work

JIM, eager to join a hockey game, ran through the house calling, "Mother, where are you?" Then as he heard her voice, he hurried up the stairs saying, "Mother, Mrs. Smith said I should give you this note right away." As Mrs. Lansing read the note, Jim noticed that she had been cleaning the guest room. The air and sunshine coming through the open window made the room smell sweet and clean. Some of his mother's prettiest sheets and pillow cases were on the bed.

"Who's coming?"

"Our pastor. His wife's mother is very ill. He's just returning from a visit to her. His wife and children will stay a little longer. Our Ladies' Aid decided to surprise her by re-papering the bedrooms while she's gone. So I've asked our pastor to stay with us a few nights."

"Oh, good! Then maybe he'll play hockey with us. He's a keen skater, Mother."

"He won't be here until after you're in bed. He'll get back just in time for choir rehearsal. After that, the church council meets."

"Oh well, maybe he'll play with us before school."

"No, he'll be in his study all morning. You probably will see him tomorrow noon, and then you can ask him to play. It would be good relaxation for him."

"I didn't know a pastor would have to study all morning."

"He doesn't use the whole morning for study. He has his private devotion early so as to start the day with God's help, and with the assurance of the promise, 'Lo, I am with you always.' Then he studies several hours in preparation for sermons, Bible classes, Sunday school teachers' meetings, talks, and the like. Even after he's finished college and a special school for pastors called a seminary, and even after he's called by a congregation to be its pastor, he has to be a life-long student. He never has time to be lazy. A part of his morning, he uses for reports and church records. He often says the mornings aren't long enough."

"Why doesn't he use the afternoons, then?"

"He gives his afternoons for his people. It's then he visits the sick and those who don't go to church, comforts the sad, helps the needy, and welcomes those who have moved into town. Sometimes he has funerals or private baptisms. He's learned he gets more done if he follows a schedule."

"What does he do evenings?"

"There are organization meetings every evening. He likes to visit each organization often enough to know exactly what it is doing, and to inspire and encourage the members to further work by a message from God's Word. After the devotion, he leaves to make calls, because the best time often for the pastor to reach both the husband and wife is in the evening."

"And I used to think a pastor had an easy life—that all he had to do was preach on Sunday!"

"Preaching and telling the people about Jesus, of course, are his most important work. But he doesn't preach only in the pulpit. You remember Daddy's telling you about St. Francis of Assisi. Here's a story about St. Francis that I like:

"St. Francis said to a young monk: 'Brother, let us go down into the town and preach.' So they went forth, the venerable father and the young man, talking as they went. They wound their way down the principal streets, around the lowly alleys and lanes, and even to the outskirts of the town, and to the village beyond, till they found themselves approaching the monastery again. Then said the young monk, 'Father, when shall we begin to preach?' St. Francis looked kindly at his young companion and said: 'My child, we have been preaching while we were walking. We have been seen, and looked at; our behavior has been remarked, and so we have delivered a morning sermon. It is of no use to walk anywhere to preach, unless we preach as we walk.'

"It's a good story for everyone to remember. Take it with you now when you go out to play hockey," continued Mrs. Lansing.

"Oh, say, I'd forgotten the hockey game. So long, Mom," and Jim rushed out of the house.

That night, Dr. Lansing asked, "Whose side won tonight, Jim?"

"Oh, they did," said Jim. "But just wait until tomorrow. I'll ask Pastor Harvey to be on our side, and then we'll win."

Then Jim continued seriously, "Why did Pastor Harvey become a minister, anyway? When he plays hockey or ball, I forget he's our pastor. We all seem to have more fun, too. He's such a good sport."

"In other words," said Mrs. Lansing quietly, "he is preaching good sportsmanship while out there on the ice."

Jim grinned at his mother. "I remember. The St. Francis story."

"When your pastor was young," said Dr. Lansing, "he prayed that he could serve Jesus all his life. One way to serve Jesus is to be a minister. Pastor Harvey told me he had felt called to the ministry from the time he was a boy."

"What do you mean by saying he was called to be a pastor?"

"Just as Jesus called His disciples, so the Holy Spirit calls men today. He speaks to the hearts of men through God's Word. A man who is called into the ministry feels a very definite urging, a definite call from God. The more he knows God's Word, the better the Holy Spirit can help him to know God's will. That's important whether he is to be a pastor or in any other work. Men who enter the ministry without a call from God have a low view of their office. They act as though they were servants of the members of their congregation only, instead of God's servant. They aren't a blessing in God's service."

"Aren't mistakes made, though, sometimes?" asked Dale.

"Yes, mistakes are made because even pastors are human. The main reason for mistakes, however, is because people do what they wish without seeking God's will. Sometimes, too, men become pastors even when they know they are unfit because they don't have a sound body, a well-trained mind, good common sense, moral courage, or a sympathetic heart.

"However, God uses many different kinds of people to do His work. Some have many talents. Some few. That makes little difference just so they obey God's will.

"I remember reading a diary of your great grandfather. He was a humble man. The work in his congregation was blessed in an unusual way. He couldn't understand it, especially when he thought about some of his fellow pastors with more talents who seemed to be struggling and seeing few results. One morning, he arrived at his church earlier than usual to find in his sacristy three of his young men kneeling in prayer asking God to bless him and his work. Then he wrote in his diary, 'Now I know why God is blessing my work. I have helping me a power house of prayer that is performing miracles.' "

"That reminds me of a story I read the other day," said Mrs. Lansing.

"A pastor dreamed that his church was a stage coach. He said to the members of his church, 'How shall we get the coach to the top of the hill? For there is no horse.' The people answered, 'You pull and we'll push.' For awhile, the heavy coach moved slowly but surely up the hill. Then the weight became heavier and heavier. The pastor could no longer pull it. He turned to see all his helpers sitting in the coach. They had become tired of turning wheels and pushing."

And then she concluded, "Prayer for the pastor, and the people, and work of the congregation is the best way of turning wheels and pushing. How else can you turn wheels and push by being kind to our pastor?"

"I'll pick some flowers and help you take care of his room," said Dorothy.

Jim added: "I'll ask him if I can run some errands for him. Then maybe he'll have time to play hockey with us. Mother said that would be good relaxation for him."

"I'll let him hold Annabelle," said Joan importantly.

Before anyone could laugh, Mrs. Lansing said seriously: "I'm glad you'll share your best doll with our pastor. I hope you'll always share your best gifts, Joan."

Dale looked disappointed. "I'll just keep my eyes open to see what I can do when he gets here."

"Dale, that's a good resolution," commended Dr. Lansing. "Your pastor is the best friend you have next to Jesus and your family. Keep your eyes open to see what you can do to help him not only now while he is in our house, but every day. Then you'll be sharing in the greatest work in the world. You'll be helping your pastor to work for Christ among His people."

BIBLE STUDY

1. Memorize Ephesians 4:11
2. Find what the Bible says about leadership in the church: Acts 14:23
3. What does the Bible say about pastoral care: Jer. 3:15; Eph. 4:11-13
4. Union with Christ in the church results in spiritual life and health: John 5:24; John 20:31; Hebrews 3:6, Matt. 18:20; John 15:4, 5

131

Dr. Lansing

Dale

Mrs. Lansing

Chapter 18

My Home

DALE felt very unhappy inside. His stomach hurt. His throat seemed to choke him. "I'm glad Mother and Dad don't do that," he thought, as he absently stroked the setter puppy's head.

Finally, he burst out: "Mom, I was just over to Larry's house. Larry and I were going to get his skis and have fun. But his mother and father were mad at each other. They used bad language. Why do they do that? Larry never wants to play after a fuss like that. He goes off by himself. Why don't his parents 'cut it out'?"

"It's only Jesus who can help them to be good to each other. Add Larry's parents to your prayer list, Dale. Pray that they will permit Jesus to enter their home. Then they'll be kind and loving to each other and Larry. Now I'll tell you what to do. Find Larry and invite him to our house to play ping pong and to have supper."

"O Mom! You're swell!" Dale hurried outside, a happy boy again.

"Isn't it too bad," said Mrs. Lansing to her niece who was home from college for a week-end visit, "that Larry's parents quarrel in Larry's presence? God has given them a rare jewel in their sensitive, artistic boy, but they're doing him a great harm by their unhappy home life. The most precious thing parents can give their children is the knowledge that they deeply love each other.

"The strange part of it is that Larry's parents do love each other. But they've got into the habit of being unkind. She hurts him by what she says and does and then he does the same to her. If only they will let Christ enter their lives, I'm sure they can still make a happy home. They make me think of the rhyme:

Jim

Joan

Dorothy

"We have careful thoughts for the stranger
And smiles for the occasional guest
But oft for our own, the bitter tone
Though we love our own the best."

"I'm glad, Aunt Sally, that you've invited me to make your home mine since Mother died. I've appreciated being a part of your family and seeing how you and Uncle prove your love for each other in many acts of kindness and thoughtfulness. So many of the girls in my college class are cynical about married life. But because I've had the privilege of living with you, I can hardly wait until Bill and I can be married. We are going to try to make our home a Christian home just like yours."

Mrs. Lansing smiled at her niece. Then washing her hands, she said: "There, Corinne, those cookies are done. Now we'll go and sit before the fireplace while I mend Dale's stockings."

Then Mrs. Lansing asked thoughtfully: "Corinne, what's the difference between a house and a home? Two houses may cost about the same. Both may be models in the community for attractiveness, orderliness, neatness, and cleanliness. And yet, one may be stiff and cold, and the other warm, livable, and cozy. What's the difference?"

"You just told Dale that Christ's presence changes it from ugliness to beauty. I suppose He also changes a house to a home."

"That's right. If Jesus is a constant guest in the home, and if every member of the family tries to do God's will, then it will be a place of peace, rest, and love. I imagine you and Bill have spent many happy hours planning your home. When the time comes to actually make your home, it may help you if I warn you now that it is not easy. It takes all the Christianity and talent you possess. It takes hard work. It means that you and Bill will have to be forgiving and unselfish. Happiness in a home

133

doesn't just come. Each member of the household has to give up much for it, has to share and work for it. Especially is that true when the greatest of all blessings is given a home in children. Then home life becomes still more complicated."

"Why is that?"

"Each individual has a will of his own. One of the parents' privileges is to help each child to make his will obedient to God's will. Another reason life becomes more complicated when children enter the home is that then it is necessary for parents to make more choices. Because their lives are examples to the children, consecrated, unselfish parents can't do things they don't want their children to do. Religion and child training are *caught* probably more than *taught*."

"Is that why you have pictures of Jesus in many of your rooms?"

"Yes, these beautiful pictures of Jesus are a constant reminder that Jesus is with us, watching and listening to us. It helps. Just take gossip for example. It is easier to teach children to speak about others only in truthfulness and kindness when the beautiful eyes of Jesus seem to look down on them from a picture. It is easier for all of us to remember to dedicate our lips to Christ's service.

"For the same reason, we've chosen our books, magazines, and music carefully. Not only children but grown-ups absorb the atmosphere and surroundings of the home. After all, the home gives the first and most lasting influence in Christian education to the children."

"A person certainly doesn't realize all the thought that goes into making a home," said Corinne, thoughtfully.

"You should have said thought and prayer," corrected Mrs. Lansing. "I've found that the best way to start the day is with prayer. Then no matter what the day has in store for me, I feel that God is at my side. It is easier, then, to rule the children with kind firmness instead of anger. It is easier to be as courteous to the children as I expect them to be to me."

"But isn't it hard to find time for prayer in the morning?"

"Yes, of course it is. There's one thing after another that comes up in the morning and that seems to require immediate attention. But everything worth while is worth striving for. I've learned from experience that the best way for me is to set my alarm early enough so that I can have my quiet hour before the day's work begins. If I feel tired, and think I'll get it done after the children

134

go to school, other things always come in the way. So, I don't permit any excuses. It's a part of my daily schedule."

"I suppose that's the secret of your having won your children's confidence. They tell you so freely about their experiences."

"There are three other things that have helped a great deal in winning the obedience and confidence of the children. For one thing, we have tried since they were small to answer all their questions truthfully. If there isn't time to answer the question when asked, we try to do so during the children's hour."

"What do you mean?"

"The children's hour is not necessarily sixty minutes long. It may be only ten minutes. It may be more than an hour. But it's that time of every day that is given to the children. Then is when we answer questions and problems, read stories together, have our family devotion and family hymn sings, learn to use the Bible, and have our family prayers. It is a splendid time to lead the many 'whys' of children to God. It is the time when respect for the Word of God, reverence in prayer, and love for Jesus can be caught by the children as they watch us. It's the time when the children learn that:

> "A home is, first of all, a place
>   Where, each and every day,
>   The love of Jesus Christ is found,
>   And where the people pray;
>   Where sacrifice for others is
>   A joy that is sincere,
>   'Tis there they'll find real happiness
>   Each day throughout the year."

"Thirdly, we try to plan many good times together. It always makes a hike, picnic, or trip more of an event if all of us go together. We also try to plan good times at home here, and make the children feel that their friends are welcome. Before we—"

"Oh Mother, here's a new girl who lives in the next block," exclaimed Dorothy as she came skipping into the room with a shy playmate. "Her name is Maxine. I want her to hear Corinne's story about her trip with the debating team to another college and all the funny things that happened on the way."

"All right, Corinne," laughed Mrs. Lansing. "It's your turn to take the center of the stage now while I finish preparing supper."

BIBLE STUDY

1. Memorize: Eph. 6:4
2. Look up the following on child training in the home: Prov. 22:6; John 21:15; Deut. 6:4-9

Chapter 19

Good Reading for Everyone in My Family

THE living room was unusually quiet. Only the howling of a blizzard, the crackling of the logs in the fireplace, and the sound of turning pages could be heard. The Lansing family was absorbed in reading.

Jim was scanning the church weekly. Ever since Jim was eight and Mrs. Lansing had arranged through a missionary for correspondence between him and an eight year old Chinese boy, he had eagerly looked at the pictures in the foreign mission section of the weekly church paper. Usually when he finished that section, he would scan or read parts of the rest of the paper. Jim was learning more about his church than he realized.

On the rug, Dorothy was re-reading one of her favorite books. Probably you'd think it was a very strange book. Mrs. Lansing had made it from Sunday school papers Dorothy had saved for the year. Sometimes Dorothy just looked at the pictures. Often she looked at page 576 where there was a letter she had sent the editor. She especially liked the continued stories which now she could finish by just turning a few pages instead of waiting till the next Sunday.

Dale was all goose-flesh. For he was in far-away Africa. Suddenly, out from the bushes a lion had rushed at his hero. Dale could hardly read fast enough to find out whether his hero was saved. Suddenly he relaxed. Once again Christ had fulfilled His promise. David Livingstone—for he was the hero—was saved by his men who killed the lion.

Mrs. Lansing was in Germany, breathlessly reading about nine nuns who made their escape through a window to a wagon where they were hidden in empty herring barrels covered with cloth, and were driven to Wittenberg and safety. Among these nuns was Katherine von Bora who later became Luther's wife.

"Poor Annabelle! What's the matter? Can't you sleep?" crooned Joan as she hugged her doll. "Then I'll show you some beautiful pictures. See this one. That's David. And that's the wicked giant David killed. Here's Ruth. Isn't she pretty? And this man with the lions all around him is ————."

"Well, well, doesn't this look cozy?" said Dr. Lansing who

had just returned from sick calls. "Everyone reading! How do you like your new book, Mother? And yours, Dale? I'm glad my family's all at home. This is a stormy night."

"You have often talked about the traveling you'd like to do," continued Dr. Lansing. "It's fun to plan, even if you may have to stay home all your life doing your job. And yet, even then, you can travel through reading. A comfortable chair, a good light, a book—and presto! You're off to far away lands and places, in long ago times, among interesting people of many races in just a few minutes. Wouldn't it be fun if you could just press a button like you do an electric light switch, and all the characters in your books would come before you? Whom would you like to see?"

"David Livingstone," shrieked Dale. "Paul! Athanasius! Luther! Muhlenberg! Robinson Crusoe! Tiny Tim!"

"I'd love to see the mother of Jesus, and Ruth—and Esther," added Dorothy.

Little Joan said sleepily, "David, too—and Jesus, and Little Bo Peep."

Mrs. Lansing smiled and asked, "What about you, Jim?"

"Oh, there are so many. I'd like to see all the people Dad's told us about—St. Francis and Polycarp, and also Hudson Taylor, King Arthur, and Abraham Lincoln, and—"

"You've certainly made a great many worthwhile friends," interrupted Dr. Lansing. "I'm very glad. It makes me feel amply repaid for the money and time Mother and I have spent in carefully choosing books for our library. I think already you know how to make good friends in books and magazines. Most people wouldn't think of associating with gangsters and wicked people, but they don't seem to realize that when they read about them they are with them.

"I hope the Christian friends you've made through good books will also make you choose to read only those 'funnies' that have well-drawn figures and teach honesty, respect, loyalty and good habits.

"The friends you make in books and papers mold your life just as much as the friends you make in school. As you can be judged by the friends you have, so you can be judged by the friends you make through your reading.

"You don't need many books, either. Often it is better to have a few very good friends than many acquaintances. Lincoln had only a few books, but he knew them well by re-reading them often. His favorite book was the Bible and so the people of the Bible became very good friends of his."

"Where did you get all our books, Dad?" asked Jim.

"Many of these are from the publishing house of our church. You can be quite sure that books purchased from publishing houses under church control are among the best of Christian books. Some I've purchased direct from the publishers. A good rule is never to buy books until you have read them and know that you will want to read them over and over again."

"Does the publishing house print all these books?"

"No, it specializes in printing hymn books, Sunday school text books, church papers, and Christian books. But on the shelves of its book store, it has many of the finest books of other publishing houses, too.

"When I was in the city a few weeks ago, I went to the publishing house. The manager introduced me to the author and artist of a new graded Sunday school book that will be out next fall. Both were working many hours a day to write and illustrate the book. After they finish their work, there are still many people who work on the book. The next page will show you some of the workers who prepare your Sunday school books.

"In much the same way, magazines and books are written for your Sunday school teacher, your pastor, church organizations, and for everyone. Therefore, just as early traveling missionaries spread the Gospel to people in many lands, so publishing houses of our churches today are helping to spread Bibles and Christian literature to people all over the world. I hope that some day you can visit the publishing house of your church and can see good reading material being made up for everyone in your family."

BIBLE STUDY

1. Memorize Rev. 1:3 or John 20:31
2. Can you see any reason for Job's wish (Job 19:23), and God's act (Ex. 31:18)
3. Whom does God tell to write books in the following: Ex. 17:14; Jer. 30:2; Rev. 1:11

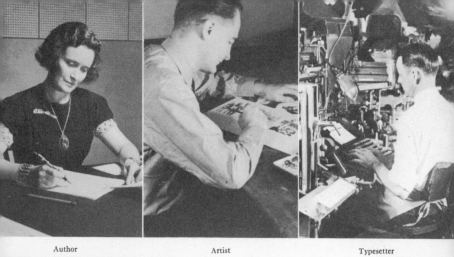

| Author | Artist | Typesetter |

| Compositor | Make-up man | Printing press |

| Folding | Machine for gathering pages | Binding |

בָּרָא אֱלֹהִים אֵת הַשָּׁמַיִם וְאֵת הָאָרֶץ ²וְהָאָרֶץ הָיְתָה תֹהוּ
וְחֹשֶׁךְ עַל פְּנֵי תְהוֹם וְרוּחַ אֱלֹהִים מְרַחֶפֶת עַל פְּנֵי הַמָּיִם
יֹּאמֶר אֱלֹהִים יְהִי אוֹר וַיְהִי אוֹר ⁴וַיַּרְא אֱלֹהִים אֶת הָאוֹר

For a long time the Old Testament and New Testament were written in scroll form. The Old Testament was originally written in Hebrew. Above are a few lines from a Hebrew Bible.

Chapter 20

The Greatest of All My Books

" 'What are they doing with him?' exclaimed a young man as he joined an angry mob at the dungeon.

" 'He's getting what he deserves, at last. We are tired of hearing his warnings. And so the princes received permission from the king to cast him into this hideous dungeon. See! Those men have been letting him down with cords. We don't have to listen to him any more. He can't live long after he begins to sink in the muck and mire at the bottom. I could almost pity him if he were any other man. It's such a filthy dungeon!'

"It wasn't long before word of the prisoner's treatment reached a servant of the king who hurried to persuade the king to permit him to get rags, worn out garments, and 30 men.

"Now why do you suppose he wanted worn out garments and so many men? Was he a friend to the prisoner? If he was, would he be able to rescue the prisoner in time?"

H Dad," interrupted Dale, "I wish you'd finish the story. Tell us what book it's in. Could we read it?"

"Yes, that story and many more exciting, thrilling stories are in one book. I left the book on the end table by the wing chair. Will you get it for me, Dale?"

"Why Dad," said Dale when he came back carrying his father's Bible, "Do you mean that story is in the Bible?"

"Yes, you'll find it in Jeremiah 37 and 38."

Holding the book that was so precious to him, Dr. Lansing said seriously:

"Just last night, we were talking about the kinds of books you should read. Among all the thousands and thousands of books that have been written, there is only one that is very important to you and to everyone. That is this book—the Bible.

"The Word 'Bible' grew out of the Greek word 'biblia' that originally meant 'Little Books' but later came to mean 'The Book.' It is believed that the word 'Bible' was first applied to the sacred books by Chrysostom.

"The more you study the Bible, the more you will think of it as 'The Book.' The contents of this Book will prove it to be 'The Book.' I shall illustrate what I mean.

ϵΝΟΙϹΟΥΚΩΨϵ ΧΩΝΥΜ'
ΛΗΟΗϹΑΝΟΗΙϵΡΙ ΤΟΝΑΗΟ
ΗΑΤΟΥΝΙϹϹ ΙϵϹΙΝΑΙ

The New Testament was originally written in the Greek language and in scroll form.
Above is a facsimile of a few lines from the Codex Sinaiticus

"It took 50 years to build the marvelous Dome of St. Peter's Cathedral. The architect was dead 30 years before it was finished. Then how did it become so perfect? Because Michelangelo, the architect, left behind him such complete plans that no mistake could mar the beauty and perfection.

"Now let us suppose that 40 different builders, living 1500 years apart, should each one in his own land hew and chisel out a number of stones, each utterly ignorant of the other's work. In later years if these stones were brought together, what could you expect to find?"

"Just a pile of stones," said Jim.

"But now suppose that from these stones there arose a cathedral as perfect as any that Michelangelo planned.

"That's exactly a picture of the Bible. The Bible is composed of 66 separate books written by at least 40 different writers, some of them living 1500 years apart and in countries separated by hundreds of miles. They wrote in three different languages— Hebrew, Aramaic, and Greek. Some of them were skilled and well educated. Some were common people. Among them were farmers, fishermen, tax-gatherers, and a doctor just like me. Moses, about whom you've read many stories, was one of the authors. Some wrote in palaces. Others wrote in tents. Few knew each other. When one wrote, he did not know that anyone else was writing, or what he was writing.

"Now in after years when these writings were brought together, what would you expect to find? Just a pile of books, of course.

"But instead, when after careful, continued investigation, the writings of these 40 men were selected from other writings, and were arranged and put together they made a complete Book, a Book without a single contradiction if rightly understood.

"The contents of this Book cover the widest range. There is not a human interest that is not touched. No matter what you like to read best, you can find it in the Bible: prose, poetry, adventure, history, stories about people who really lived, hymns,

141

Et ut pfecerũt oĩa fcdm legem dũi: reuerfi funt ĩ galileam · ĩ ciuĩtatem fuã nazareth . Puer autẽ crefcebat et

A facsimile of a portion from the Latin Bible printed by Gutenberg from movable type

inspiring sermons, and drama. In it you'll find light, strength, comfort, and help according to your need. It is the traveler's map, the soldier's sword, the Christian's chart. It should fill the memory, rule the heart, and guide the feet."

"But, Dad, how can the Bible be so perfect when so many different people wrote it?"

"It is so perfect because God was the architect. He planned the book. Every part of each of the 66 books was inspired by Him (II Tim. 3:16, II Pet. 1:21). As in the British navy, all rope that is used has a red strand that runs through the center, so the Bible's message is like a red strand that binds together all the books from Genesis to Revelation. This unifying message is that Jesus is the Christ, the Son of God, and that believing, you may have life through His Name.

"But it isn't only the contents that make it 'The Book.' This book has great influence. Queen Victoria said, 'The Bible is the secret of England's greatness.' Most of the early immigrants to our country built first the church and then the school. From this humble beginning, educational institutions have been started by people who loved the Bible and whom the Bible inspired with a love for learning. In Shakepeare, there are 187 actual quotations from the Bible and 551 allusions to it. Great masterpieces in literature, art, and music cannot be appreciated apart from a knowledge of the Bible. We might mention Handel's 'Messiah,' Mendelssohn's 'Elijah,' the paintings of Raphael, Da Vinci, and Durer, and the sculpture of Thorwaldsen.

"'The Book' also transforms lives. Countless examples could be given to prove this. I'll just take time to quote the words of a native chief of New Zealand—'My father and I were once blood-thirsty cannibals. On that stone, we slaughtered, roasted, and devoured human beings. We are Christians now. What raised us from what we were to what we are now? The Bible.'

"Since the Bible is 'The Book' with the power of transforming lives, it must be used and studied so that you learn to know Jesus as your best friend."

A facsimile of a section of Martin Luther's German Bible

"The other day," said Mrs. Lansing, "I read Luther's rule for Bible reading:

" 'First, read one book carefully; then study chapter by chapter and verse by verse, and lastly, word by word. For, it is like a person shaking a fruit tree—first shaking the tree and gathering up the fruit which falls to the ground, then shaking each branch, afterwards each twig, and last of all looking carefully under each leaf to see that no fruit remains. In this way, and in no other, shall we also find the hidden treasures that are in the Bible.' "

"The remarkable thing about the Bible," continued Dr. Lansing, "is that you never will know all there is to know in the Bible. Charles Elliot was a life-long student of the Bible. He re-read the Bible many times. In his 77th year, just a month before he died, as he sat reading the Bible his daughter asked, 'What are you reading?'

" 'I am reading the news,' he replied.

" 'The Book' has been compared to a remarkable exhibit which is to be found in the Dresden art gallery. The exhibit is a silver egg. When you touch a hidden spring in that silver egg, it opens to disclose a golden chicken. When you touch the golden chicken, it opens to disclose a crown of glittering gems. When you touch the crown, a magnificent diamond ring is disclosed. In the Bible, you can find beauty richer than the gems in any art gallery.

"The more you know of the Bible, the more you will want to share it with other people. That is why the first translation was made. It was called the Septuagint translation. It was a translation of the Old Testament from Hebrew to Greek because Greek had become the language of the people. It was made some time between 280 and 180 years before Christ. From that time on, there have been many translations until in 1938, the world celebrated the thousandth translation of the Bible.

"Sometime, you can study a history of the Bible. It would be interesting for you to take a trip to Rome, St. Petersburg, and London to see the oldest Bibles in the world. It would be interesting for you to see the Bible books written as scrolls, and on expensive vellum, to see the hand decorations, and the carefully written manuscripts. Some of the oldest copies would be hard

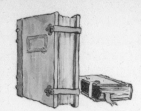

A facsimile of a few lines from the King James Bible

for you to read because only capitals with no spacing were used. For instance, the first words of John 3:16 in our language would have looked like this:

FORGODSOLOVEDTHEWORLDTHATHEGAVE

"It would be interesting for you to see copies of the Bibles you've already heard about: Wycliff's, Tyndale's, Luther's, King James', and the first copy of the Bible printed by Gutenberg's press.

"Just translating the Bible or printing it, however, is not enough. It must be spread to the people.

"As early as the time before the Council of Nicea, a learned, wealthy pastor, Pamphillus of Caesarea, circulated numerous books of the Bible (in scroll form, of course) as loans or as permanent gifts. This caused a wide circulation.

"Bible societies were a result of the Reformation and were organized in all lands for the purpose of translating the Bible and distributing it cheaply.

"In 1698, 'The Society for the Promotion of Christian Knowledge' was organized in London for the purpose of circulating the Bible among the common people who couldn't afford to buy it. It now works in foreign fields too and has become the 'Bible and Tract Society of the Anglican Church.'

"In 1699 a similar society was organized in Scotland.

"In 1719, the Canstein Bible Institute was organized in Berlin by the wealthy Baron Canstein in connection with Francke's institutions. It became the pioneer of Bible Societies.

"In 1804, the largest and most influential Bible Society was founded in London and called the British and Foreign Bible Society.

"I haven't time to mention all the Bible Societies but there is one more that I do want to mention: The American Bible Society organized in 1815.

"How thankful you can be that you live in a time when Bible societies make it possible for you to own your own Bible. It is a privilege that few people had before the invention of the printing press.

"I've told you now a few things about the Bible. I hope it has helped you to realize that one of the reasons the Bible is the greatest of all the books you own is because it has been preserved during all these years of warfare, persecutions, and trials, and

† NEW TESTAMENT – GREEK
† OLD TESTAMENT – HEBREW

has been translated and spread to many people. God wants everyone to have His Word with all its messages and promises, among which is 'Lo, I am with you always.' There is much more that is interesting about the Bible. There are more books written about the Bible than about any other book. There are more translations of the Bible than of any other book. The Bible is the world's best seller.

"No wonder Sir Walter Scott, the world's great literary genius, surrounded by a library of 40,000 books, said, as he lay dying: 'Lockhart, bring me "The Book."'

"When asked what book he meant, he replied, 'There is but *one* Book. Bring me the Bible.'"

BIBLE STUDY

1. Memorize Ps. 119:105
2. The Bible is of divine origin—Deut. 31:9; Jer. 30:1, 2; Gal. 1:11-12; II Pet. 1:21; II Tim. 3:16
3. The purpose of the Bible—Acts 20:32; II Tim. 3:15-17; John 20:30, 31; Rom. 1:16
4. Find the different names given to the Bible in the following: Gal. 3:22; Psalm 119:105

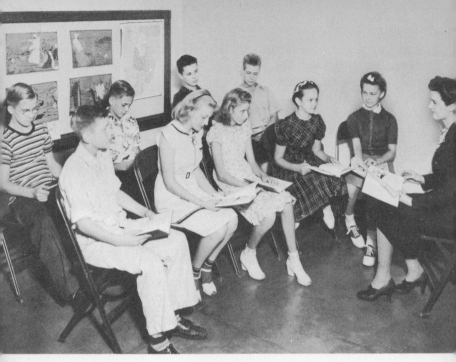

Chapter 21

My Sunday School

SUCH a thing had never happened before!

"Dad," said Mrs. Lansing, "just imagine! It's a whole half hour before Sunday school, and Dale and Dorothy have already left. It's very different from last year when I asked Dale to recite his memory verse, 'Be ye doers of the word and not hearers only,' and he exclaimed, 'But we don't do anything, Mother! We're just sitters of the Word. Why do I have to go to Sunday school?'"

Soon Dr. and Mrs. Lansing, Jim, and little Joan were a part of the group on the way to Sunday school. Dr. and Mrs. Lansing belonged to the Bible class. Rosy-cheeked Joan whose little fat legs had a hard time to keep up with her daddy was a member of the class of three-year-olds.

When the whole family was back home again and together at the dinner table, Dr. Lansing decided to have his curiosity satisfied. So he asked: "What did you do in Sunday school to-day, Dale?"

"Oh say, Dad, you should be in our class! We have exhibits

and pictures, and displays just like at school. If we get there early, she lets us help her get the displays, or the sand box, or the pictures ready, and she answers all our questions and tells us many things she doesn't have time for in class. It seems like our class time just flies by. We're always *doing* things this year. She also shows us how our lessons can help us to live better *right now*. Next Sunday we ————."

"And when she smiles and her eyes shine, she's so pretty, Dad. She never sits down and reads the questions from the book, either. She seems to know the whole lesson by heart, and she is so happy when we know our lessons, that we just want to know them," interrupted Dorothy.

"Next Sunday, Dad," continued Dale, "she wants someone to tell her when Sunday schools began. Do you know anything about it?"

"I might as well tell you something about it right now. Sunday schools, of course, are for the purpose of Christian instruction.

"The people of Israel were God's chosen people and they were careful to teach their children about God and His commands.

"In the days of Samuel, prophets taught young men, in schools that must have been something like our seminaries. At that time, children were taught in the home by the parents.

"During Nehemiah's time, synagogue schools appeared. These schools consisted of elementary day schools in which the Old Testament was taught from little parchment rolls especially prepared for the children. There were also higher schools of learning. In connection with the synagogue worship on the Sabbath, there was a Sabbath school for children. It is considered the oldest Sunday school, even though it was very different, of course, from the Sunday school of today.

"In the early Christian church, children were taught in the home and in catechetical schools. Justin Martyr and Clement—you've already heard about them—taught in catechetical schools.

"When monasteries became common, monks often took care of the instruction of the young.

"You remember Charlemagne who was like a light in the dark ages. He encouraged parents to teach their children in their homes. In 804 A. D., he had a law passed requiring parents themselves to learn the creed, the Lord's Prayer, and the words of the institution of baptism, and to teach them to their children and to those whom they brought to Holy Baptism.

"After he died, people again lost interest. Again they became careless about Christian truths. They did not even know the Lord's Prayer, the Creed, or the Ten Commandments. Luther became very sad at the ignorance of the people, and so he wrote a 'little Bible,' called the Catechism, which contained some of the most important truths of the Bible. He taught the Catechism to children and grown-ups. This was called Catechetical instruction. Then he encouraged parents to teach the Catechism in their homes, and pastors to teach on Sundays, either before or after services.

"The modern Sunday school had its beginning in 1780 when Robert Raikes (1735-1811) of Gloucester, England, who had been reading the Bible and providing teachers for prisoners, became discouraged and turned to the more hopeful task of dealing with children. He was appalled at the ignorance and vice of many children in the poorer sections of the city. He decided to gather these children on Sundays and provide them with much needed instruction. His school was at first called the 'ragged school' because of the ragged, dirty, ignorant waifs that became the first pupils of the Sunday school. Cleanliness was particularly stressed. Because education was not free then, as it is today, both secular and religious subjects were taught. In time, however, the Sunday school became a school for teaching Christianity.

"The first teacher was Mrs. Meredith who conducted class in the kitchen of her home in Sooty Alley. Later, Mrs. Mary Critchley started a Sunday school in her home which was near Mr. Raikes' home. Mr. Raikes paid her salary. She taught from 10:00 to 12:00, from 1:00 to 3:00, and sometimes until 5:00.

"After a few years of experimentation, Raikes published a report about his work. Immediately many people went to Gloucester to see the work he was doing. The result was that the Sunday school movement spread rapidly, especially in America.

"The first Sunday school in America was organized in Philadelphia in 1790 and was known as 'The First Day Society.' It was not a church undertaking. It was a Sunday school society organized to teach reading, writing, and spelling, as well as Christianity.

"Now there are Sunday schools in many places in the world. Since 1889, world Sunday school conventions have been held regularly every four years in various parts of the world.

"The Lutheran church has always laid great stress on the training of the children in the Christian religion. Most Lutherans who came to America brought with them the Catechism, Bible, hymn books, and devotion books. One of the earliest successful attempts at Sunday school work in the Lutheran church was at St. John's Lutheran Church in Philadelphia, in 1821.

"In the last ten years, the number of children attending Sunday school in the Lutheran church has increased a great deal, and the growth is more rapid each year. A very important improvement is the Bible class department where parents can have instruction too. When teachers are trained, prepared, conscientious teachers like yours, then the Sunday school can be a great blessing in winning and holding souls for the Kingdom.

"And so, Dale, you can now see that Christ's promise, 'Lo, I am with you always,' has been true for children too. It has been fulfilled from earliest times through Christian education."

BIBLE STUDY

1. Memorize Mark 10:15 or Luke 18:17
2. How do the following apply to the lesson: Prov. 22:6; Mark 10:14; II Tim. 3:16; Deut. 4:10; Acts 18:11

The First Communion

Chapter 22

Three Great Questions for Me To Answer

JIM was very much impressed. Twenty-seven young people had just gone before the altar. Each in turn had answered the pastor's questions:

Dost thou renounce the devil, and all his works, and all his ways?

Dost thou believe in God, the Father, Son, and Holy Spirit?

Wilt thou, by the grace of God, continue steadfast in this covenant of thy Baptism, even unto the end?

Especially was it a solemn, sacred moment for Jim when big, strong, fun-loving, athletic Bob gave his answers in clear, serious tones. For Bob was the object of Jim's hero worship.

Later at the dinner table, Dr. Lansing said, "This was a great decision day for those young people. It doesn't seem possible that you will be in the next Junior confirmation class, and that in two years, Jim, you will be one of a group at the altar publicly confessing your decision to live with Christ. That will be a great day for our family."

"Has there always been confirmation, Dad?" asked Jim.

"Just a few days ago, I told you about religious instruction having been given children from earliest times. The first mention of the Catechumenate was during the time of Justin Martyr. He refers to it in his first great Apology (140 A.D.). There was, however, no confirmation such as we have it now until after the Reformation when it was encouraged by Luther.

"Martin Bucer, who died in 1551, is called the father of confirmation. He was one of Luther's followers and co-workers. Bugenhagen, another friend of Luther's, introduced confirmation into Pomerania. It was not long before most of the churches in Germany gave confirmation instruction. During the Thirty Years' War, however, it disappeared in many of the churches.

"It did not become popular again until the time of Spener. He had been favorably impressed by confirmation as practiced in Hess, Germany. He considered it an excellent means of teaching the young and of confirming them in true Christianity. He wrote an explanation of Luther's Catechism. It contained over 700 questions and became the text book of the confirmands. Because of his enthusiasm for confirmation, it was gradually adopted by the different Lutheran Churches of Germany. From there, it spread to Denmark and Norway, where it was made compulsory by law in 1736. One of the great educational leaders in Denmark was Pontoppidan about whose explanation you have already heard. It was based on Spener's but had about 200 less questions. This explanation, the hymn book, and Luther's Catechism were the text books used in schools.

"In Sweden, confirmation was introduced in 1811.

"Lutheran immigrants to our country valued confirmation so highly that they continued it in this country."

"But why do we have confirmation?"

"As you receive Christian training at home, in church, and in Sunday school, you learn more and more about Jesus, your Savior. And then all too fast you grow up, finish grade school, and get near to the time that you will go away from home to college, or go away to work. Then your parents and teachers can no longer be with you. And so it is very important that you know what you believe and how you want to live, whether as a Christian or not. Jesus not only wants you to grow up as a Christian, but to remain one as long as you live. That is also the wish of your parents and church. So a special, intensive course of instruction called confirmation has been provided in the Lutheran Church.

"This instruction aims to give pupils a better understanding of God's Word, to show how God's Word can be a guide in daily living, and to give them a vision of what a glorious thing life with Christ can be as He walks beside them—a comrade, a protector, and a victorious Savior who says, 'Lo, I am with you always.'

"When the course of instruction is completed—and after all, the instruction is the chief value of confirmation—then comes the public examination, confirmation day with its public confession, and the partaking of the Lord's Supper. Therefore confirmation day becomes a confession day, a consecration day and a witnessing day.

"There are many sacred, beautiful, important days in a person's life—days that are mileposts along the road of life. I like to think of, though I don't remember it, the day of my baptism. That was a great day. I thank God and I thank my parents for that day— the day in which my life was linked up with Jesus according to the promise of these words: *'For as many of you as were baptized into Christ did put on Christ.'* My name was then written in God's great Book of Life. Another red letter day was my confirmation day when before the congregation I made confession of my belief in Christ as my Savior. *Everyone therefore who shall confess me before men, him will I also confess before my Father who is in heaven.*

"Have you ever heard about the Jewish nation's greatest confirmation day? Joshua called the whole nation together and said to the gathered multitude: *'Choose ye, this day, whom ye will serve, . . . As for me and my house, we will serve Jehovah.'* That answer, *'We also will serve Jehovah for He is our God,'* was no different from the confirmation promise.

"One day Jesus asked His disciples, *'Would ye also go away?'* Peter answering for the group said, *'To whom shall we go? Thou hast the words of eternal life and we know and have believed that Thou art the Holy One of God.'* That was a confession of faith similar to the one you make on your confirmation day.

"But there's another side to confirmation. There is God's side, too. Through the instruction preceding confirmation, through the prayers of the congregation, and through the pronouncing of the benediction, God confirms the faith of the confirmand and his purpose to live as a disciple of Jesus Christ."

151

"What books will we study?"

"The principal books will be Luther's Catechism, an explanation to the Catechism, a Bible history, the Bible itself, and also the hymn book from which you will learn hymns that will sing the truths of the Gospel into your heart, and that will give you something to sing while you work."

"But Dad, how can anyone be sure he can 'continue steadfast to the end'?"

"That's exactly what one always wonders. Will you, when you so seriously and honestly make your confession on your confirmation day, be able to remain true to it to the end of your life? What about tomorrow, next year, and twenty years from now? Your confession on confirmation day does not give you the final victory.

"Every day is a day of choosing, a day of decision. Jesus Christ is the great divider of human lives—you must either turn to Him and accept Him or you will turn from Him and reject Him. A nation can remain neutral in war. A citizen may refuse to commit himself on a political issue. A jury can disagree. Thousands of questions can be answered with an evasive 'I don't know.' But you either believe in Jesus and take Him as the Savior of your soul, or you do not believe His Word, and you disobey Him. There is no middle ground.

"The choice or the decision is one thing. Abiding in that choice is much more. But it can be done."

"How?"

"By trusting in Jesus Christ and obeying His will. He will keep you as He has promised. *'My sheep hear My voice and I know them, and they follow Me: and I give unto them eternal life, and they shall never perish, and no one shall snatch them out of My hand.'* Of the early Christians it is told that *'they continued steadfastly in the apostles' teaching and fellowship, in the breaking of bread and the prayers.'* Do as they did and the Lord will keep you steadfast until death."

BIBLE STUDY

1. Memorize Joshua 24:15
2. How do the following apply to the lesson: John 6:67-69; Gal. 3:27; Matt. 10:32; John 10:27-28; Acts 2:42

Augustana
South Dakota

Concordia
Minnesota

Luther
Iowa

St. Olaf
Minnesota

Pacific Lutheran
Washington

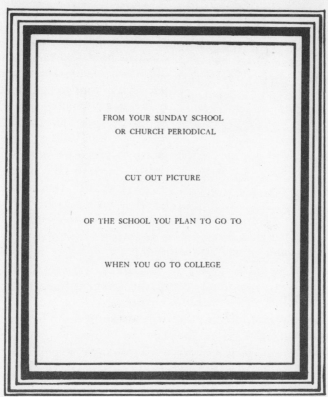

FROM YOUR SUNDAY SCHOOL

OR CHURCH PERIODICAL

CUT OUT PICTURE

OF THE SCHOOL YOU PLAN TO GO TO

WHEN YOU GO TO COLLEGE

Name of School

Chapter 23

The Schools of My Church

I WAS early," said Dr. Lansing, "so I waited outside. I shall never forget the picture—scores of feet tramping the sidewalks; little fellows hugging their books; little girls with rosy cheeks; older boys and girls reciting memory verses; the church door opening; the children entering."

"That's right," said Pastor Harvey who had joined the Lansing family, "your Bible class visited the different Sunday school classes last Sunday, didn't it?"

153

Augustana
Illinois

Gustavus Adolphus
Minnesota

Bethany
Kansas

Augsburg
Minnesota

"Yes. How I enjoyed it! I especially noticed the carefully planned lessons, the modern methods used, and the beautifully illustrated text books. I came to one class in time to hear the teacher say as she pointed to an interesting chart on the blackboard, 'Here is the Road of Life. I'm going to give each one of you a similar chart to take home. Try to discover the right road and travel it each day this week. Be careful of the side roads.'

"At another class, I watched a Bible drill. I am glad to see that Sunday school pupils are beginning to use their Bibles when they are as young as eight years old. By the time they reach confirmation age, they should know the Bible well enough so that it really will be 'The Book' for them."

"How fortunate we are that we can study the Bible, and that we can worship God in the way we believe is right," mused Pastor Harvey. "We don't stop to think often enough about how fortunate we are that we live in a country where church and state are separate.

"We also are fortunate that we live in a state, the legislature of which has passed a law allowing children in the public schools to be dismissed a certain number of hours each week for Christian instruction in their own churches. This week-day instruction in the churches accomplishes more than the Sunday school. It seems more like real school, too, since classes meet during school hours.

"In some places, Saturday school takes the place of week-day school and is very effective."

"We have much to thank you for, Pastor Harvey," interrupted Dr. Lansing. "Before you came, we had never taken advantage of the law which permitted us to have week-day schools. Now our children who go to Sunday school, week-day school, and summer vacation school are getting a foundation that should make them intelligent Christians."

"Yes," added Pastor Harvey, "all these opportunities for Christian education are a blessing. Our church has always been a

154

teaching church. It has always tried to keep its teachings pure and true to the revelation it has received from God. The Lutheran church has always realized that its teaching influences everything else in the church—its spiritual life, its worship, its organizations, and its service here at home and abroad.

"That's why, in the early beginnings of our church, schools were built as soon as churches."

"Dad has told us about the early beginnings of our church," interrupted Dale. "Why doesn't our church build schools now?"

"It does, Dale, but in a different way. At first, there were no public schools. Usually, therefore, each church had its own parochial school. When cities and towns saw the importance of education, public schools were built. It wasn't long until the first amendment to the constitution was enforced in schools. Religion couldn't be taught where teachers, and pupils were of different faiths. So public schools taught only secular subjects, and each church provided Christian education for its people.

"That's why the Lutheran church has always emphasized Christian training and family worship in the home where the child gets its deepest, most lasting impressions. That's why the Lutheran Church stresses Sunday school, week-day school, summer vacation school, and confirmation.

"But it does more. The Lutheran church, with the interest and strength of many individual churches banded together, supports more than 125 academies (high schools), and colleges where many thousands of Lutheran young people receive a higher education as thorough and up-to-date as that given in any school in the land. Besides an education which will fit young people for their life work, church colleges surround them with a Christian atmosphere, with Christian friends, with opportunities for Christian activity, and with Christian teachings. Your church colleges stress that the God of the Bible, the Father of Jesus Christ, is the God that created heaven and earth; that there is therefore no contradiction between what He tells you in history and nature, and what He tells you in the Bible; and that it is only man's ignorance or unbelief that finds contradictions. In your church colleges, young people have a splendid opportunity to receive an education harmonious with the Bible, to experience Christ's promise, 'Lo, I am with you always,' and to become men, and women who joyfully take their place in the work of the church.

"And then your church does still more. Many of the boys of church colleges and state schools wish to prepare themselves to be pastors and missionaries. The church needs thoroughly trained and thoroughly Christian pastors and missionaries. And so the Lutheran church has built seminaries. You remember the first one built under church control was Gettysburg. Now there are more than thirty Lutheran theological seminaries in America. Boys who feel called to become pastors finish their four years of college and then study at least three years at a seminary.

"So you see, Dale, there are many opportunities for Christian education in your church schools. When you . . . "

Pastor Harvey was interrupted by the quick opening of the

155

door, the sound of running footsteps, and a cheery, "Hi, everybody!"

"Why, Corinne, I thought you were a hundred miles away at college."

"Some girls and boys were driving this way and asked me to come along. We've had the busiest week! We put on our class play, Monday. Yesterday, I gave my voice recital. And the last three days, we've had mid-semester exams. So I decided to come home and rest until tomorrow. It's surely good to be here." And with a happy sigh, Corinne sat down in the wing chair.

"We've just been talking about church schools," said Dr. Lansing.

"I'm so glad I'm at a church college. I've made so many good friends and we do have such good times. It was at college I met Bill, too, you know. I can't tell you how much it's meant to me. I really am sorry I'm graduating in June. I can hardly believe it. It seems like yesterday that Aunt Sally told me to write for college catalogs. How I waited for the mail the next two weeks! How much fun Aunt Sally and I had studying the different catalogs to find out which college offered the best course for what I wanted to do. How thrilled I was when it was decided that I should write a letter of application. I still have the cordial letter I received in reply, telling me I was enrolled in the Freshman class."

"Now I must go," said Pastor Harvey. "It's like an answer to prayer that you came tonight. Miss Lane was unexpectedly called home this afternoon, and I've wondered whom I could ask to substitute as teacher on such short notice. Will you do it?"

"Of course, I'll be glad to. Show me the Sunday school lesson and I'll prepare it right now."

When Pastor Harvey left, Dr. Lansing said, "Corinne, I'm happy about you. You could have said you were too tired or given some other excuse. Thank God for young people who come from church schools, and in gratitude to God for their great privileges, go out into congregations to use their talents in service for His kingdom."

BIBLE STUDY

Memorize Proverbs 9:10

The following describe the value of knowledge and wisdom: Prov. 3:13; 8:11; 16:16

The following were instructed in knowledge and wisdom: Acts 7:22; II Tim. 3:15

156

Chapter 24

My Father Serves

"DAD, Dick said that his father said that a man can't be a Christian and amount to anything. That isn't true, is it?" asked Dale.

Dr. Lansing looked at the puzzled expression on Dale's face, and wondered how he could best explain away this statement that seems to be so often thrust at young people.

"Oh, I don't mean the men you've been telling us about all year," added Dale. "I know they amounted to something and were Christians. I mean men living now."

"You've put the cart before the horse, Dale. You should have said they amounted to something *because* they were Christians. Probably Dick's father was thinking in terms of dollars and cents. There are many who become wealthy even though they are not Christian, it is true. But there are many Christians who become wealthy, too. However, financial success is not the only kind of success. Christians must not do as the world does—measure a man's value by the money he has made. Christ made no money. He did not even have a bed of His own. Think of the men in our country who have had one crop failure after another, and still have kept their faith in God, and in the promise, 'Lo, I am with you always,' and have proved it by service in the church. They put to shame many who have never known a crop failure.

"Real success is doing something worthwhile for others— making life a little easier or a little happier for others. Even though a man is poor, he can build a Christian home, live a God-fearing life himself, be kind and helpful to others, work to make their burdens lighter, and help them to withstand temptation. When a Christian man uses his talents in some form of service, he becomes a powerful influence for good.

"The millionaire who owned the Dollar Steamship line was a Christian. He decided that one way he could serve Christ was to transport Bibles, Testaments, and Christian tracts for the American Bible Society to all parts of the world, free of charge on his ships.

"Dr. Wilfred Grenfell could be a wealthy city doctor, but he is unselfishly giving his time and abilities to the poor people of Labrador.

"Albert Schweitzer, who is one of the world's greatest organists, could be making thousands of dollars by giving concerts, but he, as a medical missionary, is devoting his life to the people of Lambarene, Africa.

"In order to do things for others, a man has to have courage to take a stand for what is right.

"I remember dashing to an elevator one particular day.

" 'Going up?' I asked, and then said, 'Twentieth floor, please!'

"I entered the offices of the .... Fifteen men besides myself sat around a table. Before us lay piles of papers.

" 'No, Mr. President, I cannot agree to this proposition. I do not believe the deal is thoroughly honest,' said Mr. Howell. 'If we do this thing, we shall put a stain on our reputation and worse than that, we shall do an injustice both to our customer, and to one of our competitors.'

" 'But it means millions to our firm.'

" 'I know it, but I'd rather lose millions than take part in a shady deal.'

"Mr. Howell is a member of a Christian church. Its teaching has given him the courage to take a stand for what is right.

"That sort of thing occurs hundreds of times daily. Sometimes, it is about a big contract. Sometimes, it is about a small bargain. Sometimes, it is a matter of not telling a lie. But always it is a question of living up to the teachings and principles of Christ."

"But, wasn't he afraid the men might laugh at him or might not like him?" asked Jim, who was an interested listener.

"I imagine everyone is afraid of other people's opinions. No one likes to be laughed at, either. That's why so many don't take a stand. But there is one thing that will give courage. That is prayer. Remember, too, after you've once taken a stand, it's easier the next time.

"Long ago, I made my way through high school by working Saturdays and vacations for a Mr. Thompson. One day I saw him sitting with his face buried in his hands.

" 'Something must be wrong,' I thought. So I went quietly to his side. 'Is there something I could do for you?'

" 'No, nothing. That whole run yesterday was wrong. Since I'm, foreman, I've had to take the responsibility. I've been trying to think it through and it helps, you know, to stop for a moment of prayer.'

"That last phrase was a surprise to me. 'So that's what he was doing when he had his face buried in his hands,' I thought. I respected him much more after that.

"Some may laugh, and become enemies if you take a stand. But often there's someone who will respect you, too, or someone who will be helped in his own life because you took a stand.

"Now, so far, I've been telling you that to be a success, whether it's farming or taking care of sick people, a man must use the talents he has to the glory of God. He must have courage to stand for the right. Furthermore, he must be a man of prayer.

"But a man's life is three-fold. Besides his work, he has his home and his church. He must not become so busy making a living that he neglects his home and his church.

"In his home, the man is the head of the house, and as such, he should set an example in unselfish thoughtfulness for the members of his family. He should take time to know and enjoy his family. He should feel it his responsibility and privilege each day to gather his family about him to read from the Bible and then to lead in song and prayer.

"As for the church, you know, from what I've told you this year, that men have had a very important part in its history. All of Jesus' disciples were men. In the early days of the church, men were always given the positions of leadership. That does not mean that women are not equally precious in God's sight. It does seem to mean, however, that in God's plan, men should be given the places of heaviest responsibility.

"There is much work for the men in the church today. Therefore, men should prepare themselves, by studying the Bible, by regular attendance at services, and at the Lord's Supper, and by learning to know their church through reading the church papers.

"More than ever before, the church today needs witness-bearing Christian men. Millions of men all around us do not know Christ. No one can do so much to reach them as other men."

"But what is there for so many men to do?"

"Most important of all is that they witness for Christ in their home and at work—wherever they are. Then, too, there are many kinds of special work. More and more men are teaching in the Sunday schools. There is also the sacred office of deacon, through which a man helps his pastor in visiting the sick and those in spiritual trouble, and also helps his pastor decide what to do with important spiritual problems of the church. Furthermore, there is the office of trustee, which takes over the responsibility of the financial problems of the church in a way pleasing to God. The trustees relieve the pastor of concern over money matters, so he can give himself entirely to spiritual duties. Another growing activity for men is the Lutheran Brotherhood."

"Oh, I know about the Lutheran Brotherhood," exclaimed Dale. "It started Boy Scout work in our church. I can hardly wait until I'm twelve so I can be a scout."

"Yes, the Brotherhood is very interested in boys, and tries to make them feel that the men of the church are their big brothers. It tries to do what it can to keep the boys true to their Lord, and their baptismal and confirmation covenant. Boys sometimes are tempted to feel that they cannot be like real men and be Christians, but that idea soon disappears when they see the men of the church unashamed of being Christians.

"The Lutheran Brotherhood has an interesting story. In quite a few places, men had organized in much the same way as women. Often their organizations were called Men's Clubs, or Laymen's Leagues. Then in 1917, representatives of different Men's Clubs met and organized the Lutheran Brotherhood of America. National Conventions were held. In 1927, the Lutheran Brotherhood of America became the present American Federation of Lutheran Brotherhoods. To it belong Lutherans of the United Lutheran Church and of the American Lutheran Conference (See p. 109). The Federation emphasizes four activities:

Devotion—that is, the use of the Word of God and prayer.

Fellowship—that is, the friendly association of men with other men of the same hopes, plans, and ideals.

Education—that is, the acquainting of the men with their church so they become intelligent workers.

Service—that is, that every man serves the church in some way according to the talents he has. Service in the church trains for leadership, and so the Brotherhood aims to have all its members have the privilege, the responsibility, and the joy of serving in different capacities. If this aim is to be fulfilled, no one person can hold the same office for as many as ten or twenty years.

"There are many other places where men can serve. Some work may not seem important. That makes little difference if it is done well. There is something for everyone to do if he really loves his Lord enough. Every man has been given at least one talent by God and ought to use it."

"Well, Dale," said Jim, seriously, "after all Dad's told us, no one can ever tell me again that a man can't be a Christian and amount to anything. It seems to me a man can't be a Christian without amounting to something."

BIBLE STUDY

1. Memorize I Cor. 16:13.
2. God wants every man to do His part—II Tim. 2:2; I Cor. 3:9; I Tim. 2:8; Deut. 16:17
3. A man of courage will follow Paul's advice—Eph. 6:13-18
4. The worker's reward—Matt. 25:34-40; Rev. 14:13

Chapter 25

My Mother Does Her Share

"HOW strangely still the house is," thought Dr. Lansing. "Not a sound but the ticking of the clock. I must have fallen asleep."

Suddenly a door slammed. Dale ran into the house. "Mother, oh, Mother! Guess what's happened," he shrieked, and then in a whisper, he added, "Oh say, I forgot. She's at Ladies' Aid."

"Dale, come in here," called Dr. Lansing.

"Oh, Dad, I'm sorry," said penitent Dale. "Did I awaken you? Mother told me this noon that I should be quiet. I was so excited because I'm on the regular team now that I wanted to tell her right away. I forgot she was gone."

"I've had a good sleep, Dale. I'm very glad you made the team. "When you——"

"Hi, Dad," interrupted Dorothy. "Doesn't the house seem *empty* when Mother's gone? I'm glad you're here."

"Yes, I am, too," said Dr. Lansing. "I was quite rebellious at first, when I learned I'd sprained my ankle and would have to stay off my foot for a while."

"But Dad," exclaimed Dale in a thrilled voice, "Mrs. Lane says you were a real hero, that if you hadn't jumped so quickly to help her, she surely would have fallen and hurt her hip again."

"Nonsense! She probably wouldn't have fallen anyway. But I've been glad to be home these two days. It's been like looking into the other half of the world. It's over fifteen years since I've had a whole day at home. I've been learning things."

"What, Dad?" asked Dale and Dorothy, in surprise.

"I've been learning how true Dorothy's statement is that the house seems very empty when Mother's gone even a few minutes. Now, why do you suppose it does?"

Both children looked at Dr. Lansing to see if he really expected an answer. They hadn't done any thinking about that question before.

"It seems kind of cozy for a fellow to come home and find his mother humming and making good things to eat that make the whole house smell yummy!"

"Oh, Dale," laughed Dr. Lansing. "You're a typical boy— hungry all the time."

"What's this? A family council?" asked Jim as he came into the room and put several books on the table.

"I just asked the twins why the house seems so empty when Mother's gone," answered Dr. Lansing.

"I'll tell you why," said Jim. "She's such a good listener. Most people seem to think about all kinds of other things when I talk. But Mother really listens, and so there's so much I want to tell her all the time, that I'm disappointed when she isn't here."

"Yes, and I know why that is," said Dorothy, thrilled with such grown-up talk. "She *cares* so much. She's just as glad as we are when something nice happens to us. She's so disappointed when we don't know our lessons well, or when we do things that are wrong, that it makes me feel good way down to my toes when Mother smiles and is happy about something I do."

"Those are all good answers. But I've noticed other things these two days. I've watched you sent to school with clean, neat clothes, and I've thought of the time Mother has spent to wash, press, and mend your clothes so they would be ready for you to wear. As she's cleaned the house, I've tried to count all the steps she's taken. Have you ever noticed how comfortable and colorful our home is? It's something to be thankful for, because sur-

162

roundings are a powerful factor in shaping character. But surroundings that seem to breathe a Christian atmosphere don't just come. Money alone can't buy them. It means that Mother's put a great deal of thought and work into making our home what it is. However, I imagine that so far, this is a description of almost every mother in every home.

"But something happened last night, that doesn't happen in every home. Just before Joan was put to bed, I watched Mother gather all of you for the 'children's hour,' as she calls it, when we have our devotion and she answers questions she hasn't had time to answer satisfactorily before. Even though I have always tried to be here at that time, my work often makes it impossible. Therefore, it has been Mother's responsibility to include such a time in every day. It has meant much to you. It will mean still more to you when you leave home, not only as a memory, but because during all these years it's been teaching you to trust in the power of God to keep and protect you. It has also been making you acquainted with the Scriptures as your guide through life.

"There are many other things I've noticed that I hope will make me kinder, more appreciative, and more understanding from now on."

"We'll try harder, too, Dad," said Jim earnestly.

"But, Dad, what are Ladies' Aids good for?" asked Dorothy.

"The Ladies' Aid is an organization of women whose purpose is to help the church spread the Gospel to all people."

"Were there Ladies' Aids way back in the time of Christ, too?"

"No, there haven't always been Ladies' Aids, so-called. But there have always been women who have given of their talents and means to help spread the Gospel and through whom Christ could fulfill His promise. During the time of Christ, there were women who had been healed by Him *who ministered unto them* (Christ and the apostles) *of their substance*.

"Also there was a widow whose devotion to the Temple as the house of God was excelled only by the Savior. If Anna had been absent on the day of the presentation, she would have missed one of the happiest days of her life. Because she was there, she saw Jesus and became the first of a long line of women missionaries. Anna commenced her mission work, of spreading the good news about Jesus, at Jerusalem.

"A little later, Dorcas was busy in Joppa giving to the poor in gifts and in labor. The Bible says she *was full of good works*. She has been the inspiration for numerous Dorcas Societies in Christian churches. The program of these Dorcas Societies is practical Christianity.

"Still later, in a heathen town, Lydia, a successful business woman, closed her shop on the Sabbath and became the leader of a prayer group which is the only religious meeting for women recorded in the New

163

Testament. When Paul came to Philippi, he met with this prayer group, told them about Jesus, and won them for Him with the result that Lydia and her household were baptized. Lydia invited Paul and his co-workers to stay at her home as her guests and friends while they worked in Philippi.

"It was not, however, until after the interest in foreign missions was aroused, as a result of the Pietistic movement, that Ladies' Aids, as such, came into being. In almost all cases, Ladies' Aids were organized for the purpose of sewing and working for missions in order that the Gospel might be spread. Usually, the beginnings were humble. A few women would take their spinning wheels on their backs, and carry their cards and sometimes an extra bundle of wool, and walk long distances to a neighbor's house. Then for a long afternoon, there would be the scraping sound of cards working wool, the whirring of spinning wheels, and the swift movement of knitting and sewing needles. Clothes, quilts, and fancy work would be made and sold, and the money sent to missions. The movement spread over entire countries and became a source of great help for missions. This movement has followed our own Lutheran church to this country, and has developed into the well-organized Ladies' Aids, Dorcas Societies, and Mission Societies of today.

"Individual women's groups have banded together into federations called Women's Missionary Federations or Women's Missionary Societies. The united efforts of women in these federations have broadened the views of women and developed a feeling of responsibility."

"That's a great many things to keep straight," gasped Dorothy.

"Yes, it is. Life for women, nowadays, is complicated. But women, too, have to remember to put first things first. First comes the home, then the church, and, then if she has strength and time for more, there are the parent-teachers' organizations and other community or cultural organizations which need Christian members in order to be of service to the community.

"Now, run out and play for an hour. As it is good for Mother to get away from home and have outside interests, so it's good for children to get some fresh air in their lungs. I'll call you in time so you can each prove your appreciation of having a mother like yours."

BIBLE STUDY

1. Memorize—Proverbs 31:30
2. The following are referred to in the lesson: Luke 8:1-3; Luke 2:36-38; Acts 9:36-42; Acts 16:14-40
3. What is said about women in Proverbs 31:10-31

Chapter 26

My Older Brothers and Sisters Do Their Part

"ALL Junior boys and girls are urged to come to the Junior Luther League meeting this week," Pastor Harvey announced. "Our boys and girls are doing fine work in this organization."

At dinner that Sunday, Jim asked, "What is this Junior League business, anyway? Will anybody care if I go?"

"That would be fine, Jim," said Dad. "But look here, you have a while to wait before you're eligible for League, haven't you?"

"Yes, you have to be in the confirmation class to be eligible," Mother said. Being Mother, she couldn't help smiling at Jim, because nothing made her happier than to see her children interested in things connected with the church.

165

Jim smiled at his mother, too. "Okay, then," he said. "I suppose that's just another thing I'll have to wait for until I'm older."

"It's just a few months more, now, Jim," said Mother.

"Say, Dad—"

"Yes, Jim."

"I don't suppose there were Junior Leagues when you were my age, were there?"

"Well, no. In fact, we didn't have Senior Luther Leagues, either. At least, not like the one we have in our church now."

"Wasn't there any organization for young people?"

"Oh, surely, Jim. A 'Young People's Society,' it was called. I was one of the officers when we first organized it."

"Were you, Dad? Swell! How did you organize it?"

"There wasn't much organization to it, son. The pastor talked about it to some of us. We liked the idea of having a Young People's Society in the congregation. So we started to plan. At the first meeting, we elected our officers. Then we appointed a committee to work out a constitution, but as I remember it, we never did get a good constitution until finally we changed our society to a Luther League."

"But why did your pastor want a Young People's Society?"

"He was interested in young people and wanted to keep them loyal and willing to serve the church. He realized that even when people are very young, they often make a decision to live for Christ.

"Bernard of Clairvaux, from his earliest years, lived a pious, chaste life devoted to Christ.

"Ansgar was only 14, when he entered a monastery.

"Luther from early childhood was deeply anxious to attain the grace and favor of God.

"Hudson Taylor was scarcely 15 when he came across the words: 'The finished work of Christ' and thereafter praised his Savior by a life powerful in prayer.

"He realized that young people are very important because they are the church of tomorrow. Others have realized the same thing.

"Martin Luther was much interested in young people. As early as 1524, he wrote: 'I pray all of you for the sake of God and of youth not to think slightingly of educational problems. For it is a serious and great matter, at the heart of Christ and all mankind, that we help and advise the young folk.' Luther blazed the trail which later led to our public school system.

"But for three hundred years after Luther, little was done for youth.

"Here in America, work among the youth began with singing schools, temperance societies, young people's Bible classes, young people's mission societies, devotional guilds, and Young Men's Christian Associations.

"As early as 1848, the first Baptist Church of Rochester, New York, had a young people's society.

"Then in 1851, Dr. C. F. W. Walther, who had always been interested in young people, wrote in the 'Lutheraner' urging a federation of young people's societies, with the result that in 1854 an organization was completed. The young people's society which Dr. Walther started was the first successful attempt in the Lutheran church in America.

"The late 80's and 90's seem to have been the years for a general youth awakening in the various churches. Those were the years when almost all Lutheran churches in our country organized young people's societies. In 1881, Pastor Francis E. Clark founded the first Christian Endeavor Society in the Williston Congregational Church in Portland, Maine. In 1889, the Methodist church founded the Epworth League.

"The influence of these pioneer groups spread. Local leagues met for devotional, educational, or social programs. Gradually, circuit, district, and national organizations were formed."

"What did you do at your young people's societies?"

"There were readings, and solos, and 'remarks by the pastor.' That was fine, of course, but it would have been better if we'd learned to give talks the way young folks do now in the Luther League."

"I noticed by the Church bulletin that there was a whole program made out for the Junior League—speakers, a devotional leader, and a discussion leader. All Juniors on the program. But, Dad, don't they do anything besides have programs?"

"Yes, a great deal more. Circuit, district, and national leagues have various projects. Missions, and missionaries are supported. Reading projects are encouraged. Interesting socials are planned. Also, a great deal of student work is done."

"What do you mean by student work?"

"In 1918, a Lutheran Students' Union was organized in the N. L. C. A.

"A 'Lutheran Students' Association of America' was organized at Toledo, Ohio, in 1922. It aims to include every Lutheran student on the campus of every school of higher learning in America. The organization gives to these students opportunities for Christian fellowship and activity.

"And then there are Bible Camps and——."

"Oh, Dad, I've heard Art and Mary and Bob talking about all the fun they had at the Bible Camp this summer, and about all they learned in their Bibles, and how they're already planning to go next summer. Do you suppose I can go, too?"

"Yes, Jim, that's something you can plan for."

"Did you have Bible Camps, too?"

"No, but I've visited several these last years. Bible camps started here in America as summer schools of Bible Institutes. Congregations here and there copied the idea by taking the young people of the congregation, usually to a lake, for a week's study of the Bible and for recreation. Many Lutheran churches then joined forces to carry on the Bible camp work. It's been a powerful influence in the lives of many young people."

"Was it at Bible Camps that Pocket Testament work began?"

"The Pocket Testament Movement had its origin with a thirteen-year-old high school girl in Birmingham, England. Her father, the late Richard Cadbury, a wealthy chocolate manufacturer and Christian philanthropist, encouraged his daughter, Helen, to give expression to her newly found faith in Christ, by interesting her friends in reading the Bible. During her last year in high school, a group of 60 girls pledged themselves before God and to one another to read and carry God's Word, daily. However, the Pocket Testament Movement grew slowly, for many years.

"But 'God works in a mysterious way His wonders to perform,' and He so guided and directed Helen Cadbury's life that she married the well known evangelist, Charles Alexander, who toured the world many times and made the Pocket Testament Movement known over the world. In 1914, he opened headquarters in London, and God used this office as an agency to distribute millions of Testaments among the soldiers and sailors during the World War. In 1916, he rented a large room in New York for the same purpose. Since then, headquarters have been established in many countries. The Luther League of the N. L. C. A. (see P. 108) joined the world-wide Pocket Testament League in 1932. Since then, other Lutheran young people's groups have joined the Pocket Testament League, too."

"Oh, I think it's just wonderful," exclaimed Mother, "that we live in a time when we can have our own Bibles and Testaments."

"It seems as though the young people have done a great many things since they organized," said Jim.

"Yes, your older brothers and sisters in the Lutheran churches all over the world have proved that they can be used to carry out Christ's promise, 'Lo, I am with you always.' But there's much left to be done. So, I'm glad, Jim, that you're looking forward to doing your share."

BIBLE STUDY

1. Memory verse—Eccl. 12:1
2. Similar Bible verses are—Ps. 71:5; Eph. 6:1-3; III John 4
3. Who turned to the Lord when young—II Chr. 34:1-7

Chapter 27

My Moments for Christ

WHY do boys have all the good times?" Dorothy wondered, as she shook her red curls in vigorous rebellion. There was Dale, her twin, who could do such splendid things—play on the Sixth grade basketball team, go on long hikes, and now he and some other boys were being made "cubs" by the Boy Scout committee. "It just isn't fair," she thought. "There isn't *anything* for me to do."

"Dorothy," called Mrs. Lansing, who seemed to read her daughter's thoughts, "if you'll help me, I can finish this trunk that I've been cleaning, before I start supper."

"Do you mean the trunk with all the dresses and albums in it?" Dorothy immediately forgot about "cubs" and hikes.

How Dorothy enjoyed that trunk! It was full of stories. Every dress and every picture had a story. Dorothy remembered rainy days when Mother had dressed her in some of the beautiful clothes her grandmother and great-grandmother had worn, and had told her the story of each.

Suddenly Dorothy noticed a box she had never seen open before. She hadn't even known it could open. In it were small trinkets.

"Mother, Mother, where did you get this beautiful flower?" exclaimed Dorothy.

"That's an edelweiss pin. Do you want to hear the story?"

"Oh, yes—please!"

"Long ago, in a quaint village, far up in the mountains of Switzerland, lived an old man who had spent his life working in ivory. His hair was as white as the ivory flowers he made; his shoulders were bent; but his eyes were bright and his hands were very sure as he used tiny tools in making the petals of daisies, violets, edelweiss, and buttercups.

"From his window, he could look far out over the valleys for miles and miles. He needed that long look to rest his eyes, but he needed it more as an inspiration for his own life. As he watched the storms come up the valleys; as he saw the shadows creep over the mountains; as he enjoyed gorgeous sunsets, Hans Klatt saw God's handiwork, and it was always beautiful, always different, always perfect. Every day was a new beginning to this worker in ivory.

"One day, a visitor was choosing six of his flowers to take back to the girls of her Sunday school class in America. As she placed them against the soft velvet of her dress, they seemed so real that she exclaimed enthusiastically, 'They are perfect, just perfect. How can you make them so?'

"'No, lady,' was his reply. 'They are not perfect. I wish I could make one perfect one. I have been trying for thirty years to make one like God makes them out-of-doors, but something is always a little bit wrong. When I bring His in, mine seem very imperfect. But I have honestly tried, and it is worthwhile giving one's life to make a perfect thing, don't you think?'

"The lady bought the pins, and later tried her best to give to her class of girls the message and the spirit of the Swiss mountaineer. 'Remember,' she said, 'that as every day was a new beginning for him, so it is for you. Try to give each moment of every day to Christ as a new beginning.'

"I was one of those girls. At first, I continually wore my edelweiss pin. Then a few years ago, the clasp broke, and somehow I never had it repaired. And yet it is one of my prized treasures. I cannot be a perfect mother. I cannot hope to have perfect children. But during all these years, this pin and the story back of it, have challenged me to try. Now that you know the story of this little edelweiss pin, I'm going to give it to you. We'll have the clasp repaired. I know the pin will be a challenge and an inspiration to you, too."

"Oh, thank you," said Dorothy as she hugged her mother. "But it seems as though nothing important ever happens until one is old. There's *nothing* to do *now*."

"But Dorothy, that really isn't so. No one has ever accomplished great things who hasn't first accomplished a great many little things. You remember hearing about Michelangelo.

"One day he explained to a friend what he had done on a statue since the friend last saw it. 'I have retouched this, polished that, softened this feature, brought out that muscle, and given more expression to the lips.'

"'But these are such little things,' exclaimed the friend.

"'Yes, they are little things,' answered the great sculptor, 'but little things make perfection, and perfection is not a little thing.'"

"But, Mother, there aren't even any *little* things for me to do."

"Aren't there? You still feel the same, then, as last night. You're still living in the land of 'Going to Be Sometime.' "

"Why, what do you mean?"

"Last night, I overheard you and Jane talking.

" 'When I get big,' Jane said, 'I'm going to live in a bea-u-ti-ful house and I'm going to drive my own car, and have a *gor*-geous office downtown.'

"And then you chimed in: 'When I get big, I'm going to wear long dresses, way down to the floor—pink net dresses with yards and yards of material in the skirt, and velvet ribbons all over the waist—and I'm going to dress up every single night—and in the daytime, I'm going to have a big house, and take care of poor people like that Jane Addams we've been reading about in school.'

"That was living in the land of 'Going to Be Sometime.' Let's try living in the land of 'Right Now,' shall we? Let your edelweiss pin help you. Make each moment of 'Right Now' as perfect as you can. Of course, Dorothy, you can never make your days perfect by yourself, no matter how determined you are. But if you love Jesus very, very much and ask Him to help you to forget yourself and make somebody else happy, then I wonder if you won't be helped in making the moments of your life more perfect. I wonder if you won't realize Christ's promise in your life: 'Lo, I am with you always.'

"You've been making me happy by helping me this afternoon.

"You can make Daddy happy by not foolishly spending the money he gives you, since he has to work hard for it; by finding something quiet to do when he is tired or wants to read; and by being cheerful.

"You can make your friends and brothers happy by taking care of things they lend you; by never taking credit for things you have not done; by defending them when others talk about them.

"You can make your neighbors happy by respecting their houses, gardens, and trees; by looking for the good in them and not the bad. Why there are all kinds of things, Dorothy, that you can do every day, even now before you grow up."

"Oh, Mummy, I know something to do right this minute. I've been thinking about it all week. There's a new boy and girl in the house on the corner. They're in my room at school. I'd like to ask them to come to Sunday school with me. But—the boy doesn't seem like the kind who'd go to Sunday school. Really, I don't know if I have the nerve to go, even yet. He might laugh at me."

"Dorothy, it isn't 'nerve' you need. It's power. You know that

171

God doesn't wish you to do these things without His help. Have you asked Him for help?"

"No—no, I haven't," confessed Dorothy.

Dorothy, and her mother knelt in prayer on the attic floor.

"Now I can do it, Mother," said Dorothy as she skipped down the stairs and out of the house.

Mrs. Lansing closed the trunk, locked it, and prayed a short "thank you" prayer that once more she had been guided in helping her daughter.

Dorothy was late for supper and Mrs. Lansing wondered.

Finally, Dorothy came hurrying into the room. Her face was so radiantly happy that Mrs. Lansing silently offered another "thank you" prayer.

"Oh, Mother, Daddy, everybody, guess what! I asked Art and Peggy to go to Sunday school with me next Sunday. And they didn't laugh at me. They were *glad*. And their mother invited me into the house, and asked me many questions about Sunday school. And oh, they have the prettiest little baby. You should see her dimples, and black eyes. Oh, oh, it was *fun*," and Dorothy stopped exclaiming long enough to give her mother a quick hug.

"And, Mother," continued Dorothy, "after dishes are done, I'm going over to Maxine's house. She's had trouble with her eyes, and has to stay in a dark room. You know how she loves stories. I'm going to read to her."

"What a busy girl you are today," exclaimed Dr. Lansing.

Dorothy looked at her mother and smiled. "It's all because of a story about an edelweiss pin that Mother gave me."

"Sounds very mysterious," said Dr. Lansing mischievously.

"Oh, tell them the story, too," begged Dorothy.

So once again Mrs. Lansing told the story of Hans Klatt whose beautiful ivory flowers had inspired a teacher, a mother, and now a daughter to try to make little things perfect, and to give the moments of every day to Christ.

BIBLE STUDY

1. Memorize Prov. 23:26
2. There is power and help in prayer—John 16:24; Jas. 1:5
3. Give your moments to Christ—Phil. 1:21; Gal. 6:9, 10; John 9:4
4. Joy comes in service—Matt. 25:31-46
5. Jesus set an example in service—John 13:3-17

Chapter 28

My Neighbors Who Don't Go to My Church

FOR six days, he had forgotten about it. And now it had a foremost place in his thoughts, because Sunday had come around again. In fact, Dale had thought about it all morning, and was still thinking about it when he came home from Sunday morning services.

"Dad," he finally said, "why are there so many churches in our town? Harry's the best friend a fellow ever had. Since we're in the same room at school, we're together all week, but Sunday mornings he has to stop at the Episcopal church for Sunday school, and I have to go on alone to our Sunday school. *Why* can't we go to the same Sunday school?"

"Just a minute, Dale," said Dr. Lansing, "let's answer your first question, now, before you ask any more questions.

"The reason for the beginning of the church was God's love for sinful man. *For God so loved the world, that He gave His only begotten Son, that whosoever believeth on Him should not perish, but have eternal life.* The foundation of the church was laid by Christ when He came. *For other foundation can no man lay than that which is laid, which is Jesus Christ.* Pentecost, as you have heard, marked the beginning of efforts by the church to bring the Gospel to those who didn't know it. The beginnings of the church were simple when compared to church life today. Gradually, its power spread over the greater part of the civilized world, and its organization became complex. It was spoken of as the Catholic church. Catholic means universal. After the Eastern and Western groups separated in the 11th century, the former was called the Greek Catholic, and the latter the Roman Catholic church. Then, as you remember, certain evil practices and false doctrines in the Roman Catholic church brought about the Reformation of the 16th century. A division occurred in the Protestant church which resulted in many Protestant churches. You have heard about Calvin, Knox, and Wesley and the beginning of the Episcopal, Presbyterian and Methodist churches. (See pages 70, 71, and 78 and also the map on P. 70.) From these churches resulted others because of different interpretations of the Word of God. That is the reason we have so many different Christian churches, each teaching some doctrine according to its own particular views. The following chart will show you various Christian churches:

"Like a mighty army, members of these various churches crossed the ocean to America where they built churches as soon as they built their homes. By the time of the Revolution, the people of America possessed a larger degree of religious freedom than was found among any other people. As the American colonies grew, the church followed the people westward until in every town and often on the highest hill in town, Christian churches, with spires pointing heavenward, could be seen."

"Aren't all churches Christian?" asked Jim.

"No, there are many churches and sects which are not Christian. Of course, within these churches, too, there are members who are Christian, but they then are Christians, in spite of the teachings of their church."

"That sounds as though there are Christians in all churches."

"As a rule, yes. But that doesn't say that all churches are true Christian churches. To be Christian, a church must 'search the Scriptures,' must accept the Bible as the Word of God, must believe in the teachings of the Bible, as summarized in the Apostles' Creed, must use the means of grace in public worship, and must be interested in promoting a life lived according to God's will as revealed in His Word. The Book of Ephesians and I John in the Bible give a very fine picture of Christian churches. Of this you can be sure—wherever the Gospel is preached in a church, there you will find Christians. For Christ, then, is in their midst. All who believe in Christ make up the communion of saints or the true Christian church. In Christ, they are bound together with a tie closer than blood relationship."

"What do you mean by the *true* Christian church?"

"Probably you are thinking of the church as the building erected by men's hands. There are many such visible churches. That isn't what I mean by the true Christian church. Neither do I mean congregations.

"Men and women are drawn into the visible church because of many different motives. Church membership does not, of itself, bring men into right relations with God. It offers opportunities for fellowship, study, worship, and service. Those who make use of these opportunities become the invisible church or the 'true Christian church' which includes the true Christians of all time. Even though this church is invisible to you, God can see the communion of saints because He searches the heart.

"Of the division of a large army, in long drawn-out battle line, one division may dash into conflict, overwhelm the enemy and be waving the flag of victory, while another division, delayed by a longer route, may be just swinging into battle array. But they both belong to the same army. They have the same commander-in-chief. So it is with heroes of the faith who comprise the communion of saints or the invisible, true Christian church. The battle against sin is continual, while time lasts. But those who follow Christ as commander-in-chief will stand with the crowned host above—as the Church Triumphant.

"Of course, even true Christians are not perfect. And yet a man who

174

Catholicism

Greek Catholic

Roman Catholic

The Reformation — Lutheran Church

−1517 A. D.

Protestantism

Calvinists
Scotch Presbyterians
Irish Presbyterians
Dutch Reformed
Christian Reformed

Anabaptists
Baptists
Mennonites

Church of England
Quakers
Puritans — Congregationalists
Pilgrims
Methodists — Salvation Army

is a Christian can not live like one who is not. However, Christians often make mistakes, and are often found guilty of being caught napping by the tempter. The true Christian regrets his mistakes, asks forgiveness through Christ, and realizes that that which makes him a member of the communion of saints is not his own, but Christ's righteousness. Even though the true Christian church is not a pure church here, it will be, when it becomes the church triumphant. Then it will be a glorified church, singing praise, because it is the church of forgiven sinners.

"Outside of faith in Christ, our Savior, no one can belong to this true Christian church. However, no church has the right to say, 'Ours is the Church of Christ. Outside of it, there is no salvation.'"

"Isn't it important, then, to which church you belong?"

"Yes, it makes a great deal of difference. You will hear people say that it doesn't make any difference what you believe, or to what church you belong since all churches are working toward the same goal anyway.

"Don't let these people fool you. It *does* make a great deal of difference to which church you belong. You should belong to that church in which you find the truth, or the largest measure of truth. Children, of course, almost without exception belong to the church to which their parents belong. However, when you are older, you should not proceed blindly, or on man's say-so, in this most important relation of your life. There are dozens of answers to the same question, but they are not all right.

"Probably an illustration will make it clearer. Suppose for some reason,

175

you need to make a hurried trip to New York. You are offered a Model T, a Model A, or a new V-8. You could get there in any of them, of course. But which would you choose?

"You *can* find Christ, as your Savior, in all Christian churches. But some Christian churches have the Gospel so much hidden behind all kinds of tradition and custom that it is difficult to receive the Gospel message. Some Christian churches have a social program that leaves very little of the pure Gospel. The Lutheran church, however, has always been the 'Church of the Open Bible.' The Lutheran church has always tried to teach as the Scriptures teach, and has always abided by the Word 'as it is written,' without putting man-made constructions on those parts of the Bible that seem contradictory, or difficult to understand. This is not boasting. It is a matter of record.

"Since the welfare of the church is bound up with the purity of the Gospel, and since God wants all men to continue in the Word of Christ (John 8:31), you want to belong to the church which is the church with the purest Biblical teachings. That church—I believe—is the Lutheran church, the 'Church of the Open Bible.'

"But, be sure to always remember this next sentence. Even though the Lutheran church defines the true church as the congregation of saints in which the Gospel is rightly taught and the Sacraments rightly administered, *the Lutheran church claims that human traditions, rites, or ceremonies instituted by men, do not have to be everywhere alike.* And so, true Christians in Lutheran churches know that there are many true Christians besides themselves, in different churches, and of different races and times. Behind the strongly-marked denominational barriers, there is an invisible bond of unity. Faith in Christ, and love for Him, besides binding men to Christ also binds all true Christians to one another.

"This thought ought to destroy the ugly spirit which so often is exhibited by different branches of the church to each other. For as Paul said: '*Love suffereth long and is kind.*' The Christian church is the loveliest creation of God's love. And so you should love all people of all churches. Follow the example of the early Christians of whom it was said: 'See how they love one another.' There should be such praise and thanksgiving in your heart, because Christ was willing to become your Savior and because He keeps His promise, 'Lo, I am with you always,' that you will be a soul-winner. For, by being a soul-winner, you can have a share in increasing the number of those who will be among the communion of saints in the Church Triumphant. Jesus said: 'A new commandment I give unto you, that ye love one another.'"

BIBLE STUDY

1. Memorize—Luke 17:20, 21
2. Christ loves the church—Eph. 5:25
3. The love of Christ binds together all believers in Christ—II Cor. 5:14-15
4. A Christian church will have the Word of God preached—II Tim. 4:1, 2
5. True Christians will search the Scriptures—Acts 17:11
6. How should Christians treat each other—Eph. 4:1-6; John 13:34; I Cor. 13:4-10

Chapter 29
My Neighbors Who Know Little About Christ

I T was ten minutes to ten on a Thursday morning when the mail man came whistling down the street and dropped a fat letter into the Lansing mail box. But no one was there to receive it. Mrs. Lansing had taken Joan with her to a nearby town for a circuit meeting of the Women's Missionary Federation. The other Lansing children were invited out for dinner.

That evening as the Lansing family gathered about the fireplace for the children's hour, Mrs. Lansing said enthusiastically, "We had such interesting programs at our W. M. F. meetings today. I wish all of you could have been with me. The topic was 'Home Missions.'

"In the morning a pastor told us about the work that is being done to give the Gospel to the deaf, mute, and blind."

"And some children did like this," exclaimed Joan as she moved her fingers in imitation of sign language.

"He had with him several deaf-mutes," continued Mrs. Lansing. "They put on a demonstration to show us how they sing our hymns. It was very interesting. There was no sound—just the movement of fingers in rhythm. Then the pastor spoke to them in the sign language. They watched him with interest. We watched them, as well as the pastor. It was wonderful to see their faces become eager and alight as he explained the glad tidings of great joy to them.

"I was also interested in a few Bible books in Braille that he had with him. Braille, you know, is a system of printing invented by a blind Frenchman in 1829. The characters are represented by raised dots and points which enable a blind person to read by feeling the raised characters.

"This afternoon, our program was an illustrated lecture, showing us 'home mission' work done by Lutheran churches. It was just like having a grand trip all over our continent. First, we were shown movies of mission work among the Eskimoes. The pictures were taken in a town within the Arctic Circle."

"I saw Eskimoes going to Sunday school—just like me," interrupted Joan again.

"Yes," continued Mrs. Lansing. "The Eskimo children waited for the chapel bell to ring. Then they filed into the school room to be taught by Eskimo teachers. The lessons were learned in English, but the teacher explained the hard parts in Eskimo, the speaker said, since small children know Eskimo better than English. After they have attended the mission school, they understand English better.

"From Alaska, we were taken to New York, Chicago, and Minneapolis, where we saw work being done to give the Gospel to the Jews.

"Then, we were taken to coast cities, where as the large fleets came into harbor, we saw missionaries from our seamen's missions visit the seamen aboard their ships, give them Gospel tracts, and invite them to the mission. Then we saw the sailors gather at the mission to use the free reading rooms, where there were papers and books in many languages. At the mission, they were also given spiritual and material help as they needed it.

"From the seamen's missions, we were taken to Indian reservations to see that the red men, too, are being given opportunities to know the Savior who died for the sins of all people of all time.

"Then we left the Indians for the Southland, to see Negroes and Mexicans also being won for Jesus through efforts of 'home missionaries.'

"As you've heard, it takes real courage to take the stand a Christian should. It's taken courage for home mission pastors to start religious education and training among the Negroes. I know of a Lutheran pastor in a large city in the South who offered to become a pastor among the Negroes. The congregation of Negroes grew in size. A large church was built. Many Negroes were won for Christ by the pastor's love and courage. But the pastor has had to suffer because of taking his stand. His children are not allowed to go to the school of the white children, and so they have to go to the school of the Negroes. It isn't easy for him to know that other white people in town look down upon him because of his associations with Negroes."

"That isn't fair," rebelled Dale, "I'd just like to—"

"Just a minute, now, Dale! It's easy enough to think what you would do if you were there. But every day, here, you have chances to do just what this pastor to the Negroes is doing, and then it isn't so easy. Probably someone of another race will come to your school, and your classmates will say thoughtlessly, 'No, we can't have any Chinks playing on our team.' Then have you courage to defend him? Probably some boy or girl from down by the tracks who lives in a shanty will be made fun of because he wears his father's old coat and shoes that are too big for him. He's another one for you to defend, and to whom you can be kind. There are many such things that happen. Maybe it's a bully 'taking it out' on someone smaller. Or, maybe it's someone who is teasing another."

"But Mother, are those things 'home missions,' too?"

"Yes, you know that mission work refers to the winning of souls for Christ. It is divided into home and foreign missions. 'Home missions' refers to soul-winning here on the North American continent. It means loving Christ so much that your love overflows into kindness and love to all those with whom you come into contact. It means winning your next-door neighbor who doesn't know Christ."

"Do you suppose there's *anybody* in our neighborhood who doesn't know Christ?"

"It isn't likely that they haven't *heard* about Christ. I mean that they don't love and serve Christ. There are many such."

178

"How do you know?"

"They don't live or act like Christians. They curse and swear. They don't take any interest in the work of the church."

"How can a person win people for Christ if they aren't interested?"

"The best way is to pray God to fill your heart with such love for all people that you will be willing to try and try again to win them. Prayer in behalf of others helps a great deal.

"Oh say, Dorothy, there was so much to take care of when I got home I forgot to give you this fat letter you received in the mail today. Open it while I take Joan upstairs. She's sound asleep. It isn't so good for little girls to go without naps, but she insisted she wasn't sleepy this afternoon and sat through the whole program like a grown-up."

"Why, Mother," exclaimed Dorothy when her mother returned, "this sounds like 'home missions' too. Do you want me to read my letter?"

"Sure," said the boys. "Anne's letters are always interesting."

THE COULEE RANCH

MONTANA

Dear Dorothy:

So many changes have taken place in these last months that I can hardly believe that I live on a cattle ranch in the "wild and wooly" west. One scorchingly warm afternoon, when the thermometer registered 102°, and we sat reading in the house because it was dangerous to be out in the sun, the quiet was suddenly broken by galloping feet coming over the hills. We rushed to the door, to see a cowboy from a neighboring ranch coming quickly toward us. He dismounted, and with a flourish of his large hat, gave Dad a white envelope from the postmaster in town.

Dad read the note, and then exclaimed: "It's an answer to prayer. Tell the postmaster, 'yes.'"

Then Dad went on to tell us that the postmaster had received word that a home mission pastor was being sent out to our town to look over the field.

Dad was very happy as he rode into town that night.

The result of that meeting was that we have a pastor of our very own. He don't have to go forty-two miles to the nearest church, any more. Since our ranch is close to town and we have a guest-room in our house, it was decided that the pastor should stay here.

It's been so much fun. He's young and interested in everything around here. He starts out early in the morning — sometimes on horseback and sometimes by car — and then travels all day finding people who haven't gone to church for many years. Some have become uninterested. Some are so poor that they don't feel they have proper clothes to wear to church. We haven't had crops here for eight years, you know.

In one community, he found a white family living among families of Indians and half-breeds. The white woman and her husband had come from Christian homes in Minnesota. And just think! In spite of hardships and lack of companions of their own kind, they had held firmly to their faith, had started a Sunday school, and even had succeeded in interesting the people to come together for services. They were real missionaries, the pastor said, and the finest heroes of faith he'd ever met.

One day, he came home and told about a family he'd found way off in the hills. Their small boy was very sick, so he'd asked, "Would you like to have me tell you a story about Jesus?"

"Haven't heard of Him! Sure! Go ahead."

I couldn't believe there could be anybody in our country who'd never heard of Jesus. But he said it isn't so strange that this boy didn't know about Jesus. He lives far away from churches, and had never seen a pastor before. And then he went on to say that it is worse when people who have every opportunity to learn to love Christ aren't even interested enough to read His Word. He said that last year, in a University, a Bible examination was given and that the papers were discouraging. Eleven said Abraham was the son of Isaac; seven that

180

Jerusalem is in Egypt; six that Christ was crucified in Gethsemane; and ten were unable to name the mother of Jesus. What do you think of that?

To go back to the boy. That boy now is baptized. The mother and father and two older brothers are in an adult confirmation class.

We have thirty in our Sunday school now. We are getting more all the time. Some come on horseback as many as twelve miles. Some of the Sunday school members have interested their parents in coming to church.

And now what do you suppose has happened?

Dad and some other men met one evening and decided to write to the Church Extension department and ask for a loan so we can build a church. Dad just heard today that we will get the loan. So now he is sending word to the men and they are going to meet here tomorrow to make plans for a new church. It will be just a small church, but it will be so wonderful to have our own.

Now I must close because Dad and Mother and "Doug" want to send letters too, in my envelope.

Write soon.

Your loving cousin,
Anne

"Oh, I'm disappointed," said Dorothy. "I thought this fat letter was all for me."

" 'Home mission' work is a great work," mused Mrs. Lansing. "An interesting thing about 'home missions' is that most churches, at least in their beginnings, were home mission churches. Many, like Anne's church, were given help by the Church Extension department so they could be built. Then for a while their pastors' salaries were paid, in part, by the Home Mission department. Then, when the churches became self-supporting, they, in gratitude, did their share, by supporting, praying for, and furthering the work of 'home missions,' so that other Lutheran churches could be established. One church alone can't do much, but when several, or many churches work together to support home missions, then the Lutheran church can spread the Gospel in widening circles. Through 'home missions,' Christ has fulfilled His promise in the lives of many people who otherwise might have been neglected. The best part of it is, it isn't only pastors who can do 'home mission' work. Everyone, everywhere can find someone close to him to win for Christ. That's 'home mission' work."

BIBLE STUDY

1. Memorize—Lev. 19:34
2. Every person should be a witnessing Christian—John 4:28, 39
3. Every Christian should love his neighbors—Gal. 6:10

Chapter 30

Making Disciples of All
the Nations

DAD," said Jim, "if there's so much 'home mission' work to be done, why isn't that finished up first, instead of so many missionaries being sent to foreign countries?"

"Christ's command makes the first great task of the church the Christianizing of all men rather than the concentrating on people in one place," replied Dr. Lansing. "The aim of missions is to make Jesus Christ known to all men as the Savior from sin.

"Since you have asked about foreign missions, this will be a good time to tell you its story," said Dr. Lansing. "It's a glorious story showing how Christ has kept His promise to be with His people always. Let's start at the beginning.

"Forty days after Jesus' resurrection, He led His eleven disciples out of Jerusalem to the Mount of Olives. He knew He was soon to go to the Father. So He probably said something like this: 'Come a little closer. I have something I want to tell you. You have been walking and talking with Me now for about three years. You have seen Me heal the sick, give sight to the blind, and raise the dead. You have seen Me die on the cross for the sins of the world. You know that I arose from the dead. Now I shall soon go to My Father. But I'm not going to leave you alone. In a short time, the Comforter, the Holy Spirit, will come to you. Wait in Jerusalem until He comes. He will give you power to be My witnesses. Then do as I commanded you that day on the mountain in Galilee when I told you to go and make disciples of all nations. Tell them who I am, what I have done, that I live forever, and that I give eternal life to all who believe in Me. Some of you stay in Jerusalem and be My witnesses. Others of you go to Judæa and Samaria. Some of you go to Asia, Africa, Europe, and unto the uttermost parts of the earth.'

"When Jesus finished saying 'unto the uttermost parts of the earth,' He lifted His hands in blessing. The Bible says Jesus was received up into heaven, and sat down on the right hand of God.

"Two angels with shining garments suddenly stood by the disciples and said: *'Ye men of Galilee, why stand ye looking up into heaven? This Jesus who was received up from you into heaven, shall so come in like manner as ye beheld Him going into heaven.'*

"Then the disciples were comforted. They remembered what Jesus had said, and they returned to Jerusalem with great joy, worshipping their risen Savior. In Jerusalem they waited, praising God with prayer and song, until the Holy Spirit came upon them on Pentecost day.

"Then as you know, the disciples were given power to carry out Christ's command. Peter became the leader of the Christian Church in Jerusalem.

182

Peter and John taught and preached in many of the Samaritan villages. When Philip had finished his work in Samaria, an angel told him to take the road going from Jerusalem to Gaza. Philip obeyed. It was along this road that Philip met the Ethiopian to whom he explained the 53rd chapter of Isaiah, and whom he baptized. It was this Ethiopian who then went on to his own country in Africa as the first missionary among his people. The disciple, Thomas, went to the East, and even today, there are three million Thomas Christians in India.

"Even while the apostles lived, and from then until the time of Constantine, God made the cruel persecutions good for something, by making them a means of spreading the Church. (See chap. 2.)

"You also remember how Saul became Paul, the greatest of all missionaries. (See P. 31, 32.) He worked in Antioch which had succeeded Jerusalem as the center of Christianity. From Antioch, he started out on his three missionary journeys. By the time that Paul was martyred, there were Christians in Southern Europe as far west as Spain.

"And then you remember the missionaries, Patrick, Columba, Augustine, Boniface, and Ansgar, who left their monasteries to go out to heathen lands in Northern Europe to win followers for Christ. (See Chap. 4.)

"Now we'll skip several hundred years and come to the year 1664. That year, an unusual thing happened. An Austrian baron, *Von Welz,* a Lutheran, wrote three pamphlets which expressed his ideas about the missionary duties of the church, and pleaded for the founding of a missionary society, and a college to train missionaries. His pamphlets brought him a great deal of ridicule, so he left his home country to go to Holland. There he was ordained as an 'Apostle to the Gentiles.' He then set sail as a missionary to Dutch Guiana where he wasn't able to work long because the climate made him ill, and he soon died. However, Von Welz has the credit of giving the first general missionary appeal to the church. In a few minutes, I shall tell you how 128 years later, his pleas, labors and prayers for a mission society were fulfilled.

"The Pietistic Movement began missions such as we have them today. (See P. 79.) The University of Halle became the center of the strongest missionary influence, and the birthplace of the first organized foreign mission effort. The first mission resulting from these foreign mission efforts was the Danish Halle Mission to India to which Ziegenbalg was sent.

"Another man from the University of Halle who was connected with this mission was *Christian Frederic Schwartz* (1726-1728), the founder of the native church of India. He was pastor in India for forty-eight years.

"It was from the Pietistic Movement that the Moravian Church received its missionary call. It began in 1732, by sending out two missionaries. During the next 150 years, the Moravian Church sent out more than 2000 missionaries. While the Protestant Churches, at large, are sending one missionary to every two or three thousand, the Moravian Church sends

183

one to every ninety-two. The Moravian Church now has three times as many members in their foreign missions as in their home churches.

"*William Carey* (1761-1834) is called 'the father of modern missions.' Before his time, missionary undertakings had been isolated, spasmodic efforts by individuals, or small groups. Because Carey's parents were poor, he had learned the trade of a cobbler. Besides making a living as a cobbler, he studied evenings until he became well educated. When he was 18, he became a preacher, but even then, he kept on with his work as a cobbler, because his salary as a preacher was very small. At one of the first pastoral meetings he attended, Carey proposed a discussion of the duties of Christians to spread the Gospel among the heathen.

"An old man said, 'Young man, sit down. When God pleases to convert the heathen, He will do it without your aid or mine.'

"But Carey didn't become discouraged. On May 31, 1792, Carey preached his famous sermon from Isaiah 54:2, 3, in which he gave to missions, the mottoes: 'Expect great things from God,' and 'Attempt great things for God.' Those who heard the sermon were so impressed that a Baptist Missionary Society, the first Protestant Missionary Society in the world was founded. Carey offered himself as the first missionary. The next year he landed in Calcutta, India.

"There are two other great missionaries to India that I shall take time to just mention, even though there are many more that I hope you can read about when you are older.

"*Adoniram Judson* (1788-1850) was a missionary to Burma, India. It was during the discouraging early years while he was learning the Burmese language, and waiting for permission to begin preaching, that Judson was asked about the outlook for successful work, and replied: 'It is as bright as the promises of God.'

"*John Scudder* (1793-1855), a medical missionary, also worked in India. All of his family and his descendants for four generations followed his example by devoting their lives to missionary service.

184

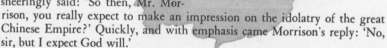

"Now, let's go to China. The Protestant missionary pioneer to China was *Robert Morrison* (1782-1834). He, too, was a shoemaker and acquired a good education and several languages by persevering study. He was sent by the London Missionary Society to China. On the way, a ship owner in New York sneeringly said: 'So then, Mr. Morrison, you really expect to make an impression on the idolatry of the great Chinese Empire?' Quickly, and with emphasis came Morrison's reply: 'No, sir, but I expect God will.'

"*J. Hudson Taylor* (1832-1905) was one of the greatest men of prayer who has ever lived. God used this man of prayer to found the China Inland Mission, the first and the largest of a number of missionary move-

ments called 'faith missions' because there is no direct solicitation of funds for work. The workers are guaranteed no fixed salary, but trust the Lord to supply their needs through the voluntary offerings of His people in answer to prayer. Its work has extended into the remotest parts of inland China.

David Livingstone

"In South Africa, *Robert Moffat* (1795-1883) was one of the pioneer missionaries. His daughter, Mary, became the wife of the best known and best loved of missionaries to Africa, David Livingstone.

"*David Livingstone* (1813-1873) worked in Africa over thirty years as a doctor, explorer, and discoverer, as well as a missionary. You have already heard a little about him. (See P. 136.) There are many books written about this great missionary who loved the Negroes so much that he stayed in Africa even when his friends urged him to go back to England. One morning, he was found on his knees beside his bed. He had died while at prayer.

"The story of missions is more wonderful than any fairy tale or any tale of Oriental magic. It seems almost unbelievable that what was given as a command by Christ to a group of eleven disciples in a far away land could grow into a mission movement that has spread into all the world and won followers for Christ among all people. If anyone wants proof that Christ has kept His promise: 'Lo, I am with you always,' he needs only to read the story of the growth of foreign mission work."

BIBLE STUDY

1. Memorize Acts 16:9
2. What does this describe—Acts 1:8-14
3. The following tell about the apostles' work—Acts 8:25; 8:26-40
4. The conversion of Paul is told about in Acts 9:1-22
5. Find William Carey's mission text

186

Chapter 31

Heroes of Faith Who Have Died for Christ

"YOU have just heard about heroes of faith who were so filled with love for Christ that they went out to tell others about Christ," said Dr. Lansing. "It sounds exciting, adventurous, and interesting.

"It was all of that, and much more. It meant the missionaries had to explore unknown lands in which there were dense forests inhabited by wild animals, winding paths through grass six or seven feet high in which poisonous snakes and ferocious animals might be hiding, and low swamp land which was an excellent breeding place for malarial mosquitoes; had to become accustomed to different climates; had to fight strange diseases; had to learn difficult languages, and often also had to formulate an alphabet so the language could be written; had to build hospitals to take care of the many sick who are always in heathen lands;

187

had to teach the heathen how to have sanitary communities, how to farm, and how to use their natural resources. Furthermore, it often took a long, long time to win the unfriendly heathen, who were superstitious, idol-worshipping, fighting savages, living in drunkenness, and other sins.

"It isn't any wonder that often missionaries would become very discouraged. It should encourage you, however, to know that missionaries were so strengthened by knowing that Christ was with them always, that they were glad to go through trials, and sufferings, in order that the Gospel could be given to all people.

"What a rich reward it was for missionaries when they could live long enough to see the Gospel message of the risen Savior transform communities of unhappy, dirty, fighting savages, to joyous, clean, witnessing Christians.

"However, winning the heathen to Christianity is not only a trying, discouraging, difficult task which requires much patience, and guidance through prayer, on the part of missionaries. It often results in suffering, trials, and periods of testing for new converts, also.

"The statement that the blood of the martyrs is become the seed of the church is usually used in connection with the persecutions of early Christians during apostolic times. Often, people do not know that this statement has been true in recent times, also.

"Christianity obtained its first foothold in Madagascar during the reign of Radama I, a chief of the Hova tribe, who succeeded in unifying the country. He was friendly to Christian missionaries, not because he believed in Christ, but because the missionaries taught his people. By the time of his death in 1829, missionaries had established several schools, had completed a Malagasy written language, and several of the Malagasy secretly believed in Christ.

"Radama's nephew should have succeeded him to the throne. But a woman, by the name of Ranavalona, cruelly put to death all rivals for the throne, and was crowned queen. At first, she permitted the missionaries to continue teaching. The first group of converts—20 of them—were baptized in 1831.

"But her chief advisers were heathen priests. Gradually, she hardened her heart against the Christians. After a few years when the Christian church had grown to 200 members, she suddenly prohibited all natives from becoming Christians. By 1836, all the missionaries and their families had been driven out of the country, but before their departure, the first complete Malagasy Bible came off the press and 70 copies were distributed secretly among the Malagasy Christians. The queen then banned the sale of Bibles, and ordered existing Bibles to be burned. However, many Bibles were hidden. (One of these hidden martyr Bibles was found in a cave and now is in the British Museum in London.)

"The hatred of the queen for Christianity resulted in cruel persecutions. In a short time, great numbers were put to death for worshipping the true God. But during this time, the Christians continued meeting together. Many private homes became churches where believers were strengthened for any fate that might befall them. Others gathered in caves to worship so they could not be seen by their enemies.

"At first, persecution was in the form of fines or slavery.

"The first Christian martyr was a young girl by the name of Rasalama. She had met occasionally with the Christians, but had not fully accepted Christ. When she heard of the government's hatred toward Christians, she betrayed some of the leaders into their hands. When she saw the courage with which they met arrest, and trial, she regretted her act, and openly confessed Christ. She was then arrested, and threatened with death unless she would renounce Christ. But she replied: 'The gods of our ancestors are no gods at all. I will not worship them, nor will I give up the worship of Jehovah.'

"She was flogged, imprisoned, and tortured, but she still remained true to her faith. Then she was chained so that her head, knees, and elbows were pressed together. Finally she was carried out for execution suspended from a pole, being too weak to walk the short distance to the execution ground. She sang praise to God with her last breath, and so inspired the Christians that many were made bold in their confessions. The heathen, witnessing the scene, marvelled that the Christian faith could, in such a wonderful manner, take away the fear of death from the heart.

"Among those who watched Rasalama die with a prayer on her lips, was a little girl called Ramona upon whom this scene made a lasting impression. In the last part of this chapter you will hear more about Ramona.

"But Rasalama's death was only the beginning of more cruel persecutions, the most severe of which came when 37 evangelists with their wives and children, and 42 who were in possession of Bibles, were condemned

189

to life-long slavery; 2,000 were fined and robbed of their personal property; and 18 were killed.

"A holiday was proclaimed. The people came out to watch the fate of those who opposed the orders of the queen. Four nobles were carried up to a hill to be burned. They were fastened to stakes above a pile of firewood. When the flames were rising, they prayed. One said: 'Lord Jesus, receive our spirits, and lay not this sin to their charge.' The falling rain put out the fire, but it was rekindled by the queen's soldiers. Then a large triple rainbow appeared in the sky, one end resting upon the spot where the martyrs' spirits were departing. Some of the crowd fled in terror.

"The other fourteen were taken to the top of a 150 foot cliff. As they were hanging there before several thousand witnesses, they were asked again to deny their Savior and cease praying. One by one they all refused, and on their word of refusal, the rope was cut and they fell to their death below. One was able to speak to his captors as he was about to be thrust over the cliff: 'You can only cast my body over the cliff. My soul goes to God in Heaven. Therefore I rejoice in dying in my Master's service.'

"During these cruel persecutions, Christians, who could, fled to the mountains and lived in forests or caves. A few Christians were able in a most miraculous manner to escape from the capital, and fled toward the coast. The whole army was sent to hunt for them. But the Christians were able to escape their would-be captors during a grueling flight that lasted for about two weeks. When they came to the coast, a British ship was lying at anchor a couple of miles out in the harbor. A Christian soldier was able to divert the attention of the harbor guard long enough so the Christians could slip into boats and reach the British ship. Some were taken to England where one of the most rousing mission meetings of all time was held, and the rest went to a near-by island to do mission work among those of their race who had been sold as slaves. So again we see that persecutions spread the church. As the Christians fled to new communities, they became the means of winning new converts.

"Even the queen finally had to admit the truth mentioned to her by some of her officers: 'The white man's religion has this peculiarity, that the more one kills, the more followers it has.' But even this did not stop her. General persecution was carried on with more zeal than ever. Some were sawed to pieces, others stoned, some beheaded, others chained permanently together with heavy chains and sent to the fever-districts of the island where most of them died. This cruel hatred continued till the queen lay on her death-bed in 1861.

"Her son succeeded her, and the very day of his coronation, he gave freedom of worship to all people. For the first time in 29 years, the Christians could fearlessly come together for worship.

"Then began a period of rejoicing that perhaps has never been equalled. From all directions, Christians who had been in hiding came back to their homes. There were many happy family reunions. Even though there had been no missionaries to guide the people for 25 years, the church had increased from a few members when persecutions began, to over 10,000 when they ceased.

"This king did not live long. Again a queen was elected. She was the Ramona who had watched the martyrdom of Rasalama. She was the niece of the queen of persecution, and had been brought up under her supervision. The defeated pagan priests were now hopeful that the Christians would again be driven out. Therefore, the Christians met her day of coronation with the greatest anxiety. They spent the days before the coronation in prayer. No indication was given them as to which way the 'wind would blow.' But they held fast to their trust in God.

"Again a holiday was proclaimed. The people were ordered to come for the coronation. The throne was veiled with a heavy cloth. Everyone wondered what the queen would decide to do. They knew she had decided to call herself Ranavalona II—the same name as that of the queen of persecution. It was a name the Christians feared. The young queen stood ready to ascend the steps. It was just a moment now before the people would know the queen's stand. Everyone was tense. Then the curtains were pulled aside.

"Revealed before the people's eyes was the Scripture passage, 'Glory to God in the highest, and on earth, peace, good will toward men.' On the table before the queen lay the Bible beside the crown she was now to wear. She and her minister of war were soon baptized. The temple gods were burned, and idolatry forbidden. In a short time, the ruling group of the people, the Hovas, became Christians. In spite of persecution, Christ had won a victory. The blood of the martyrs had become the seed of the church in Madagascar. This persecution in Madagascar is considered the worst persecution of Christians since the time of Nero."

BIBLE STUDY

1. Memorize II Tim. 3:12
2. What does the Bible say about persecutions in II Cor. 12:10; Rom. 8:35-39

191

Chapter 32

The Gospel Changes Lives

STRANGE, interesting things happen in strange, interesting lands. However, the strangest, most interesting thing of all," said Dr. Lansing, "is what God can do in the heart of men surrendered to His will.

"You have heard that in spite of the fact that all missionaries had been banished from Madagascar during the persecutions, still the Word of God with its precious message of a Christ who promised, 'Lo, I am with you always,' gave the native Christians such courage that they remained true to their Savior. Only eternity will reveal the heroism of the millions of dark-skinned heroes, who have been faithful to Christ, and have therefore lost position, property, fathers, mothers, brothers, sisters, and all that they hold dear on earth.

"Now I'm going to tell you about the power of the Word of God to entirely change the lives of the heathen and to make them helpful in saving the lives of many of their own people. They know and understand their own people as the missionary never can learn to know them. They understand the customs of their race. They are accustomed to the climate. Because they know their mother-tongue, it is easy for them to express the Gospel message so that it will be clearly understood. It is impossible to estimate the influence of the lives and work of these native Christians upon the people of their own race. From the many heroes of the faith, I shall choose four Lutherans whom I'd like to have you know.

"*Rainisoalambo* (?-1904) lay very ill in a dirty hut of a deserted village in Madagascar. His relatives had left him to die. His body, covered with boils and sores, was hot with fever. He was unable to move. He sought help from his many idols, and charms, He was a sorcerer. But the idols failed to help him. Rainisoalambo began to weep.

"And then he began to think about the God of the Christians. He remembered the Bible teacher who had taught him to read and had influenced him to become baptized. He remembered how he had hoped to become a teacher in his village and to receive a salary from the mission, and that when he'd found that there was no money to gain, he'd lost all interest, and had returned to his charms and idols.

"Now he decided he would pray to the Christian's God and see what would happen.

"For a while he was better. Then things became worse than ever. His cattle died. He had no food. His disease caused him more pain. One evening he asked, 'God, what is your purpose in making me suffer like this?'

"That night, he dreamed that he saw a figure of light which said: 'Cast away all your charms and idols.'

"Rainisoalambo was sure it was the Christian's God who had spoken to him. He quickly picked up his charms and idols, and with unusual strength for a sick man, threw them far over the hillside. He never had felt so happy as he did that day.

"Rainisoalambo became well, tended his fields, repaired his house and fences, and read and studied the Bible. He wanted to find out the Lord's will in many things. He spoke to his relatives and friends. He prayed to God for them. One by one, his family and friends destroyed their idols and charms. Rainisoalambo placed his hands upon them and prayed, and they were healed, spiritually, and physically.

"When Rainisoalambo had done all he was able for relatives and friends, he chose 8 men to receive training and to become evangelists. These evangelists sometimes had to suffer a great deal. Some were imprisoned; some were fined. But they continued to preach and heal. Everywhere they went, hearts were won for Christ. By the time Rainisoalambo died, 50 evangelists had been sent out, and the revival had become a living power over the whole island. Rainisoalambo is sometimes called the Hans Nielsen Hauge of Madagascar.

"*Onesimus Nesib* (?-1931) was born in Gallaland, Africa. His father died when he was small. From then on, he seldom left his mother whom he dearly loved. Suddenly, one day, enemies came upon them. People who had weapons were killed. His brother and sister were taken. Someone grabbed Onesimus, but his mother held his hand and said, 'I won't give him up!'

"The man took out his sword and said, 'If you don't give him up, I will kill both you and him!'

"Then his mother said, 'It is better he becomes a slave, than that they kill him.'

"Onesimus was sold from one master to another. The price for which he was sold on one occasion was a horse, another time four cows, and a third occasion 200 pieces of salt. One of his cruel masters said that he would sell Onesimus to the cannibals, so when Onesimus saw white people the first time, he thought, 'Alas, now I am among the cannibals.'

"While he sat there trembling, a white man came to buy him from the slave dealer, and said, 'Do not be afraid, for now you will never be sold again.'

"Onesimus thought: 'He is fooling me just like all the others. Later, he will eat me.'

"The white man was a Swedish Lutheran missionary who soon realized that the serious, strong-bodied, intelligent young Galla might be used by God as a missionary to the Gallas who were so cruel, and so impossible to win that the Mohammedans had called them, 'the people who say, "No." '

"When Onesimus had completed the courses at the mission school, the missionaries wished him to attend a missionary training school. So Onesimus volunteered to work his way to Sweden. He studied for four years at the Johannelund Mission Seminary. He was then ordained as a missionary to Africa. He started working in Gallaland with two white missionaries, but he was rejected by his own people. Then he spent three years translating into Galla, a tract, Luther's Small Catechism, and a hymn book. In another seven years, he had translated the New Testament. By 1897, he had completed the whole Bible, and in 1899, it was printed by the British and Foreign Bible Society.

"When Onesimus had finished the work in connection with the printing of the Bible into Galla, he went on to the western part of Gallaland to the neighborhood of his birthplace.

"God used this educated Christian Galla to win the proud Galla race, to open his country to mission work, to give them the Bible in their own language, and to found the first mission station in his country—at Lakamte. There, Onesimus had his headquarters and grew old in the service of his master.

"*Chu Hao-jan* (1883-) was stepping off a train at Hankow, China, on the 21st of April in 1927, when he was seized and taken to the headquarters of the communists. They took his passport, a bundle of paper notes, and about $260 in gold and silver. After a cross-examination, even though they could find nothing for which to accuse him, he was led away to be bound.

" 'Why do you bind me?' asked Chu. 'I'll go where you want me to go.'

"He was taken to the river, put into a boat, and taken across to Wuchang. There he was mocked and tied to a post, his hands tied to his back, and the rope slung over a beam so tightly that his heels could hardly touch the floor. While he was tied, the guards continually pulled the triggers of their guns, and pointed their bayonets at Chu, to frighten him. The third night, he was beaten with a heavy oak stick, and then bound more tightly. Then heavy pieces of timber were piled on his back to increase the weight of his body which was practically supported by the ropes with which he was tied.

"At midnight of the third night, only a young boy was left on guard. Chu told the boy how intensely he was suffering, how he was perspiring, thirsting, and shivering. The ropes were then untied giving Chu a few minutes of rest. Then he was again tied, but not so tightly. The timber on his back was removed. Later that night, the ropes were unfastened entirely.

"The next morning he was put into a prison. He was not tied any more. He spent the time in prayer and meditation. He thought of his devout father, a weaver, who one night had heard a voice say, 'Go north,' and had obeyed immediately, taking his wife, children, and possessions, and traveling north more than 100 miles by wheelbarrow, settling in Sinyang where he continued his work as a weaver. He remembered how his father's curiosity had led him twice to go by night to the home of the foreign teacher, Daniel Nelson. He remembered the morning his father had told his family what he had done, and how horrified his brother and he had been.

" 'If people find out you are visiting the foreigners, our reputation and business will be ruined,' he had cried.

"And he remembered, even though he had determined never to have anything to do with the foreigners, how happy he had been later when all of them had been baptized, how he had entered the Union Theological Seminary and had been ordained, had married a bright Christian Chinese girl, had been called as the pastor of the congregation at Sinyang, had later been elected president of the Lutheran Church of China, composed of ten Lutheran synods, and how much he had to be thankful for in spite of the cruel treatment he was receiving now.

"At midnight that night, a sympathetic guard gave him paper and pencils. He wrote his first letter after his imprisonment. That was the beginning of a series of events which finally resulted in his release on May 28.

"Chu Hao-jan is a man of rare ability and rich Christian experience. He is a leader among his people."

"Of the five Peng brothers, little Fu was the most faithful in visiting shrines and in worshipping Chinese gods. He was very serious as he tried to imitate his parents in prostrating himself before the altar or the house shrines, and in knocking his forehead against the stone floor. He did not understand the religious ceremonies or the things his father told him about his ancestors, but he was nevertheless thrilled by the knowledge of being an important person.

"One day, Fu said to his little brother: 'When I become an ancestor, my name will be inscribed on an ancestral tablet, too:

" 'Peng Fu, born on the 29th day of the ninth moon in the fourteenth year of Kwang Hsü (1888-).'

"When Peng Grandmother became ill, little Fu accompanied his mother to the shrine of the goddess of mercy, Kwan Yin, to seek aid. Peng Mother lit candles before the goddess, burned incense, and bundles of yellow paper prayers. The priest struck a gong to send the prayers on their way. Then the priest took the 'seek-the-answer-box,' filled with numbered bamboo sticks, and told Peng Mother to shake it until a stick fell to the floor. The number on the stick was matched with a number in a book that said 'Favorable.' Peng mother gave the priest a string of brass cash. But when they arrived home, things did not look favorable. Peng Grandmother was worse.

"Then a sorceress was called, went into a trance, and said: 'In order to win the favor of the goddess, you must bring her 13 catties (pounds) of incense, 10 catties of paper money, and you must bring me a live chicken, a large piece of pork, and a good sized fish.'

"But even then, Peng Grandmother grew worse and worse. It was evident that she was dying. Then Peng Mother gave orders to dress the sick woman

Chu Hao-jan   Peng Fu

in her yellow silk burial dress and place her on a mat in an adjoining room so that her soul would not cling to the old bed, when the body was removed, and haunt those who would later sleep there. The exercise was too strenuous for sick Peng Grandmother, and she died.

"Immediately Peng Father strangled a red rooster beside the dead woman so that she would have something to ride on into the spirit world.

"Peng Grandmother was placed in a coffin which had stood by her bed for many years.

"For two years, then, there were feasts and ceremonies by Confucian teachers and Buddhist priests in order that Peng Grandmother might have a grand funeral and safely arrive. . . .

" 'When and where will she arrive?' wondered Fu.

"Years passed by.

"When Fu was ten, he dashed home, nearly knocking over a middleman who had arranged for Fu's betrothal. Fu was too excited to listen to the important matter of his engagement.

" 'I have seen a foreigner,' exclaimed Fu. 'He is ugly, bleached looking, and has a long beak. He lies down to rest like a human being. He eats. He prostrates himself on his knees, but there is no god before him.'

" 'He must have hatched from larva. These foreigners are not real human beings, I'm sure,' said Peng Mother. 'He did not cast his eyes on you, did he?'

" 'No, oh no,' replied the frightened Fu.

"But Fu saw the foreigner again, and coming years brought many changes. The little Fu, who had torn off the pretty picture covers from Missionary Knut Stokke's Bibles and had thrown the printed material away, when Stokke had to leave because of the Boxer Uprising, later entered the mission school, was baptized, and learned to love the printed message of the Bible. He graduated from the high school for boys at Sinyang, and in 1916 from the Lutheran Theological Seminary at Shekow. He then worked as evangelist in Junan until 1928 when he was ordained. In 1937, he was honored by being elected president of the Lutheran Church in China by representatives of ten Lutheran Synods. In 1939, Peng Fu visited the United States in behalf of the Lutheran Church of China. If you have seen him or any others who have been won for Christ through foreign missions, then I know you will always want to do your share that the Gospel may be preached in all the world."

BIBLE STUDY

1. Memorize Isaiah 49:12
2. The following tells about mission work—Acts 14:27
3. Jesus had power to change lives—II Cor. 3:18; Is. 60:1-3

ASIA

SOCIETY FOR LUTHERAN
MISSION IN RUSSIA

ALASKA

NORTH

SIBERIA

MONGOLIA

MANCHUKUO

U.L.C.

LUTH. FREE
AUGUSTANA
N.L.C.A.
L. BRETHREN
MISSOURI

SIAM

PHILIPPINE
ISLANDS

EAST INDIES

A.L.C.   NEW GUINEA

HAWAIIAN ISLANDS

LUTHE
OF NC
-UN
ME:
CENTRA

AUSTRALIA

PACIFIC
OCEAN

*...There are approximately 500 missionaries on the
foreign mission fields of the world who have been
sent out by the Lutheran Churches in America. On
these fields it is estimated that there are about 300,000
Christians belonging to the Lutheran Church.*

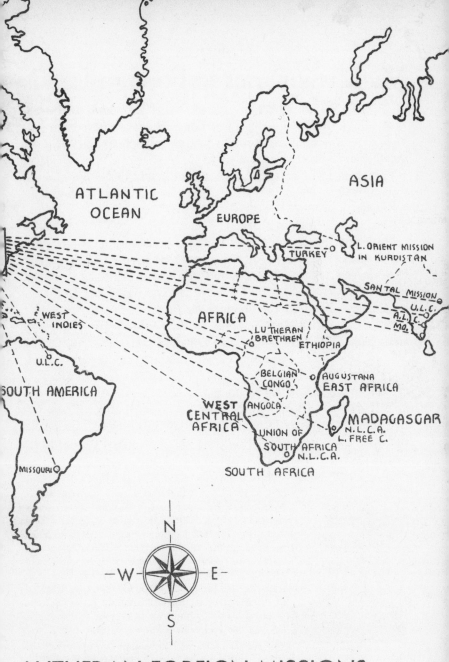

LUTHERAN FOREIGN MISSIONS

Chapter 33

My Missionaries to Foreign Lands

"THAT'S an interesting chart," said Jim, and then read, "Approximately 500 Lutheran missionaries have been sent out from America to the foreign mission fields. Who are they? Have you seen any of them?"

"Yes, Jim, at the national and district conventions of our church, foreign mission topics are usually given by men who are home on furlough."

"What does 'furlough' mean?"

"Missionaries are sent out to foreign countries for a certain number of years. Then they are given a year's vacation when they come back to America to rest, study, and to tell us in America about the work in foreign fields. By the way, can you name any Lutheran missionaries I've told you about so far?"

"There was that Austrian baron by the name of Von Welz who went here," said Jim, pointing to Dutch Guiana.

"Good," said Dr. Lansing. "He gave the first missionary appeal, you remember. Then, who was the first missionary to India?"

"Ziegenbalg," said Dale.

"All right, and Christian Schwartz was the founder of the native church in India. Of course, you remember Hans Egede, the first missionary to Greenland. Now there are a few more of our own Lutheran missionaries you should know.

"The memory of *Karl F. A. Gützlaff* (1803-1851) is perpetuated on China's wild coast, near the Straits of Formosa, by a towering lighthouse which sends out the loud cry, 'Gützlaff!' instead of 'Beware!' He was a Pomeranian Lutheran missionary to Batavia, Singapore, and many parts of China. He wrote tracts into Siamese, translated parts of the Bible into five dialects, and helped Robert Morrison translate the Bible into Chinese. He later traveled in Europe arousing mission interest. It was he who inspired David Livingstone to become a missionary. Livingstone had become interested in missions, and had resolved that he would give to missions all he could earn beyond what was required for a living, but when he read Gützlaff's appeals in behalf of China, he determined to give *himself*. Later God's guidance led Livingstone to hear Moffat and to become interested in Africa. Also, it was Gützlaff's appeals that reached the Lutheran Church in the United States, and awakened interest in foreign missions.

"*John Christian Frederick Heyer* (1793-1873) had been a home mission pastor for 23 years, traveling by foot and on horseback to carry on the work in Pennsylvania, Maryland, Kentucky, and Indiana, had been active in organizing Sunday schools, and had been a trustee of Gettysburg Seminary (See Pp. 94, 95). Then reports of Gützlaff's work in China fired the Lutherans in America with missionary enthusiasm. Heyer accepted a call to go as a missionary to India. There he founded the Guntur Mission, and became the first president of the Lutheran Synod of India. He served three terms in India, returning to India the last time when he was 77 years old. Between his second and third terms, he served 12 years as a pioneer pastor in Minnesota. He had a passion for souls.

"*Hans P. S. Schreuder* (1817-1882) had gone to Africa, hoping to win the Zulus for Christ. After learning the Zulu language, and making a long. adventurous journey, he finally reached the kraal of King Mpande, king of the Zulus, waited a week while King Mpande discussed the matter with his counsellors, and then was told that he couldn't have permission to begin mission work among the Zulus.

"Discouraged with his efforts to win the Zulus, he decided, 'I'm going to China.' When he arrived in Hongkong, he looked up the well-known missionary, Gützlaff, who greeted him with a peculiar question, 'But, how do you expect to be a missionary among the Chinese, you who have fair hair?' Schreuder learned that his fair hair and light blue eyes made it impossible for him to look like a Chinaman even when dressed like them, with sandals, robe, and queue, so he returned to Africa.

"Finally King Mpande became ill. The royal medicine men, in swaying monkey tails and full blown birds' bladders, armed with their most potent charms of human hearts, livers, and earthen jars of gall, could not ease Mpande's pains. Finally a royal delegation of Zulu courtiers, headed by a chief, came to ask Schreuder to help the sick man. Again Schreuder made the long, difficult journey over turbulent rivers, hills, and steep mountains to the king's kraal. God blessed his medical efforts, so that the king, the prime minister, a princess, and several other Zulu aristocrats were healed of their ailments. Thus God used medicine bottles to open the way for Schreuder to win the good will of the Zulu king and to receive his permission to begin mission work among the Zulus. After 14 years of patient labor, the first Zulu Christian was baptized. Now Zululand is a Christian land.

"*Lars Olsen Skrefsrud* (1840-1910), a boy with more than average gifts, joined a highland regiment as a drummer boy, fell into bad company, forgot his confirmation vows, and soon became a leader among his godless friends. One night, with his friends, he robbed a warehouse, was caught red-handed, brought to trial, and was sent to prison. While in prison, he repented of his sins, consecrated his life to his Master as a missionary, and began to prepare himself for such work. After he regained his freedom, he continued studying, and applied for mission work. He was told that because he had been in prison, he couldn't be used. It was a great disappointment to him. A friend told him to go to Germany to the Boerresen's. In Germany, Skrefsrud studied one year, and then received a call from the Gossner Mission Society to go to India. There Skrefsrud studied Santali, which then was not a written language, invented an alphabet, taught the people to read their own language, and published a Santali grammar.

"*Hans Peter Boerresen* (1825-1901) had a fine voice, and was popular with young people in Denmark. At the age of 27, when he went to Berlin to find employment, he missed his young Danish friends, and, in loneliness, began to read his Bible. One Sunday as he read the parable of the Prodigal Son, he was so touched that he knelt down in the park and dedicated his life anew to God. He and his wife left for India a year after Skrefsrud's departure. With Skrefsrud, they became the founders of the Santal Mission in India. Boerresen sang the Gospel into so many hearts that he was called the 'singing missionary.'

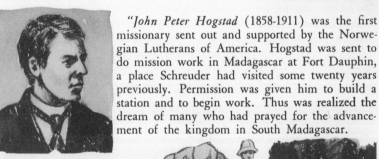

"*John Peter Hogstad* (1858-1911) was the first missionary sent out and supported by the Norwegian Lutherans of America. Hogstad was sent to do mission work in Madagascar at Fort Dauphin, a place Schreuder had visited some twenty years previously. Permission was given him to build a station and to begin work. Thus was realized the dream of many who had prayed for the advancement of the kingdom in South Madagascar.

"*Daniel Nelson* (1853-1926) was not very old when he left Norway to sail the seven seas and visit many lands. At one time, a typhoon caused the ship to be wrecked. Some of the crew drowned. Others held on to boards from the wrecked vessel. Nelson thought all hope of rescue was gone. Suddenly the night sky became lighter and off in the distance, he saw a sailboat. It wasn't long before the boat came closer, and Nelson saw that on board were Chinese fishermen. He knew the Chinese had a dislike for white men, but in times like this, color seemed to make little difference. Yellow hands threw out a rope and white hands clutched the rope. When Nelson and a few other men were safely on board, no common language was needed to express the joy all felt. When the ship landed, the Chinese fishermen hospitably gave food and clothing to the shipwrecked men. Later Nelson found out that near the place where the ship had been wrecked, was an island on which lived cannibals. He then realized that if the Chinese had not rescued them, their fate might have been worse than that of drowning.

"Years later, when Nelson was busy shingling a roof, he seemed suddenly to hear a voice say, 'Sell your farm, take your family, and go to China.' He stopped his work and said, 'Lord, if Thou wilt send me a buyer, I will go.' His wife encouraged him. He sold his farm, and in 1890, the Nelson family reached China to begin mission work. Nelson had gone to give the saving message of Christ to the Chinese who had saved his life.

"Now," said Dr. Lansing, "I have told you a little about the most important work that the church is doing. It's a fascinating story that begins with Jesus on the Mount of Olives telling his disciples to go unto the uttermost parts of the earth, and giving them His great promise, 'Lo, I am with you always.' When the story ends, that is, when Christ has been preached to the uttermost parts of the earth, then the world will end. Then Jesus will come again in like manner as He was beheld going into heaven. Then Christ will gather unto Himself all those who believe in Him. It will be *a great multitude which no man could number, out of every nation and of all tribes and peoples and tongues, standing before the throne and before the Lamb, arrayed in white robes, and palms in their hands.*"

BIBLE STUDY

1. Memorize—Matt. 9:37-38
2. The above quotation is taken from Rev. 7:9
3. What was Paul's aim as a missionary—Rom. 15:20, 21
4. Medical mission work is important—Matt. 4:23; Matt. 10:1
5. Spiritual awakening is a result of mission work—Acts 2:37, 38; 14:27

Chapter 34

The Helping Hand of My Church

D R. LANSING put down the newspaper. "Come on, boys," he said. "Let's find out if there's anything we can do to help Mother. If that roast and apple pie are as good as they smell, we want to try them right away."

"I should have opened the oven door before," laughed Mrs. Lansing as she slipped an apron over Dr. Lansing's head, and gave him the potato masher. "Now just the potatoes to mash, and supper's ready."

Dale twined his legs around the kitchen stool and watched proceedings. Suddenly, he noticed something different. "Why, Mother, what's that over the sink?"

Mrs. Lansing turned a flushed face, and smilingly said, "A reminder! Now let's eat while everything's warm."

When they were seated, Dale continued, "A reminder of what?"

"A reminder of a story I read called 'The Thank-you House.'

"A beautiful new house was being built in one of the many seaside suburbs of the bustling park-city of Kobe, Japan. A bright-eyed little girl was proudly showing everything to an American missionary.

"'How wide and shady your new yard is!' said the missionary, glancing from the lacquered veranda to the expanse of clean, white sand. 'And what is that building at the corner? It's too big for a playhouse, too nice for a barn, too foreign for a servant's house. It is not shaped like a storehouse.'

"'Come,' the child cried gayly. 'I will show you our Thank-you House!'

"'A Thank-you House?' repeated the missionary questioningly of the pretty Japanese mother who was following them about.

"'The children have called it that ever since we explained that we were building it with the new house because of all God's goodness to us. We are so thankful for all our blessings that we decided to build this small house in appreciation. It cost little more than a shrine to the god of wealth which we would have built had we not known Christ. The house is to be used as a Sunday school for the children of our village.'

" 'And what is this room with its matted floor, and sunny little porch?'

" 'Our Thank-you teacher will live there,' the child replied.

" 'Yes,' the quiet hostess said. 'We hired one less servant, and put off a tutor for Taro for a few years, so we can employ a Bible woman for this town. She will live here, conduct a Sunday school, and teach the people.'

"The missionary thought to herself: 'How many there are in my own country who have heard of Christ, and the promise He has always kept, and who have lovely homes, but who have never thought of a Thank-you House, or of giving people less fortunate a chance.'

"And so," continued Mrs. Lansing, "I cut out a picture of a lovely Japanese home to make me think of the Thank-you House. I know it will help me thank God oftener for the many blessings our family enjoys. I'm sure it will help me to pray more for others, think of many ways to help others, and do more toward the charity work of our church."

"What charity work does the church do?" asked Dale.

"There are many phases to this work. It includes all works of love done for those who are unfortunate. It's like the helping hand of a person whose heart is so filled with love and gratitude to God that he can't help but do good. It includes all things done to relieve the sufferings of men, women, and children. This work, however, is intended not only to bring relief. It has a larger purpose—to show men the spirit of Christ, and to bring them to a knowledge of the heavenly Father and of His beloved Son. Every opportunity for charity work and service is an opportunity to demonstrate the saving love and power of Christ, to bear witness of Christ, and to make known His salvation.

"One church working alone to do deeds of mercy wouldn't be able to do much. But when all the Lutheran churches of one synod unite to do charity work, then much more can be done. That's why the church synod has a charity department with workers who plan how best to do things. Then each church cooperates with funds, interest and prayers.

"The church's helping hand has many tasks to perform in many places. It reaches into the home where Christian members do acts of kindness to each other. It reaches those in the local church who are sick, unfortunate, or in need. Helping hands and thankful hearts take flowers to the sick, read and sing to shut-ins, and give clothing and fuel to the needy.

"The church's helping hand reaches out further—has founded Deaconess training schools and hospitals where women train to become missionaries, parish workers, and leaders in the care of those who are so small they need help, and those who are so old that they need help."

"That reminds me," interrupted Dr. Lansing, "of a family I've watched.

"One cold, wintry morning, one of my patients, the mother of Erick and Judith Thompson, died. She had been ill almost constantly since the birth of Judith two years before. The father, who was a hard-working day-laborer, did not know where to turn. There were no relatives to assist him. Friends and neighbors helped for a few days until he finally found a housekeeper. He could not afford to pay much. It was hard for him to find anyone who would stay any length of time. He tried placing the children with friends, but later learned they were being mistreated. Finally after he had struggled along for almost two years, I suggested that he place the children in a Lutheran Children's Home, fifteen miles away.

"After seeing the Home, and visiting several hours with the superintendent, he decided to place his children there. He could visit them weekly, and feel sure they were getting the things they should have. His income was small, but he agreed to pay what he could, which amounted to around $3.00 a week for each child. (It actually costs twice this much to run Children's Homes.)

"The superintendent of the Home explained that the Home Finding Department of the Church would send a case worker to get certain information from him; that this investigation is necessary to secure the history and background of the children as well as information concerning their health, so the workers at the Home can give the children intelligent care.

"When everything was arranged, Mr. Thompson took Judith and Erick to the Home. The superintendent was waiting to welcome them. The other children, who had been prepared for the coming of the two new children, immediately accepted them into their midst. They remembered how hard it had been when they had first come.

"Five years went by. Mr. Thompson visited his children regularly. One day, he came to the superintendent saying that he had just learned that he had a fatal disease and could live no longer than a year. He was anxious that the Church accept his children and make plans for their adoption, because an institution, no matter how nice it is, is no permanent place for children. He hoped this could be done before he died. During these years, Mr. Thompson had been brought close to his God, and said that if he only knew that his children would be cared for, he would be ready to die any time.

"The superintendent referred the matter to the Lutheran Welfare Society in the State. They prepared to find a suitable home, which is not an easy thing to do. They were looking for a Christian home which would give the children real love and affection and train them in Christian living.

"More months sped by. Mr. Thompson was on his death bed. When the superintendent of the Home came to tell him that a suitable home had been found for his children, Mr. Thompson said, 'Now I can die in peace. God has always answered my prayers, and now He has answered this one, too.

"The day came when the foster parents came to the Home to see and visit the children, who had been carefully prepared for the great event. They knew their father's wishes, and they had been told about this family who had no children, and wanted them for their own.

"Before the day was over, Erick and Judith decided they liked these people, and wanted to go home with them. It was with tears of happiness that the workers waved goodbye to the family as they rode away—Judith, sitting with her foster mother, and Erick assisting his new daddy with the driving.

"Erick and Judith were 'left alone' no longer!"

"And last week," Mrs. Lansing continued, "our Ladies' Aid chorus went out to give a program at the '———— Sunset Home.' I was touched by seeing how appreciative and happy those people in the sunset of their lives were. They are well cared for. They receive all they need to eat and wear. Most of them have private rooms. But best of all they receive what their souls need—God's Word and Sacraments. Morning and evening devotions, and Sunday services are conducted in the chapel of the Home."

"You've mentioned Children's Homes, Sunset Homes, Home Finding, and work among the sick and needy," said Dr. Lansing. "It is interesting that just as it was the church that made the first plans for education, so it was the church that first became interested in the unfortunate. Deeds of mercy are a result of the influences of Christianity. After the church had done much for education and charity, then the government also began such work. But there are other things included under works of charity."

"What are they?" asked Jim.

"There's work in the hospitals, asylums, prisons, reformatories, city missions, day nurseries, and I suppose there are still things I haven't mentioned. And of course, I mustn't forget 'box work.'"

"Oh, do you mean boxes like the one you send to Children's Homes?" asked Dorothy.

"Yes. I'm sure my little reminder in the kitchen is going to make this year's box give more happiness to others because more thankfulness, love, and real thought are going into the planning."

"Well, Mother," said Dr. Lansing, "your little reminder is ours too, now, since you've shared the story with us. We shall try to live our thanks, too, so that we can have a share in reaching out helping hands."

BIBLE STUDY

1. Memorize—Matt. 25:40
2. Read—Luke 10:30-37; Matt. 25:31-46; Mark 9:41; I Pet. 4:10
3. Where in the Bible is the Parable of the Good Samaritan?

There is now a stamp to be sold at Easter time for the benefit of crippled children similar to the Christmas seal which is sold at Christmas time to help fight tuberculosis.

Chapter 35
I Am God's Steward

"WHAT did our pastor mean today when he said he would preach a series of sermons on stewardship during the next five Sunday evening services? What is stewardship?" asked Dale.

"He meant that he is going to tell you how God wants you to use what belongs to Him," said Mrs. Lansing.

"Why, Mother, what are we using that belongs to God?" interrupted Dorothy.

"Everything you have is really God's," explained Mrs. Lansing, and then noticing the surprised expression on Dorothy's face, she added: "I think I can best explain it to you through a story.

"King Victor had defeated the rebellious knights of his kingdom. Those who had not fallen in battle were now prisoners awaiting trial and condemnation. The day of the court-martial had come. Humbled and crestfallen, the defeated knights stood before their king, knowing that he could require their lives.

"The king sat silently upon his throne, looking unhappily at those who had once been his friends and who now faced him with the guilty look of traitors in their faces.

"At last the king spoke. But instead of the expected sentence of death, he uttered words of forgiveness. Not only were the rebels pardoned, but their castles, their lands, their swords, and their rights were fully restored to them.

"The knights heard what the king said, but could hardly believe their ears. They moved about uncertainly, not knowing what to say or do. Finally, Lothar, the chief knight, stepped forward, and said: 'Your majesty, this is the most wonderful, royal proclamation my ears have ever heard. It is truly worthy of a great king. We have been rebels, but we have learned our lesson. You will never have cause to regret your great-hearted and generous act.' Then turning to his companions, he said: 'Fellow-knights, henceforth, I belong to my king. My castle is his; my realm is his; my sword is his; my life is his. If you are with me in this pledge, raise your right hands to confirm your vow.' With right hands raised, they promised perpetual loyalty to their king.

"Those knights by their new relation to the king, by the consecration of their castles, their lands, their swords, their lives, and their all, assumed the position of stewards to their king. They no longer thought of their possessions, talents, or lives as their own, but as belonging to the king.

"Man, too, became rebelliously disobedient at the fall. Therefore, God had the right to condemn you. But instead, He sent His Son to suffer punishment in your behalf. Your response should be similar to Lothar's: 'I belong to my Lord. My life, my

208

body, my mind, my time, my talents, and my possessions belong to Him.' Such a confession becomes Christian stewardship—the investment of your whole life for God."

"But what do you mean by saying that my life, my talents, my time, and my possessions belong to God?" asked Jim.

"That question requires a long answer," said Mrs. Lansing. "If you give your *life* to God as a steward, then you will look up to God, and ahead to God for guidance. You will continually ask yourself: 'Is this God's way, or am I going the world's way?' You will have a vision in everything you do. It will be as though you were conscious always of Christ saying: 'I am with you always.'"

"I know a good illustration," said Dr. Lansing.

"A traveller visited a stone quarry.

" 'What are you doing?' he asked one of the workmen.

" 'I'm cutting stone,' answered the man abruptly as if he thought the stranger should mind his own business.

" 'What are you doing?' he asked another workman.

" 'I'm trying to make a living for myself and my family,' was the reply.

" 'And what are you doing?' he asked a third worker.

" 'I'm helping Sir Christopher Wren build a cathedral down at London,' was the reply."

"That is interesting," said Mrs. Lansing. "The first two men were working the world's way. The third was working with a vision—God's way."

"I can see that," said Jim. "But I don't see how we can be stewards of our bodies."

"Long ago, during the time when monasteries were so popular," continued Dr. Lansing, "the body was considered a necessary evil that should be under subjection. Many monks scourged, tortured, and deprived their bodies of the food necessaray to keep strong, and of clothing sufficient to keep them warm, because they thought then they were pleasing God. That, however, was the world's way just as much as those who abuse their bodies by over-eating, drinking, lack of care, or impure living. God's way —the stewardship way—is to think of your body as the temple of God. *Know ye not that ye are the temple of God?* The *stewardship of the body* then, Jim, means everything that will serve its development and well being —food, sleep, exercise, work, cleanliness, and purity—so that your body will be fit to do the will of God in some form of service.

209

"*Stewardship of the mind* means reading clean literature, seeing good pictures, studying in preparation for a life lived God's way, and making every thought obedient to Christ's will.

"*Stewardship of time* is important. Edison said: 'Time is the most valuable thing in the world.' It takes time to grow in Christian faith and to serve according to God's will. It takes time to do everything worth while. Every person living has twenty-four hours in every day. A millionaire has more money than you, but he has no more time. God's way is to use time to advantage. The world's way is to waste time, to use it selfishly, and to let it slip by without being used in God's service. The world's way is: 'Time is short. Enjoy it while you can.' God's way is: 'Time is short. I must use it while it lasts in a way pleasing to God.' A certain man spent fifteen years trying to balance a pole on his chin. Which way was that? Missionary Schreuder spent 14 years trying to win his first convert among the Zulus.

"*Stewardship of talents* is being conscious of Christ's promise: 'Lo, I am with you always.' You will have the same vision as Antonio Stradivari, the great violin maker of Cremona, Italy. He believed that God and he worked together to produce the wonderful Stradivarius violins. It doesn't make any difference how few your talents are or how many. God's way is using what you have in His service. An old man had no talents, he thought. He was poor. And yet he wanted to give to the Lord's work. So he offered to scrub the church floor without charge.

"There are many who have had great talents and have used them as stewards. Because I have been telling you the story of the Christian church with an emphasis on the Lutheran Church, I shall mention a few Lutherans who have had great talents, shared their talents, and given of them in service. You've already heard about the artists—Durer, Cranach, Holbein, and Thorwaldsen; the musicians—Nicolai, Gerhardt, Bach, and Handel; the Swedish nightingale—Jenny Lind; the hymn writers—Luther, Kingo, Brorson, Grundtvig, Landstad, and Lindeman. There were also the musicians—Brahms, Wagner, Mendelssohn, Schumann, Grieg, and Sibelius; the violinist, Ole Bull; and the singer, Olive Fremstad. I should also like to mention one of the greatest choral directors the world has ever had,

F. Melius Christiansen, and the great opera singer, Kirsten Flagstad, who says that of all things that have contributed to her art, the greatest has been her religious faith. Whether you have many talents or few makes no difference. But it does make a difference in which way you use the talents you have.

"And then one more thing. *Stewardship of possessions* requires that you make a right about face. Among the first words you said were, 'That's mine.' Many people never grow up to become stewards of possessions. They spend their lives so they can *get* this and that, and so they can say, 'That's mine.' They forget God's way—the stewardship way which *gives.* You have already begun to earn some money. The stewardship way is to set apart a certain amount of everything you earn or receive for the Lord's work. The Jews of the Old Testament were required to give a tithe or a tenth to the Lord's work. You who live now are not required to give a tithe, but if you remember Christ's mission command and all Christ has done for you, you will want to give gladly and willingly your share to the Lord's work. Do you remember the widow's mite, and how pleased Christ was with her offering, because it meant loving sacrifice on her part?"

"But, Dad, how can I know how much I should give?"

"No one can tell you that, Jim. Read God's Word and you will learn to know Christ better. Then you will be glad to give in order that others may know Him. Prayer to God will help you to know how much to give.

"What a solemn, serious family," continued Dr. Lansing with a laugh. "It does sound serious, I know. Stewardship living is serious, but it's so thrilling. People want thrills today. There are more thrills in living God's way—the stewardship way—than in any other kind of life. The wonderful part of it is that the thrills of God's way last forever. St. Paul found it so. All in the 'March of Faith' have found it so. You will find it so."

BIBLE STUDY

1. Memorize—Rom. 14:7, 8
2. The following verses tell you to be stewards of what?—Hag. 2:8; I Tim. 6:7
3. God wants you to be stewards of your time—John 9:4; of your talents—Matt. 25:14-30; of your mind—Rom. 12:2
4. God wants you to be a steward of your body—I Cor. 6:19, 20; I Cor. 3:16; Ps. 139:14

Chapter 36

Lo, I Am With You Always

THE glowing embers of the fireplace were the only light in the darkening room. The Lansing family, and the setter, too, were relaxing about the fireplace, after a long hike along the river, which had been bordered here and there with apple and plum trees in blossom.

Dr. Lansing broke the silence by saying, "And now a beautiful fall, a stormy winter, and a glorious spring have passed since I began telling you the story of the Christian church. You have traveled to far away places in long ago times. You have seen the heroes of faith marching down through the ages, each one strengthened by Christ's promise, 'Lo, I am with you always.'"

"Why do you always call them 'heroes of faith,' Dad?" asked Dale.

"You understand, of course, what 'heroes' means. It's the word *faith* which is difficult to understand, because it is not a thing you can feel, or see, or reason. And yet, you have faith in many things you can't feel, see, reason, or prove. For instance, you expect, if you live, to awaken tomorrow morning to the light of a new day. Unless it is cloudy, you know there will be beautiful sunshine. That's faith. In the same way, faith trusts in God, takes Him at His Word, believes His promises, knows He will keep His promises.

"In the Book of Hebrews, Paul says: *'Faith is the assurance of things hoped for, a conviction of things not seen.'* Then he illustrates from the Old Testament, by listing some of those who had faith in God's promises of a coming Savior, and who, in faith, obeyed God's will. The list begins with Abel, who because he trusted and loved God, offered, in faith, a better sacrifice than Cain. He mentions Enoch who because of his faith was taken alive to heaven, and Noah who, by faith, prepared the ark exactly as God told him, even though there was no water in sight. He also speaks of Abraham who had a faith so great that he went to a far away land God promised him, and was willing to sacrifice his son, Isaac, when God asked him.

"New Testament heroes of faith do not need to look forward in faith to the fulfilling of God's promises about a Savior. New Testament heroes of faith believe in a risen Savior, and in that verse in the New Testament which is called the heart of the Bible: *'For God so loved the world that He gave His only begotten Son, that whosoever believeth on Him should not perish, but have eternal life.'*

"This year, I have told you about some of the heroes of faith who have been shining lights in the story of the Christian church from its beginning up to the present time. You have seen Paul, Athanasius, Augustine, Ansgar, Huss, Luther, Muhlenberg, and many others. Because of their strong faith and their witnessing lives, they have helped many others to faith, and trust in Jesus.

"Faith is like putting your hand into God's and trusting Him to lead you. Faith ends all anxiety and worry about tomorrows. Faith is like a telegraph wire which links earth to Heaven, and on which God's messages of love fly so fast that often before you pray, He answers."

"But God doesn't answer all my prayers," said Jim.

"It often *seems* that way. However, I can assure you that *God always answers prayer.* Therefore, nothing lies outside the reach of prayer except that which is not according to God's will. Sometimes, He does not answer it as you wish. He probably gives you something much better than you ask. Often, because He sees that that for which you ask would harm you, He substitutes something else. Sometimes, God delays the answer to your prayers because it may require long years of preparation.

"But never become discouraged. Continue praying. Pray in faith, believing God will answer your prayer. Open the door of your heart. Then the Holy Spirit will help you to talk to God about your needs, and your hopes. That's what prayer is—a communing or talking with God about the smallest details of your daily life, as well as your most difficult problems. God knows you and your needs better than you do. When you have told God about your needs, in prayer, then have faith that you can leave everything with Him, and He will answer your prayer.

"Jesus while He was here on earth prayed. Often, He went apart from the throng, and prayed alone to His Father. Through prayer, He received help, strength, wisdom, and all that was needed. He continually invited, prompted, and encouraged others to pray. When the disciples said, 'Teach us to pray,' He taught them the perfect prayer—'The Lord's Prayer.'

"Prayer does the impossible. It often causes miracles. During the Apostolic church, Peter was in prison; the Jews were triumphant; Herod was supreme; the arena was decided upon as the scene of Peter's martyrdom. But *prayer was made to God without ceasing.* What was the result? The prison was opened; Peter was freed; the Jews were puzzled; the wicked king was eaten by worms; and the Word of God was victorious.

"The men who have been used the most by God have spent much time on their knees.

"Martin Luther said that the more he had to do, the more time he needed to spend in prayer.

"Hudson Taylor's prayers have sent more than 1800 missionaries into inland China.

"Livingstone, who died while on his knees in prayer, is an example of faith and persistent service for others.

"In the sub treasury building in New York, there is a statue of George Washington at Valley Forge, kneeling in prayer in the woods in winter. He was a general of an army, but he needed God's help."

"I say my prayers, too," added Joan importantly.

Then Dr. Lansing continued: "The Alpine shepherds have a beautiful custom of ending the day by singing to one another an evening farewell. The air is so crystalline that the song carries long distances. As the dusk begins to fall, they gather their flocks. As they lead them homeward, they sing: 'Hitherto hath the Lord helped us. Let us praise His name!'

"Like the echoing song of the Alpine shepherds, hymns of praise resound to you from the heroes of faith who have remained faithful unto death. They have won in the strength of the Lord. As Christ kept His promise in their lives, so He will keep His promise in your life. Join in the March of Faith and follow a Savior who alone can guide you safely beyond temptations, trials, testings, and sorrows, to the final goal—the Church Triumphant in heaven.

"Now," concluded Dr. Lansing, "I'd like to close this story of the Christian church with a short prayer:

"For the sake of our precious Savior, Jesus, wilt Thou increase our faith and our prayer life so that we may strive to do Thy will and keep close to our heavenly Guide who has given the strengthening, comforting promise: 'Lo I am with you always.' Amen."

BIBLE STUDY

1. Memorize—Heb. 11:1 or Rev. 3:20
2. What does God say about faith—Matt. 17:20; Luke 7:9; Mark 11:22; Acts 16:5
3. What does Jesus want prayer to be—Matt. 7:7-11; John 15:7; Phil. 4:6
4. What does God say about prayer—Mark 11:24; Col. 1:9; Col. 4:2; Prov. 15:8; Eph. 6:18

The
History of My Congregation

....*was organized*..............
      Name of Congregation   *Date*

My first pastor was..

The other pastors who have served my congregation are (it would also be interesting to write in the years they have served):

....

....

....

....

....

....

My first Sunday school superintendent was...................

My present Sunday school superintendent is...................

My first Sunday school teacher was...........................

My present Sunday school teacher is...........................

There are .... *baptized members in my congregation*

Viking Ship

Landing of the Swedes
and Finns

The Mayflower

Hardships of Emigration

Pony Express

Locomotive

Washington at
Prayer

Lincoln

Liberty Bell

Von Steuben

Fleet of Columbus

Statue of
John Ericsson

Ship "New Netherlands"

Signing of the Constitution

Sloop
"Restaurationen"

Adaptation of
Whistler's "My
Mother"

Lutheran Firsts in America

(Continuation of the list on page 85)

1682—The first organ builder in America was Gustavus Hesselius.

1763—The first ordination of a Lutheran pastor who had been *born and educated* in America was that of the Rev. Jacob van Buskirk on October 12. He was born in 1729 at Hackensack, N. J.

1776—July 4—The sexton who rang the liberty bell was a Lutheran.

1776—The first treasurer of the United States was Michael Hillegas of Philadelphia, the son of a good Lutheran mother.

1777—One of the first American flags was made by Sarah Austin and a group of ladies, all members of Gloria Dei Lutheran (now Episcopal) church in Philadelphia and was presented to John Paul Jones. This flag received the first salute granted the Star Spangled Banner in Europe.

1777—The first elected governor of the State of Georgia was John Adam Treutlen, a Lutheran, who was deacon in his home congregation, Jerusalem Church, Ebenezer, Ga.

1781—John Hanson sits in the chair as the first "President of the United States in Congress Assembled." During his presidency of one year, the Post Office Department was reorganized with a Postmaster General at the head, the first Cabinet was organized, a National Seal was designed and adopted which is the same used today, and he issued the first Thanksgiving proclamation.

1789—The first Speaker of the House of Representatives of the United States was Frederick Augustus Muhlenberg, a Lutheran, son of the famous Lutheran clergyman, Henry Melchior Muhlenberg.

1790—The funeral services in connection with the burial of Benjamin Franklin were conducted in Zion Lutheran Church, Philadelphia.

1795—Founding of Hartwick Seminary—oldest Lutheran Seminary in the United States.

1799—The now famous words, "First in war, first in peace, first in the hearts of his countrymen," were first spoken in Zion Lutheran Church, Philadelphia, on December 26, on the occasion of the official memorial service at the death of George Washington, held for the members of Congress. They were spoken by Major General Harry Lee.